Winnifred Thomas

To my friends, the Dingman's
Feb. 1948. W.T.

THE BIRDS OF BREWERY CREEK

Photo by W. V. Crich, F.R.P.S.

YELLOW WARBLERS
"I came to like the Yellow Warblers best."

THE BIRDS
OF BREWERY CREEK

By

The Right Honourable
MALCOLM MACDONALD

Illustrated with photographs by
DR. ARTHUR A. ALLEN
and
W. V. CRICH, F.R.P.S.

GEOFFREY CUMBERLEGE
OXFORD UNIVERSITY PRESS
LONDON   TORONTO   NEW YORK
1947

Printed in Canada

ACKNOWLEDGEMENTS

I AM INDEBTED to Dr. Arthur A. Allen of Cornell University and Mr. W. V. Crich, F. R.P. S., of Toronto for providing the best feature of this book—the illustrations. They are masterpieces of the art of bird photography. I must also thank Dr. Gilbert Grosvenor, the President of the National Geographic Society, for permitting me to use Dr. Allen's coloured photographs.

I am deeply grateful to Mr. Hoyes Lloyd of Ottawa, President of the American Ornithologists Union, and to Dr. Oliver Hewitt of the National Parks Bureau for reading through the manuscript and making many valuable suggestions. All these eminent authorities have been very generous in giving me help.

My debts to the authors of various books are acknowledged in the text. Particularly useful to students of eastern Canadian birds are *The Birds of Canada* by Mr. P. A. Tavener, the doyen of Canadian ornithologists; *The Ducks, Geese and Swans of North America* by F. H. Kortright; *The Birds of Massachusetts and other New England States* by the late Edward Forbush, and Dr. A. C. Bent's monumental and still incomplete work, *The Life Histories of North American Birds*.

M.M.

The Residency,
Penang.
May, 1946.

CONTENTS

CHAPTER   PAGE

   I   BREWERY CREEK   3

  II   A BIRD'S YEAR   7

 III   JANUARY AND FEBRUARY   21

 IV   MARCH   25

  V   APRIL   51

 VI   MAY   97

VII   JUNE   148

VIII   JULY   197

 IX   AUGUST   248

  X   SEPTEMBER   272

 XI   OCTOBER   290

XII   NOVEMBER   312

XIII   DECEMBER   321

CONTENTS

I. Prologue: Choice

II. A Fresh Year

III. January and February

IV. March

V. April

VI. May

VII. June

VIII. July

IX. August

X. September

XI. October

XII. November

XIII. December

ILLUSTRATIONS

YELLOW WARBLERS   *Frontispiece*
"I came to like the Yellow Warblers best."

SAW-WHET OWL   *facing page*   6
"I never saw a Saw-whet Owl."

RING-BILLED GULLS   22
"Gather in large, close-packed colonies."

COWBIRD EGGS   38
"The all-time high record is actually a
five-storied nest."

KILLDEER PLOVER   54
"They build no structure to hold their eggs,
but merely select a slight hollow in the
ground."

PHOEBE   70
"The female is always the nest builder."

WOOD DUCK   86
"The drake is the best looking of all
North American wildfowl."

CANADA GOOSE   102
"Their marriage is a contract entered
into . . . 'until death do us part'."

COMMON LOON   118
"Its striking plumage."

RUBY-THROATED HUMMINGBIRD   126
"Its figure was trim."

SKUNKS   134
"Perhaps it had a young family in
the neighbourhood."

ix

ILLUSTRATIONS

FLICKER   *facing page* 150
"The head of a young bird stuck out of the nest."

CATBIRD   158
"Both parents . . . eyeing me disapprovingly."

CANADA WARBLER   166
"Like bright flowers fluttering amongst the woodland foliage."

BALTIMORE ORIOLE   182
"He perched on a twig on the edge of the nest."

SPOTTED SANDPIPER   198
"Kept a sharp look-out against intruders."

BELTED KINGFISHER   214
"Bold and handsome."

BLACK-CROWNED NIGHT HERON   230
"Immature birds are brown and cream coloured."

BLACK-CAPPED CHICKADEE   246
"Possession of the woods was gradually passing to regular winter birds like . . . Chickadees."

BLUEBIRD   262
"The Spirit of Happiness."

SNOWY OWL   278
"A bird of noble distinction."

RED-EYED VIREO   294
"The nests . . . were bound to each branch of the forks by the finest of all threads—cobwebs."

TREE SPARROW   310
"Braved the rigours of the season."

THE BIRDS OF BREWERY CREEK

CHAPTER ONE

BREWERY CREEK

BREWERY CREEK LIES close to Ottawa. Its waters run modestly, here between crowded shacks and there amongst grassy waste land, round the edge of the neighbouring city of Hull and eventually, about a mile downstream from the Parliament Buildings, pour themselves into the Ottawa River.

The contents of the creek are now *aqua pura*. In earlier days, however, they were liable to be adulterated with a stronger liquid. The place may not in its youth have sowed wild oats, but it certainly squeezed wild hops. Somewhere along its banks stood a brewery. The presses and vats, bottles and drays of this establishment have now disappeared. They are ghosts as airily dissolved as the froth and bubble of the beverage with which they were so intimately associated. But their memory, like the effects of potent drink, lingers long after they are gone. The creek has not forgotten the hilarious distinction which they once lent it and in pious and nostalgic gratitude celebrates the fact in its charming, bibulous name.

At its mouth Brewery Creek spreads out fan-wise and its waters flow comparatively calm and shallow before being swept into the strong, deep current of the Ottawa. The estuary so formed has the appearance of a small, placid lake roughly triangular in shape with two sides bounded by wooded shores and the third by the open river. Although the place is little more than a mile from the centre of Canada's capital city, its aspect is wild. Its shores are a mixture of rocks, mud and reeds. In spring it includes one or two marshy inlets which dry up later in the year. Its banks are covered partly with thick woods and partly by rough meadowland filled in summer with a tangle of wild flowers. Willow trees flourish by the water's edge. Scattered in the more open spaces are thickets of stagshorn, sumach, dogwood and other shrubs. On the higher ground elms and aspens, plums and cherries, hickories and ash trees grow. The woods are filled with red and silver maples.

Nearby is a street of houses with street-cars and other noisy traffic. But the estuary of the creek itself is untroubled by these sights and sounds of a modern city's sophistication. The place has been mercifully by-passed by civilization and Nature there remains undisturbed. Amongst its woodland trees stand two or three small cottages inhabited by men who tend the log-rafts moored off shore in summer. Elsewhere on the bank is an abandoned sawmill consisting of an empty shed, a broken-down chute and the gaunt ruin of a tall chimney. Not far away are some oil tanks. Otherwise the estuary is untamed.

It lies almost opposite my house, Earnscliffe. One day in July, 1944 I paddled my canoe into it and found it a pleasant haven inhabited by some interesting birds. Soon I fell into the habit of crossing to it most mornings. The expedition gave me exercise and fresh air and a daily glimpse of the peace and beauty of Nature. Moreover, I discovered that the place was truly a paradise for an ornithologist. Its variety of natural features made it congenial as a summer residence for many different species of birds and it lay on the migration routes of many others. Sea birds, river birds, lake birds, marsh birds, shore birds and land birds all came to it sooner or later. I watched them

4

from the middle of 1944 until the end of 1945. My observations were scrappy, for work kept me in an office all day and I could only cross the river for an hour or two in the early mornings, before breakfast, and occasionally for a short while in the lunch hour or in the evening. However, perhaps the best time for enjoying the hobby of bird-watching is soon after dawn, when the birds are first awake and most active. My experience in Brewery Creek at any rate seems to prove the truth of the old adage that the early worm catches the bird. In eighteen months I saw 160 different species in the estuary.

The area covers only a small space of calm water and some acres of rough ground. I did not count birds which I saw outside it, wishing to confine the study to bird life within this area. Moreover, I only counted birds of whose identity I was certain. Probably I caught glimpses of a few others—an extra Sparrow or Warbler or Duck, perhaps—whose presence was too fleeting or too elusive for indisputable recognition. Nor did I bother to paddle my canoe to the creek at the dead of night, otherwise I might have added a Whip-poor-will and one or two more Owls to my list. For example, I never saw a Saw-whet Owl, though that engaging little creature must often frequent the place. I believe that a keen observer could see about a dozen more species than I have recorded here.

I wonder how many inhabitants of Ottawa realize that more than 170 species of birds can be found during the year in a small area on the edge of the city. It is charming to know that so near the East Block, where civil servants prepare Acts of Parliament, the love life of Spotted Sandpipers is also being enacted; that within spitting distance of diplomatic cocktail parties in Rockcliffe Park many kinds of Warblers, Vireos and Finches also hold their social gatherings; and that not far from the mumble of legislators' oratory on Parliament Hill can be heard too the querulous scream of the Yellow-bellied Sapsucker.

Many people like watching and learning about birds. In the hope that the citizens of Ottawa may take an increasing interest in this pleasing aspect of the capital's life, I have written this account of the Birds of Brewery Creek through the year 1945, with a few additional notes concerning the autumn of 1944.

Photo by W. V. Crich, F.R.P.S.

SAW-WHET OWL
"I never saw a Saw-whet Owl."

CHAPTER TWO

A BIRD'S YEAR

I.

THE FIRST SENTENCE in Viscount Grey of Falloden's classic on *The Charm of Birds* reads, "This book will have no scientific value". Prudence as well as candour bid me make, near the beginning of this volume, the same unequivocal statement.

Bird watching is a hobby indulged in by countless devotees. All sorts of people from the humblest to the most exalted are included amongst them. Lord Grey, for example, was not the only renowned modern English statesman with a weakness for it. One of the endearing qualities of that much and wrongly abused Prime Minister, Neville Chamberlain, was his love of Nature. In particular he had an intimate knowledge of trees, flowers and birds. When he was Chancellor of the Exchequer and later Prime Minister he walked round the lake in St. James's Park every morning before breakfast, observing with his keen, hawk-like gaze whatever birds were present on the water and the surrounding lawns. He often reported his discoveries to me when we met in the afternoon on the Treasury Bench in the House of Commons.

Unlike Lord Grey, he never wrote a book about birds. But like many self-respecting English amateur ornithologists, he occasionally sent a letter to *The Times* recording an unusual observation. I remember reading on that great journal's centre page one morning a note which said:—

7

37, Eaton Square,
S.W. 1.

Sir,

It may be of interest to record that whilst walking through St. James's Park to-day, I noticed a Grey Wag-tail running about on the now temporarily dry bed of the lake, near the dam below the bridge.

Probably the occurrence of this bird in the heart of London has been recorded before, but I have not myself previously noted it in the Park.

I am your obedient servant,

NEVILLE CHAMBERLAIN.

P.S. For the purpose of removing doubt, as we say in the House of Commons, I should perhaps add that I mean a Grey Wagtail and not a Pied.

I at once dictated a letter to my secretary and addressed it to the Editor of *The Times*. It read:—

St. James's Park,
S.W. 1.

Sir,

It may be of interest to record that, whilst running about in St. James's Park yesterday, I noticed a Chancellor of the Exchequer walking by the temporarily dry bed of the lake, near the dam below the bridge.

Probably the occurrence of this animal in the heart of London has been recorded before, but I have not myself previously noted it in the Park.

I am your obedient servant,

GREY WAGTAIL.

P.S. For the purpose of removing doubt, as they say in the House of Commons, I should perhaps add that

I mean a Chancellor of the Exchequer and not a Chancellor of the Duchy of Lancaster.

I hoped that the Editor would print this interesting nature note next morning in the same position as Mr. Chamberlain's had occupied. Unfortunately I was busy for the rest of the day and could not attend personally to its despatch. For some ludicrous reason my secretary did not think that I intended it seriously and did not post it—a deplorable sin of omission which nearly cost her her job.

2.

Probably the initial attraction of bird-watching for most people is the sheer aesthetic pleasure of contemplating creatures so beautiful in form, colour and action as birds are. No one can pursue the hobby for long, however, without discovering other interesting aspects of bird life. He learns that a bird's existence is governed by a series of crises which succeed each other in a fixed order each twelve months, making an annual rhythm in its life. The first crisis is spring migration and it is followed in turn by the establishment of "territory", courtship, nesting and rearing young. Finally comes autumn migration when the birds return to their winter quarters.

Many fascinating biological problems arise from birds' behaviour during these various episodes and no intelligent ornithologist, however amateur, can fail to become intrigued by them. Much modern ornithological writing is concerned almost exclusively with these scientific aspects of the subject. Many of its authors are not only painstaking but also brilliant observers, who have added immensely to the range and accuracy of our knowledge of scores of individual species as well as of bird society as a whole. Their books are invaluable to serious students.

My volume does not pretend to have the same importance. It is a mere introduction to bird life in a particular, limited region and approaches the subject from the aesthetic rather than the scientific point of view. That is not to say that it ignores completely the scientific problems connected with migration, courtship and breeding. Some of them are touched upon in these pages, for the seasonal rhythm of events in the birds' year must in any case be the main theme of almost any coherent story about them. But I do not discuss these aspects fully. They are introduced only as much as may be necessary to give a comprehensive sketch of bird society in Brewery Creek. What is written about them in this narrative will perhaps give the reader a hint of the delight which awaits him when he probes into more learned works.

Since, however, no account of bird life in a district is intelligible without a general knowledge of the successive crises which face birds through the year, let me in this chapter give a brief, simplified sketch of the elementary facts of the matter. In essence they apply more or less to every species which appears in this book, so a general account of them now will cover all the birds and save much repetition later.

3·

At the opening of each year, on January 1st, birds are in their winter quarters. Many sea-birds are scattered widely over the oceans, leading unsociable lives. Other salt and fresh-water fowl, however, and most species of land birds congregate in flocks. They do this partly, no doubt, for companionship and partly to enjoy better hunting. Many pairs of eyes are more likely than one pair to discover supplies of food in comparatively scarce winter conditions.

Almost all species winter further south than their summer breeding grounds. I shall mention later some exceptions to this rule. Only the hardiest Canadian species winter in Canada. Most cannot abide cold, ice and snow and when autumn frosts bring a warning of their approach they flee into the United States. Many even go as far as the Caribbean Islands and Central and South America to find congenial winter resorts. There they stay and bask in the sun during the first two or three months of the year, like fashionable holiday-makers on the Riviera or in Florida.

With the approach of spring birds grow restless. Certain physical changes connected with their reproductive organs take place, making them wish instinctively to travel to their nesting grounds. The multitudinous movement of spring migration begins.

All birds migrate, but there are vast differences in the extent to which they travel. Generally speaking three different types of migration occur.

First there is "local migration." Sometimes the birds of a locality are popularly divided into "residents" and "migrants". The residents can be seen in the area all the year round. But in fact very few, if any, birds are resident to the extent of staying in precisely the same place through the twelve months. Even these residents shift their ground to some extent in spring and autumn, since the ideal situation for their nesting in summer is hardly ever exactly the right spot for their feeding in winter. Their movements may be of very limited scope, such as a change from the higher slopes to the lower slopes of a mountain. Or they may involve a rather wider change from one type of country to another in the region. These kinds of more or less limited movements are called "local migrations."

The second type of migration may be called "dispersals". They are as regular and in many cases as extensive movements as the more customary migration, but are different in that they do not take place from south to north in the spring and from north to south in the fall. Indeed, they may take place in any direction. They are not dictated by the birds' need to follow the warm sun north or south, but by other requirements.

Sea-birds offer the best examples of these "dispersals", which in their case are explained as follows. During most of the year the birds have the whole ocean to feed in. They are scattered over wide spaces of sea. But the sites where they can nest are limited. They cannot build safe supports for their eggs on the wild ocean waves. They must make for a convenient coast or island and become land-lubbers for some weeks or months. These journeys may take them north, south, east or west, according to the geographical relationship of their customary feeding places to their annual nesting grounds. Wherever the latter are situated the birds, impelled by the urge to reproduce, must go.

The third type of movement is the commonest and may be called "typical migration." It is the journey made by the vast majority of birds between their winter resorts in the south and their breeding grounds further north. The extent of these journeys varies greatly between different species. Some are short, others are gigantic. The World's Long-distance Champion Migrater is the Arctic Tern. It breeds in the Arctic and winters in the Antarctic. Actually it spends most of its time travelling, for careful observations show that the journey between its summer and its winter resorts takes about four months each way. Some other species make equally impressive oddyseys, at any rate in relation to their size. Thus, many small Warblers travel from South America to Canada. Tiny Ruby-throated Hummingbirds fly from the Central American Republics and the Caribbean Islands to Canada, Labrador and even Alaska.

How are the travellers guided on these immense flights? Many remarkable cases of unerring, uncanny direction-finding exist. The Golden Plovers of the Pacific Coast, for example, cross 2,000 miles of trackless ocean, without even an island or rock to serve as a landmark as they fly. Again, the parent birds in many species start their autumn migration before their offspring are ready for the great adventure. In due course the inexperienced, untutored and unguided youngsters find their own way. How do they chart their passages through the skies? We do not know. Much study of bird mechanism is still necessary before we learn this fascinating secret. It remains largely a mystery.

Though the journeys are usually accomplished with remarkable accuracy and success, they are made at great cost. The casualties are many. Storms may arise and destroy large numbers of the travellers as they make their way, dashing them to the ground or blowing them far out of their course. Again, the weaker birds making broad sea crossings may fail and never reach the further shore. Or again, tired birds are less capable of escaping the attacks of enemies, such as birds of prey. The toll of lives on migration is heavy.

A movement which repeatedly defies the risk of such

destruction must be impelled by a deep purpose. It is, of course, the strongest instinct in all animals, the urge to reproduce. Each bird species requires certain conditions of climate and territory for breeding. It is particular about the temperature in which it lives, it likes a certain minimum amount of daylight every twenty-four hours, it requires special conditions of vegetation for nesting, and it needs certain types of food to support itself and its young through the summer. These various causes combine to dictate the regions where this or that species shall nest, and they are the motive forces behind the great northward and south-ward journeys of millions of birds in spring and autumn.

To describe the subsequent sequence of events in a bird's life I shall take as an example an individual bird. Let it be any small passerine or perching bird: a typical, common or garden creature like a Bunting or a Finch. With variations of detail in some respects, the general process applies to all such species.

In winter it is a member of a flock, roaming contentedly with many companions through their feeding areas. Cocks and hens mix indiscriminately in these parties. No passions or jealousies disturb the flock's harmony, for in winter their sexual instincts are quiescent. Peace and good fellowship prevail.

With the approach of spring this happy state of affairs begins to dissolve. The cocks show a tendency to quarrel. Little rivalries break out amongst them. This change is produced by the beginnings of a physical change in the birds. Their generative organs slowly develop potency. For a while longer the cocks continue to associate in flocks together, but their brotherly relations show a marked deterioration. Gradually each cock becomes more independent. It occasionally wanders away from the flock, doing this more and more frequently.

Then the cocks start on their spring migration. Generally, amongst passerine birds, they travel ahead of the hens. The same does not apply in the case of wild-fowl. The passerine cocks travel north in loose flocks, but all the time the individual's sense of unity with its companions is waning. His instinct makes him more self-sufficient and self-assertive, leading to the time when he must set up an individual, separate establishment of his own for the supreme purpose of mating and rearing young.

The journey north may take several weeks, being accomplished in stages. Most migrants travel by night, feeding and resting during the days.

As soon as the males reach their breeding grounds they take the first step towards finding homes. The flock now disperses and individual birds scatter widely over the countryside. Each takes to himself an area of ground in which to settle and wait for the arrival of a mate. These areas are called "territories". They vary in size for different species and also according to the numbers of a species who settle in any particular region. The average extent of a Song Sparrow's territory, for example, is about half an acre.

These territories are only established, and their respective boundaries fixed, as a result of much quarrelling. Rivals for the same territory settle the issue by combat. This is not always violent, as I shall explain later. Eventually, these various trials of strength resolve the problem. The whole area is parcelled out into numerous territories. Each cock has its own little domain with exactly defined boundaries well-known to itself and to its neighbours. The intrusion of one cock into the territory of another immediately provokes a chase or struggle between them, which does not end until the intruder has withdrawn to his own land.

Each cock is thus in effect a landed proprietor. Nor is he passive in this role. On the contrary, he is active in proclaiming land-ownership and alert in defending his rights. He announces his ownership by song. The principal cause of spring song is the desire of each individual to advertise his ownership of this or that territory and to warn rivals to keep away.

Not all the males succeed in finding a territory. In an overcrowded area there is no room for all the contestants and the weaker birds fail to secure any rights. Without territory (*i.e.* a nesting ground) they cannot win a mate. Some of them lead a disconsolate, bachelor existence throughout the summer, but others may be so fortunate, later, as to find hens whose partners have suffered accidents and died. The lucky ones woo the widows, inherit their territories and thenceforward enjoy all the pleasures and responsibilities of married life.

As I have said, the males of a species generally arrive on their breeding grounds ahead of the females. Sometimes a few hens come in this first wave of migration, but the great majority follow several days after the cocks. They arrive when their partners-to-be have settled their territorial quarrels and are ready for the next step in the business of procreation. This is an example of the ingenious ways in which Nature arranges the economy of animals' lives.

As soon as the hens arrive flirtations between them and the cocks begin. The strange antics called "courtship displays", calculated to attract one sex to the other, are indulged in. Before long the pairs sort themselves out.

16

Each cock has not only a territory but also a mate to share it with him. The preliminary flirtations soon end in mating and their domestic life together begins. The hen starts to build a nest. In due course she lays eggs and the process of hatching and rearing young proceeds.

Often a cock will return year after year to the same territory or to a near-by territory. Sometimes a cock will also find the same mate in successive seasons. Their reunion after a winter's separation must arouse in them pleasing emotions.

Ownership of territory is one of the fundamental features of a bird's existence. It is as essential a part of "the annual rhythm" of their lives as are migration, pairing and nesting. All breeding birds have territory in one form or another. Even where sea-birds congregate in a crowd, almost a mob, on the limited space of a cliff-ledge each pair has its own particular square foot or so in which its egg or eggs are laid. The parents are as resentful of intrusion by a neighbour into this small scrap of private property as are the owners of more extensive estates.

The existence and importance of territory in the economy of avian society have only comparatively recently been properly appreciated. A few early ornithologists noted that pairs of this or that species seemed jealous of any visitor near their nests. But it was left to an English ornithologist, Dr. Elliott Howard, to expound some forty years ago the universal nature of the system, and to attempt an explanation of it. Since then many scientific bird watchers in various countries have added important information to our knowledge of the subject and have developed the theory of its reason. The exact and full explanation of "territory" is by no means yet established. There is still

17

room for conflicting arguments and controversies. I shall not trouble the reader with an account of these, for anyone who wishes to learn about the subject can easily do so in the works of more experienced and knowledgeable ornithologists than myself.

I will only say that, in general, the establishment of a territory in which each pair can produce and hatch eggs unmolested is necessary for the orderly and successful reproduction of a species. Nor does the need for this end with the safe hatching of chicks. The youngsters have to be fed and this involves securing an adequate food supply. The area of a pair's territory works out roughly at the space which is required to provide food for a bird family. Each pair has a monopoly (so far as its own species is concerned, but not with regard to other species, which may in whole or in part share its territory) of the provisions in its own property. It forages exclusively there, being driven back into its own territory if it seeks to poach on a neighbour's preserves.

This need to make territories more or less coincide with units of food supply only exists in the case of land-birds. Sea-birds do not nest on the ocean, but on shore. For feeding, however, they have the whole sea. Their nesting territories and their feeding grounds are thus separate from each other. This explains why sea-bird's nesting territories are small and enable these species to gather in large, close-packed colonies. The same is true of other birds who nest in colonies, like Herons, Cliff Swallows and English Rooks.

Birds remain organized on a territorial basis throughout the summer, as long as the requirements of rearing young demand it. Between different species there are variations in detailed practice. Some produce only one set of eggs a

18

year whilst others produce two, three or even four. Again, in most species the hen incubates the eggs whilst the cock keeps guard over her and the nest. In other cases both birds share the duties of incubation and in a few species this function belongs to the male. Generally both parents join in the labour of feeding their chicks after hatching. But again, practice may differ.

At the end of the nesting season territory ceases to be important. It has done its job. The reproductive organs in the birds become passive again. The urge to pair dies and parental duties are over for another year. So families break up and the boundaries between territories cease to be observed. Once more the birds begin to mix freely and indiscriminately with their kind. Flocks are formed.

The summer ends. Autumn chills invade the air. Warm-weather birds feel uncomfortable in the north and the fall migration begins. Soon birds are flying south in millions, retracing their routes to their various winter quarters. Arrived in them, they form regular winter flocks. Thus the annual rhythm of a bird's life has been completed. The seasons have gone full cycle. Only when spring returns in the following year will the process which I have described commence all over again.

4.

We are now ready to review the birds of Brewery Creek. Only a few more explanatory sentences are necessary before we begin. I should explain that this book does not attempt to tell the life history of every species which flies through its pages. It is not a collection of full-length portraits of all the birds in the creek, but a mere sketch of bird life there as a whole. A sketch is a work of art in which only certain characteristic features are selected for portrayal. Many details are omitted. The following pages therefore contain a broad picture of Brewery Creek's bird society. Although every species which I saw is at least mentioned, some receive less attention than they deserve. Amongst the crowd, however, I do select several representative species—such as the Phoebe, the Northern Flicker and the Spotted Sandpiper—for more complete treatment. The events of their lives throughout their stay in the creek are described in detail.

The arrangement of the book prevents these life stories from being written in each case as a continuous tale. Successive chapters deal with successive months. Therefore the affairs of Phoebes, for example, are related in a series of episodes distributed through several chapters. In March the Phoebes arrive in the creek (Chapter IV); in April the hen builds her nest (Chapter V); in May she is incubating her eggs (Chapter VI); and so on. This arrangement may annoy readers who wish to peruse the story of a species as a continuous narrative from beginning to end. May I point out that these earnest students can in fact satisfy their desire by selecting the section in each chapter dealing with a species and perusing them one after the other? In the case of the Phoebe it can be done by picking out Chapter IV section 8, Chapter V section 7, Chapter VI section 5, Chapter VII section 4, Chapter VIII section 4 and a paragraph in Chapter XI. In the case of Northern Flickers, to give another example, it can be done by reading Chapter V section 6, Chapter VI section 4, Chapter VII section 6 and part of Chapter VIII section 5.

That is enough by way of introduction. Let us now start on the journey to the creek.

CHAPTER THREE

JANUARY AND FEBRUARY

IN WINTER Brewery Creek lies asleep beneath thick coverlets of ice and snow. It does not stir nor make any sound in its slumber. The ripple of water is silenced, the woods are quiet and all the customary small noises of living earth are hushed. Many natural features of the place which are familiar in spring, summer and autumn are obliterated. Rocks, tree stumps and tumbled logs lie beneath snowdrifts. Most of the shrubs too are hidden, only the tops of the taller ones protruding. Even the land and water are indistinguishable from each other, for it is difficult to tell where the shore ends and the estuary begins. Both are buried under a vast snowfield, clothed in a common shroud, sharing the same winter grave.

Only the larger landmarks jut from the snow—the deserted saw-mill, the oil tanks, a couple of shacks and the silent ranks of leafless, woodland trees.

I often gazed from Earnscliffe across to Brewery Creek. The view had romance and beauty. The atmosphere was usually brilliantly clear and often the sky was blue and cloudless. Bright sunlight gave a sparkle to the white landscape. Occasionally two or three small, black human figures appeared, trudging on skis or snow-shoes along the river. Sometimes they stayed for a while to cut ice or to fish through an ice-hole. Except for them nothing stirred in the scene. Everything seemed inanimate, from the frozen, snow-covered Ottawa River in the foreground, across Brewery Creek and the farmlands in the middle distance

21

to the shaggy Gatineau Hills along the horizon. They all looked like objects in a gigantic Christmas tableau.

One afternoon in early February I crossed the river on skis. For three months or more the ice stays a foot or two thick, overlaid by a deep snowfall. In a normal year you can drive a heavy lorry across the river any time between early January and mid-March. It would be an ideal highway for driving a team of dogs. I have often deplored my lack of imagination and enterprise in not acquiring a sleigh and half-a-dozen huskies during my first winter in Ottawa, and learning to drive them on the river. It would be appropriate for a High Commissioner to ride down river by this means when going to pay his respects to the Governor-General at Rideau Hall, or up river to discuss affairs of state with the Prime Minister on Parliament Hill. If by ill-luck—as would probably have happened—the dogs had got mad one day and torn me to pieces, it would have been too bad. But whether in the end I disciplined them or they disciplined me, between us we would have saved a little gasoline, that precious fluid which was needed then in such large quantities to fight the enemy.

However, I thought of that too late; so when I crossed the river to Brewery Creek at the beginning of February, 1945 I went on skis. The place had the stillness and peace of death. It was a cold day, the thermometer recording several degrees below zero. I carried my field-glasses, but in vain. No sound, not even a Starling's chatter, broke the frosty silence. The world was birdless.

Things might easily have been different. On another day in January or February I might have seen any or all of a number of species which pay Brewery Creek occasional visits in the winter. However, I did not bother to make

Photo by W. V. Crich, F.R.P.S.

RING-BILLED GULLS
"Gather in large, close-packed colonies."

more journeys at that time. Darkness still obscured the earth before breakfast and I was not free at any other time. I was not greatly concerned at this, expecting that when longer days came with March, ice and snow would still bind the river. Then, as the mornings grew lighter, I would cross to the creek and study its winter bird life.

Spring, however, came suddenly and soon. When I crossed the river early in March, winter was already breaking up. Alternately caressed by sunshine, driven by wind and beaten by rain, the snow was rapidly melting. Such bird visitors from the far north as usually dally in Brewery Creek at that season had fled.

Probably I should not have seen more than half-a-dozen species which cannot be seen there at other times. A flock of Redpolls would certainly have passed by sooner or later. One or two kinds of Grosbeaks no doubt would have come that way. I might have caught sight of an Arctic Three-toed Woodpecker scrambling up a tree, or of a Northern Shrike impaling its prey upon a thorn. The Shrike, which is the fearsome Butcher Bird, has another accomplishment. Even when snow is still on the ground it is a lusty singer. The combination of its taste for butchery and music reminds me of W. S. Gilbert's verse,

> When the enterprising burglar's not a-burgling
> And the cut-throat isn't occupied in crime,
> They love to hear the little brook a-gurgling
> And to listen to the merry village chime.[1]

At best the list of winter species in Brewery Creek would have been short. One bird in particular I had hoped to see.

[1] From *The Pirates of Penzance*, by W. S. Gilbert. By permission of the copyright owner.

23

I knew its cousin in northern Scotland and had looked forward to meeting the Canadian member of the family. The Snow Bunting is the borean member of the Sparrow tribe. Indeed, it is an Eskimo among birds, breeding northwards from Labrador and Hudson Bay on Arctic shores and hillsides. It is a familiar visitor to the door-steps and window-sills of the furthest north, bringing cheer in those solitary regions for fur traders, missionaries and Royal Canadian Mounted Policemen.

The bird's summer dress is a mixture of jet-black and snow-white, in which white greatly predominates. When it comes south in winter the purity of this plumage is marred by rusty edges to many feathers. Nevertheless, the impression when it flies is still of an almost wholly white bird. Snow Buntings in winter travel in large flocks. They are unconcerned by inclement weather, whirling about gaily in high winds and storms of snow. They feed on the seeds of plants jutting from the snowfield. Like an army foraging in inhospitable country, a flock will hurl itself on a crop of these and demolish them. They are restless creatures, forever flitting and running over the snow, clinging for a few moments to the dead flower stalks whilst they rob the seed-clusters, then taking wing again to fly to further stalks. The rear ranks of a flock rise, flutter forwards over the backs of their feeding comrades and alight on unattacked weeds ahead. So they progress in a series of movements like snow flurries. Their lightness and whiteness and continual whirling have earned them their prettiest and most descriptive popular name, "Snowflakes".

I was sorry that when I visited Brewery Creek at the beginning of March these snowflakes had melted.

24

CHAPTER FOUR

MARCH

I.

MARCH CAME IN like a lamb, skipping in innocently with mild weather. Warm sunshine, gentle breezes and showers of rain followed each other in succession. Lacking reinforcements of snow from Heaven, the snow on Earth could not maintain itself against these powerful foes. A sudden, prodigious thaw began.

Even so, it takes time for several feet of snow to disappear. On March 5th I crossed the river on snow-shoes. The only birds in Brewery Creek that morning were a few Starlings gossiping together in a group of elm trees. I need not write much of them. They are such inveterate advertisers of their own virtues and vices that no-one else need dwell on the subject. But perhaps I should mention this: the Starling is not a native Canadian. It arrived in comparatively modern times from Europe. In an unfortunate moment in 1890 sixty specimens of the breed were transported across the Atlantic Ocean and introduced to New York City. In the following year another forty came. They made good settlers, prospered and have since spread far and wide in North America. The present immense population on the continent springs from that original hundred introduced less than sixty years ago. Starlings are now familiar residents in many parts of Canada. Their habit of nesting in tree holes brings them into rivalry as householders with some native species, like Bluebirds. This is a wretched misfortune, for the most up-to-date orchard methods—such as

lopping off rotten branches and filling holes with concrete—
had already reduced the number of suitable nesting places
for those beautiful creatures. We must hope that the invasion
of North America by Starlings does not do to the indigenous Bluebirds what the invasion of the continent by the
white man did to the native Redskins.

People once hoped that Starlings would not survive the
rigours of the Canadian winter. But that proved a vain
hope. Although most of them migrate, many Starlings are
impervious to cold and remain here happily through the
cruellest hardships of December, January and February.
They are like those crazy Englishmen and Scotsmen who
stroll through the streets of Ottawa hatless and coatless
when the temperature is 20 degrees below zero. Damn the
impertinence of these immigrants!

On March 7th a Crow joined the Starlings amongst the
elms. Most Crows winter further south, but occasionally a
few remain all the year in the Ottawa neighbourhood. This
particular bird may therefore have been either a winter
resident or a spring migrant.

On the following day a wandering band of about twenty
Pine Siskins visited the creek, flying with gay chirpings on
to the scene. Snow still lay thick over most of the ground,
but a few patches of bare earth revealed a crushed mass of
last year's dead grass and weeds. The small, brown-striped
birds flew in bunched formation straight to the largest
patch, alighted, scattered over the ground and started feeding. Siskins are irregular winter visitors to the Ottawa
district, so their appearance, like that of the Starlings and
the Crow, was not necessarily significant of spring's
approach.

By now, however, the snow on the river had almost
completely disappeared, leaving bare, slippery ice. Snow-

shoes slithered awkwardly on its glassy surface. To get a
grip I took them off and walked in mocassins. Occasionally
I heard a low, mysterious whistle close beside me. Sometimes it made me halt and look around to see what strange
bird was accompanying me. But there never was a bird.
The sound was deceptive, connected no doubt with the
impending freeing of the river. The ice floor beneath me
was cracking. Sometimes it emitted a louder and more
sinister explosion of sound, but I could still reach the opposite shore in safety.

2.

The early retreat of winter brought the first definite
evidence of bird migration several weeks earlier than usual.
The vanguard of the great host which started moving from
the south arrived in Brewery Creek on March 9th. Early
that morning I walked across the river and snow-shoed on
its further bank. The silence of the wintry world at sunrise
was broken only by the chatter of some Starlings in the elm
trees. A pair of solemn Crows flew silently overhead. Then
I noticed a movement on a patch of bare ground amongst
the snow. Studying the spot through field-glasses, I discovered a bird which was strange to me—rather larger than
a Sparrow, brown-backed and white-chested, with a black
gorget, yellow throat, black and white masked face and two
black tufts like a pair of horns growing from its head. A
Horned Lark!

I soon saw three others in the immediate neighbourhood. They moved quickly over the ground in a series of
short, hurried runs, keeping to the patches of bare earth,
which were now considerable. When they wished to pass
from one such area to another they spread their wings, flew
low by the shortest route across the intervening snow,

landed quickly and promptly chased after more food. They seemed to be reluctant fliers—almost earth-bound. Occasionally they addressed each other in gentle, confidential, scarcely audible whispers, as if they were anxious not to attract the attention of other creatures.

On the following day they were still there. One of them strolled over the ground singing a sweet song in a voice and accents reminiscent of an English Skylark. Perhaps it was tuning-up for a flirtation. In the courtship and nesting season the male Horned Lark puts on a spectacular aerial display accompanied by music. Rising in a wide spiral by a series of upward flights, punctuated with snatches of tinkling song, the bird almost disappears from sight. Shortly afterwards he swoops towards the ground as if to dash himself to death, but pulls out of his dive close to earth and alights quietly beside the female. At this time the larks appear anything but earth-bound and their conduct is even more reminiscent of Skylarks.

By the next morning the Horned Larks had left Brewery Creek, hastening further north. These birds are amongst the true pioneers of spring settlement. They are frontiersmen in bird society, making their habitations on the new year's virgin soil without even waiting for the snow to disappear. Their nests are built of wisps of grass in natural hollows on the ground amongst the snowdrifts. In them soon appear four or five grey, brown-spotted eggs.

3.

For several days after that I was away from Ottawa. When I returned the ice on the river had worn so thin that its passage on foot was dangerous. On March 18th I made an attempt to cross, but when I had proceeded a quarter of the way an ominous sound of cracking made me hesitate. A Herring Gull flew past, crying a warning that pools of open water were not far distant. This was emphasizing the obvious, for I could see a miniature lake of clear water about half a mile away. Overhead I heard a shore bird's musical whistle and, looking skywards, saw a swift-flying Killdeer Plover—a herald trumpeting in the spring. I beat a hurried retreat.

Three mornings later, on March 21st, I crossed the river in a canoe! The break-up was the earliest on record, occurring two or three weeks before the normal date. Most of the river was already clear of ice, although loose chunks of ice, and occasionally large islands of it, floated downstream. A brisk breeze had blown a mass of ice-floes against the further shore. When I came to it I succeeded in thrusting the canoe for some distance along narrow channels of open water between the shifting slabs of ice. But beyond that they were jammed so tight that I had to step out on to an ice-floe, lift the canoe from the water and walk from ice-floe to ice-floe lugging the craft behind me.

On shore snow still predominated, although the patches of bare earth had increased in number and size. Since my last visit several spring migrants had arrived and the place was lively with bird calls. The usual company of Starlings and Crows had been joined by American Goldfinches, Song Sparrows, Bronzed Grackles and American Robins. I shall write of all these birds later; but let me comment at once on the American Robin. I say "American" advisedly, for the bird is so different from its English namesake. The Yankees' boast that they build things far bigger than other people do is certainly justified by the size of their Robin. It has a breast as red as an English Robin's, but a body as large as a Thrush's. Indeed, the American Robin looks like what an English Robin would feel like if the latter got thoroughly drunk. The truth is that it *is* a member of the Thrush family, misnamed by early settlers in the New World who saw its red bosom and enthusiastically christened it after the Redbreast of the Old World.

In the creek that morning, as on the river, the central channel of water flowed open and free. But wide margins of unbroken ice stretched out from each bank and a broad barrier of jumbled ice-blocks across the creek's mouth barred the way to the river. In the open water fragments of ice floated like miniature icebergs. The creek was half ice, half water.

Bright sunshine gave a glitter to the scene. As I gazed upon it a wild duck flew along the creek. It drooped its wings to break its flight and landed on a lump of ice floating downstream. There it travelled unconcernedly, like an Arctic explorer marooned on the ice-pack. The bird was a female American Merganser, its body brown, grey and white. A few moments later I noticed through my field glasses that an object in the water nearby, which my naked eyes had mistaken for another bit of ice, was also a living creature. It was a Merganser drake, fully adorned in his dramatic snow-white, cream and black plumage. Beyond him swam a second duck.

This was handsome proof of the fact that "in the spring these hardy birds are the very first of our water-fowls to start on the northward migration. They follow the retreat of winter and by March and April are well on their way to their summer breeding range"[1]. Ice and snow have no

[1] A. C. Bent, *Life Histories of North American Wildfowl*. The United States National Museum.

terrors for them. They like to spend the winter as far north as they find open water and several stay through the cold months near rapids on the Ottawa River.

Presently I noticed other heroically early starters in the new drive northwards. Further up the creek four American Golden-eye were swimming and diving. The male birds looked particularly spick and span. Their black jackets and white vests were immaculate, but their most distinguishing mark was a large white spot on each cheek of their otherwise black heads and faces. Like American Mergansers, some of them spend the winter on pools of open water near Ottawa.

As I watched these two parties of wildfowl something startled them and they took wing. The Mergansers lifted themselves heavily and with apparent difficulty from the water. First they skimmed swiftly for several yards along its surface, then rose slowly and even laboriously into the air, like heavily-laden sea-planes taking off. The Golden-eye made a much quicker get-away, freeing themselves more easily from the water, climbing at a stiff angle and circling to gain height. The sharp whistle of their wings beating the air was eloquent of will power. This thrilling sound is characteristic of the bird's flight and has earned it the nicknames "Whistler" and "Whistlewings".

Nature never seemed to me more exhilarating than when I saw these beautiful creatures at home in that keen, crisp, wintry landscape.

4.

In the succeeding days several other members of the great procession of spring migrants arrived on the shores or in the air of the creek. On March 24th a Cowbird, on the 25th a Red-winged Blackbird, on the 26th a Phoebe and a small flock of Pintails, on the 27th a Northern Flicker and some Tree Sparrows, and on the 30th[1] a Meadowlark and a Belted Kingfisher appeared. I first saw most of them soon after sunrise on the dates mentioned. Many birds migrate at night and probably most of these had actually arrived in the creek only an hour or two earlier.

During several nights at that time the air remained windless and the temperature fell so low that a thin veneer of ice formed over the calm river. It lay there at dawn like a sheet of fragile glass. When I drove my canoe through it the ice cracked and broke in all directions, as if I were smashing a vast window pane. An hour or so later, as the warmth of the sun spread over the earth, the ice melted and disappeared. For almost a week this infant ice was born each night and murdered afresh each morning.

Day after day the sky was serenely blue and the sun shone brilliantly. For another week, however, ice-floes continued to make an almost continuous ice-field round the edges of the creek, and down the central channels of both creek and river floated a succession of small icebergs. They were scattering fragments of great masses of ice which were breaking up in the higher reaches of the Ottawa. Gleaming beautifully in the sunlight, they looked like toy models of the huge icebergs which I had seen the previous summer off the coasts of Baffin Island, not far below the Arctic Circle. Amongst them the Mergansers and Golden-eye continued to swim and fish.

[1] March 30th was Good Friday and turned out to be a good Good Friday for an ornithologist. Besides the Meadowlark and Belted Kingfisher in Brewery Creek, I saw my first Tree Swallow of the year in Earnscliffe garden, my first Bluebird of the year at New Chelsea and my first Slate-coloured Junco of the year at Old Chelsea.

32

5.

On shore the snow gradually melted. It remained longest in the woods or beneath groups of trees where it was partially protected from the sun and remained a glistening carpet of sugary spring snow. Before it wholly disappeared the next phase in the cycle of bird life had commenced. In spring birds lose no time in progressing towards the achievement of the supreme aim which then governs all their activities—procreation, the renewal and preservation of their various species. No sooner have they completed migration (which might be supposed to exhaust them) than they take the next step, the securing of "territory" on their breeding grounds. This is done by the males who, as I have already said, generally amongst passerine birds arrive ahead of the females.

The most conspicuous birds on the shores of Brewery Creek towards the end of March were cock Song Sparrows. It was not their plumage that made them prominent. Their mostly brown, striped and streaked bodies, with a distinguishing dark spot in the centre of the breast, were pretty, but in no way striking. What drew attention to them was their music. A dozen sparrows were distributed over the area, each holding its separate ground. At dawn they all perched on twigs near the tops of shrubs or small trees in their respective territories, faced the sun, tilted their heads, opened wide their beaks and poured forth songs so vehemently that their throats swelled almost to bursting point.

They appeared to be singing a greeting to the rising sun. A sentimental visitor might imagine that the words of their chorus were,

"Oh, what a beautiful mornin',
Oh, what a beautiful day."[1]

But in fact the thoughts being expressed so sweetly could be more nearly translated,

"This is my territory and if any of you sons of hen-birds come near it, I'll tear every feather from your so-and-so bodies."

One of the most fascinating studies in ornithology is bird song. What inspires singing? The charming old idea that it is an expression of innocent joy has been exploded by modern scientific observers who love truth and hate sentimentality. It is true that the old theory has not been completely blown to bits. To some extent in some species at some seasons of the year song is a spontaneous, pleasurable expression of surplus energy. But primarily, especially in spring, its object is more utilitarian. It has three main purposes which animate different species in different degrees. First, it is used by a male to proclaim his ownership of a certain piece of land. Second, the male sings to attract a female. Third, each bird of a pair may use it later, when nesting has begun, as a signal to indicate to its mate its whereabouts.

The early morning chorus of Song Sparrows in March was a hearty advertisement of their respective territories. Each bird was making a declaration of land-ownership and uttering a warning to other cocks that trespassers would be prosecuted. The hens had not yet arrived. So far the cocks were concerned only with their rights as landed proprietors. It is by voice as well as by physical force—if and when

[1] Copyright MCMXLIII by Williamson Music, Inc., New York. Reproduced by permission of the copyright owner.

34

necessary—that passerine birds establish their right to the small scrap of earth in which they will later mate, build a nest and rear a family.

Other birds which now began to appear in numbers were similarly engaged. Some were more decorative than the Song Sparrows. One morning a male Red-winged Blackbird and a cock Robin perched beside one another on a branch, both proclaiming their territory. They presented a fine contrast. The former is a jet-black bird with brilliant crimson "shoulder" bars edged with yellow on the upper wing coverts. These marks are like epaulettes and one of the French names for the bird is actually *L'étourneau à épaulettes*. If I may be permitted an imaginative analogy, the bird looked like an Admiral in full-dress uniform. The Robin beside it was not unlike an officer from a brother service. Its gay, puffed-out red breast and black busby-coloured head gave it the appearance of a General in the ceremonial uniform of a regiment of the Guards. I was amused to see this gallant sailor and soldier standing side by side on the same tree.

It is a mistake to let one's imagination run away with one and to draw extravagant parallels between characters in the bird world and characters in the human world. The practice can quickly degenerate into sloppy sentimentality. It becomes unscientific to the point of utter nonsense. Yet it is sometimes tempting to indulge in it, and when a few days later I listened to half-a-dozen Red-winged Blackbirds gossiping together in some willow trees protruding from the flood waters of the creek I was again irresistibly reminded of a group of senior naval officers. The birds were all cocks, complete with epaulettes. Hen Red-winged Blackbirds are differently marked, wearing smartly striped brown dresses. They arrive some time after the males, and none appeared in Brewery Creek until April 1st.

As I say, the birds' voices that morning reinforced the illusion that they were Admirals All. They sounded like the speech of aged sea-dogs who were beginning to lose their vocal powers but retained unimpaired their capacity for swearing. A Red-winged Blackbird's favourite expression is a hoarse, quavering ejaculation giving a distinct impression of bad temper. This unpleasant noise is repeated so persistently, however, that the nautical analogy breaks down, for no one who has heard it could maintain that the birds belong to a silent service.

The Redwing is also capable of a musical whistle, as clear and strong as the stroke of a bell. But it employs this call too rarely. The Robin, on the other hand, does not often make a sound which is unpleasant. The quality of its song varies greatly between one performer and another, but generally it is the most tuneful in the early spring migrants' repertoire.

The Bronzed Grackle is another blackbird with a horribly grating voice. It might seem strange that a family whose nominal representative in England is one of the purest and most beautiful songsters should in America produce a set of execrable performers. The English Blackbird is a superb artist on the flute, but the American Blackbirds are mere adepts on the policeman's rattle. The explanation is that the birds in the two countries belong to different families, the English Blackbird actually being a Thrush. This is another case of an error in christening by the early English colonists in America. Seeing the superficial resemblance between the Redwings and Grackles of their new land and the Blackbirds of their old, they applied to the former the name of the latter.

Bronzed Grackles make up for their ugly voices by their lovely appearance. One afternoon at the end of March I watched a small party of them strutting near the water's edge. Bright sunlight lit the colours of their polished coats. It is hard to believe that in reality their plumage has no colour, being uniformly black. The feathers have a glossy, metallic sheen, however, and when light plays upon their surface it produces a series of magical, shimmering hues. The birds' shoulders appear richly bronzed and their heads turn so brilliantly purple that they might be mistaken for splendid tropical creatures. Mr. P. A. Taverner has a good phrase in which he describes the "knightly, Black Prince armour" of the Bronzed Grackle.[1] There is something knightly, courtly too about the bird's strut. But it has touches of pomposity and impudence also which suggest a court jester rather than a prince.

The Bronzed Grackles enjoyed something like a monopoly of the shore in the almost complete absence, so early in the year, of true shore birds. The latter had only one representative in the form of the Killdeer. This Plover always arrives very early in the spring, long before the hosts of other shore birds. Yet I wonder whether it has ever been seen or heard in Canada as early as it was this year. As I have already written, I first saw a Killdeer flying over the river on March 18th. I first saw one on the banks of the creek on the 24th. A pair of them appeared late that afternoon. They had not been visible when I visited the place in the morning, and it is unlikely that I would have missed either the sight or the sound of these restless, nervous, noisy birds, had they been present. Probably therefore they had moved in during the day. They certainly wore an aston-

[1] P. A. Taverner. *Birds of Canada*. Published and copyrighted by The Musson Book Co. Ltd., Toronto.

ished look, as if they were not yet accustomed to their surroundings. But perhaps that was my imagination. In the next week two or three additional pairs arrived and they all remained in the neighbourhood. For several months afterwards Killdeers were amongst the most self-assertive residents of the creek and I shall write later about their character and habits.

Birds were not the only winged creatures who, in the last week of March, carried the message of spring to Brewery Creek. Several times I saw butterflies with reddish-brown wings flitting like lost spirits through the leafless woods. When they settled momentarily on the ground and spread their wings to sun themselves, rows of blue spots and yellow margins showed on the wings. So this was the pretty creature called Camberwell Beauty in England and Mourning Cloak in America. It is the largest butterfly to hibernate as an adult, finding crevices in which to shelter and sleep through the long, bitter winter. When the ground is released from ice and snow it wakes, stirs into life and sallies forth to bring a promise of warm sunshine to the earth.

6.

During these days the trees and shrubs were still bare skeletons. The bones of their trunks and branches had no flesh of leaves. Even their buds were still small and scarcely noticeable. The woods were half-transparent. You could see through their ranks of tree trunks to glimpses of landscape beyond.

The trees looked cold so long as snow remained at their feet. But gradually it disappeared. Colour began to enliven the shoreline. The browns of crushed grass, dead weeds

Photo by W. V. Crich, F.R.P.S.

COWBIRD EGGS
"The all-time high record is actually a five-storied nest."

and bare earth, the red of dogwood stems, the grey of maple trunks and the green of willows became vivid. Sunlight and showers of rain helped the process of reviving life. Grass became green, catkins stretched and shook like lamb's tails in the breeze, pretty flowers of elms and elders opened and the willow-stems turned golden-green. Overhead the fiery sun often hung in a flawless blue sky.

These hints and suggestions of the recovery of the world from its winter slumber coincided with increasing liveliness on the part of birds. Rivalry for territory amongst the cock Song Sparrows was intense. Occasionally disputes on the subject arose. If a bird was sure of its ground, it flew at any intruder and drove him helter-skelter beyond the territory's bounds. Sometimes, however, the issue was not so easily settled. Two Sparrows on the same territory might have more or less equal claims. The matter was then decided either by a short, sharp pitched battle or else by a leisurely chase. In the course of generations this latter procedure has become curiously formalized. One morning towards the end of March I watched an example of it.

Two cocks of apparently equal strength and resolution laid claim to the same area. I shall call one the challenger and one the defender of the title to the land. When I caught sight of them the defender was chasing the challenger. They flew deliberately, one behind the other, round and round the same small piece of ground, like athletes running successive laps over a race track. They travelled low over the grass, so low that their flight rose and fell with the hillocks and dips in the ground. Seldom deviating from a set course enclosing not more than twenty square yards, they went monotonously over it again and again. At one point the route cut through some sumach bushes. Each time the birds followed, as if automatically, the same twisting line in and out amongst the sumach stems. Occasionally the challenger alighted on a branch for a brief rest. The defender followed him and alighted on another branch close by. After a few moments he darted at his opponent again. The challenger promptly took wing, dropped towards grass-level and once more started flying over their chosen course.

In one sense both birds gave a demonstration of considerable energy. The defender was unflagging in the chase and the challenger tireless in evading him. Yet the whole affair also had an artificial air, as if it were mere play-acting. Neither bird made special exertions to fly fast. Their wings did not beat swiftly or strongly. On the contrary, the beats had a rather gentle quality. The wings were stretched horizontally, almost stiffly, and in that position made quick, fluttering or quivering movements which seemed hardly enough to keep the birds in the air.

The challenger made no real attempt to escape from his pursuer, as he could easily have done. He stayed on the set course and flew only a few inches ahead of his rival. It was as if this were a rule of their game. He clearly was not compelled to do it. Had he chosen, he could either have turned and violently attacked his pursuer or have bolted altogether from the field. But he wished neither to put the issue to the test of battle nor to abandon his chance of ultimate victory. So he continued his half-hearted, leisurely retreat, hoping no doubt that it would prove to be a case of *reculer pour mieux sauter*.

His rival was in a similar mood. He was not unduly irritated by half-measures and did not press his attack too eagerly. He followed faithfully every twist and turn of the challenger, yet made no savage rushes at him. His ire was aroused, but was under control. His tactics were Fabian. He hoped gradually to wear his enemy down.

Now and then the challenger swerved off the regular course and perched in an elm tree a few feet away. The other followed him as surely as if he were a piece of mechanism attached at a fixed distance behind. A third cock, who evidently regarded this tree as standing within his territory, immediately appeared and attacked them both. They promptly beat a retreat to their own ground, where they continued their chase as if nothing had disturbed it. This happened four or five times whilst I watched.

The pursuit continued as long as I remained there. It was still proceeding—energetic yet unhurried, persistent yet prudent—when at length I turned to go elsewhere. Sometimes these contests continue for several hours. Their monotony is relieved occasionally by the birds changing places. The pursued turns and becomes the pursuer and the pursuer obligingly allows himself to be pursued. In the end victory goes to the one with the greatest powers of endurance.

7.

Now the hens of various species were arriving and the next great crisis in bird life, courtship, began. So far as my observation went, the Cowbirds started it. On March 27th two pairs of Cowbirds in one tree were moved simultaneously by the emotions of love. Trust them to make an early beginning!

Cowbirds are undistinguished in appearance and unsavoury in habits. They are the smallest members of the Blackbird family in Canada. The males have iridescent black plumage from the tips of their tails to the base of their necks. Above that they wear a snuff-coloured hood. The females are uniformly ashy-brown, except for a lighter throat. The birds' dark eyes and short beaks are in keeping with this general dullness.

In the old days in the American West they were called Buffalo Birds. This name sprang from their habit of invariably associating with herds of buffalo. They roamed about familiarly with the Monarchs of the Prairie, strolling between their feet, under their bellies and even over their backs. But now the buffalo have almost disappeared. Domestic cattle have increased in their place. The birds have therefore transferred their attentions to the newcomers and the Buffalo Bird has become the Cowbird. No one seems to know exactly what attracts them to cattle, but no doubt the succulent flies and other insects which also keep the beasts company have something to do with it.

Cowbirds are over-sexed creatures. Whenever and wherever I saw them in the last days of March males and females alike were shamelessly egging each other on to love-making. On the ground a male would waddle unsteadily, with parted legs and drooping wings, towards a female, like a drunken wooer. In the meantime she stood with her neck stretched up and beak pointed skywards, as if inviting a kiss on the throat, though she was presumably merely inviting her lover to admire its pale colour.

When these posturings were performed not on firm earth but in the tree-tops—as they often were—they appeared even more clumsy. Sometimes I watched as many as half-a-dozen pairs of Cowbirds making public asses of themselves in one small tree. The females started by calling "Chuck" (or some such encouragement) gently and coaxingly to the members of the opposite sex. They did this with their necks craning skywards, as I have described. In eager response the males cried "Zee-zee" and began bowing their heads, drooping, opening and closing their wings and spreading their tails fanwise. They lost balance on the slender branches and in their excitement could scarcely prevent themselves from falling off the tree. To recapture their equilibrium they shut their wings and tails quickly. Then the females whispered "Chuck" again. The intoxicating sound promptly made the males forget themselves once more, and the stupid unbalancing trick was performed all over again. This undignified exhibition was repeated continuously, until the birds felt so frustrated that in exasperation they spread their wings and flew away.

These goings-on have a bad ending. The fact is that Cowbirds are not at all nice to know. In the first place they are the loosest, most disreputable characters in Canadian bird society. Love with them is no more than a casual "liaison". No male of the species is faithful to a female and no female is constant to a male. They are neither polygamous nor polyandrous, but just promiscuous. A cock will pick up any hen on any tree. The "Chuck" of every female is like the "D'you remember me, dearie?" of a harlot. Their union is as brief as it is merry and as carefree as it is short. Cowbirds never pair for a season.[1] They have no need to do so, since they assume none of the

[1] I understand that the above description does not apply in all respects to the Cowbirds of some regions. Dr. Herbert Friedman in his careful study of "The Cowbirds" states that those of Ithaca, New York, where their numbers are limited, were predominantly monogamous. Observers in most other districts where the species is generally more numerous have reported otherwise. I can vouch for the fact that the Cowbirds of Brewery Creek belong to the promiscuous school.

43

responsibilities attaching either to marriage or to parent-hood.

This is the second unorthodox fact about Cowbirds. They build no nest and establish no nursery of their own. When the time comes for a female to lay an egg she deposits it in the nest of some other bird who happens to be tempo-rarily away from home. Sometimes she devours one of the owner's eggs to make room for her product. No particular type of nest is thus honoured. Cowbirds' eggs have been found in the nest of more than a hundred different kinds of birds. But usually it is in a Sparrow's, a Vireo's or a Warbler's. Sometimes the bird imposed upon recognizes the odd egg and angrily flings it out. At other times she deserts and builds again elsewhere. Occasionally she erects a second nest on top of the first, and cases have been known where a third storey and even a fourth have been added above the lower ones, in each of which a Cowbird's egg had been laid. The all-time high record is actually a five-storied nest. The clever architects of these fantastic structures are generally Yellow Warblers.

Usually, however, the foster-parent incubates the stran-ger's egg as well as her own clutch. In due course the changeling hatches. Since the period of incubation of a Cowbird's egg is generally shorter than that of others, the youngster appears before its fellow-chicks. With this initial advantage, it grows larger and stronger than they do and eventually smothers, starves or ejects them. The poor, duped foster-parents lavish upon it all their affection and care and the youngster waxes strong. In about a week it can leave the nest and make its first attempts at flight. There is some-thing tragic in the sight of a pretty little Warbler feeding a loutish young Cowbird twice its own size.

Mature Cowbird hens have sometimes been seen feeding

fledgeling Cowbirds after the latter have left the nest. But these evidences of belated maternal conscience are rare. However, it is senseless to condemn Cowbirds. No bird should be judged by human standards of morality. If the Cowbird's conduct is cruel, it is also innocent. If it is wicked, it is also unwitting. The bird is a victim of a freak of evolution. Some circumstance of its life in the dim past has determined its unusual and disconcerting habits. No one can tell what is their origin. Some earnest searchers after truth have produced the theory that it began when Cowbirds were in truth Buffalo Birds. The birds, they argue, needed the company of buffalo in order to find sufficient insects to eat. But the buffalo herds were not static; they kept moving. This mobility made it impossible for Cowbirds to build nests and rear young in any set place. So they *had* to lay their eggs in other birds' nests and trust to luck that they would be hatched.

Perhaps there is something in this notion, but it can hardly be the whole truth. It assumes that all other Cowbirds, not only in North but also in Central and South America, who have similar irresponsible habits were likewise irrevocably attached to moving herds of animals. This may or may not have been so. But the theory does not explain the similar behaviour of English Cuckoos and other birds in various parts of the world who have no such dependence on cattle. Their conduct must spring from a more subtle biological cause.

Anyway, whatever the explanation is, Cowbirds are thorough parasites.

8.

One small bird with whom Cowbirds sometimes lodge their chicks is the Phoebe. This charming little Flycatcher

45

is another of the earliest spring migrants. A cock appeared in the creek on March 25th. I think I may have seen him immediately after his arrival. When I landed that morning and passed the old saw-mill there was no sign of him; but when I retraced my steps half-an-hour later I heard his call, "Phoe-be", oft-repeated. Then I saw him flitting restlessly from branch to branch in some elm trees beside the building, exactly as if he were inspecting the place from every angle. Occasionally he flew beneath the mill itself, where it juts beyond a high, sloping bank of earth and is supported by wooden beams on piles driven into the ground. The tops of these beams are ideal sites for a Phoebe's nest and on examination I saw the remains of two old nests there. Probably they had belonged to this very Phoebe and his mate in previous springs, for Phoebes generally return year after year to the same nesting site. It may well be that this particular bird had just arrived and was experiencing his first thrill of excitement at the rediscovery of old haunts.

During the succeeding days he had the air of one who is waiting at an agreed rendezvous for a friend. He was usually perched on a branch of the tree nearest to the nesting place. He sat bolt upright, giving an occasional characteristic, nervous jerk to his tail. Whenever he saw a passing insect he dashed out with a flight as light and airy as that of a butterfly, captured the victim and returned to his perch.

Sure enough, four mornings later a hen arrived. She is a rather smaller but otherwise almost exact replica of him, with the same dull olive back and wings and shaded white breast. Phoebes are not only early migrants, but also early nesters. The hen of this pair lost no time in considering various locations for their new home. Whilst the cock kept

watch in the trees, uttering his brisk, friendly call at intervals and occasionally darting into the air to cut short the
careers of passing flies, she spent her time fussing round
the dilapidated nests on the beams beneath the mill and
inspecting another possible site, where there was also an old
nest, in a small shed nearby. She seemed uncertain which
spot to choose.

Phoebes often start building two or three nests before
deciding which one is the most suitable for their purpose.
This Phoebe might therefore make a start in any of several
sites. The mill and the shed each had what an English
house-agent seeking to secure clients would call "a wealth
of old timber" beams. Both also stood beside a secluded
little bay in the creek with good shore-mud to help in nest
building, stagnant shallows where insects would hatch
plentifully to provide a natural larder, and clear water in
which the birds could indulge a Phoebe's passion for
bathing. This latter practice is popular with them partly, I
suspect, in order that they may periodically drown some of
the bird-lice which infest their ill-kept nests and must sorely
afflict their bodies.

9.

On the water as well as on shore signs of impending
pairing and nesting were evident before the end of March.
The American Mergansers did not contribute to these. The
drake and one of the ducks soon disappeared and put in no
further appearance. A solitary, so far unattended and
unloved female was left behind, swimming forlornly in the
creek.

The two pairs of American Golden-eye, on the other
hand, stayed and were joined a few days later by others of

their kind. Their numbers varied. Sometimes three pairs, sometimes four, sometimes five and sometimes six were on the water. Occasionally an extra duck accompanied them. As I have indicated, when passerine birds migrate the majority of the males of a species precede most of the females. They settle on the breeding ground and establish their territories before looking for mates. Only after that does pairing occur. With wildfowl the practice is different. The sexes migrate in mixed flocks together and often a drake chooses his duck long before they arrive jointly at their nesting place.

The Golden-eye in the creek had not come to stay, but merely made a halt on their way elsewhere. Invariably they swam in a group together, cruising about and diving. Often the drakes added a certain amount of wooing to these more unemotional activities. Their amorous inclinations were unaffected by weather. Some days were foul, but rain could not damp nor wind cool their awakening ardour. Whether the water were calm and they floated serenely before their enchantresses, or it were rough and their poise was disturbed by the constant slapping and heaving of wild little waves, they went through the strange antics of a male Golden-eye in love.

Much bird courtship "display" is fantastic in appearance. The origins of the strange assortment of acrobatics and contortions which different species perform as an introduction, an invitation, an inducement to mating are lost far back in bird evolution. Obviously their purpose is to attract the woo-ed's attention to the wooer. To achieve this the display is usually so contrived that in its course any particularly pleasing patch of colour in the bird's plumage, or on its beak or legs, is shown to advantage. But the attraction

48

must not be just coldly aesthetic. It must be such as to arouse the conjugal instincts of the hoped-for mate. It must be whatever in bird life is suggestive. It may even appear pornographic. This is no doubt the explanation of many extravagant and even clownish gestures, which would only make human beings roar with laughter but which apparently, in the right circumstances, fill birds with sexual desire.

The display of American Gold-eyes is an excellent example of this curious aspect of bird behaviour. As early as March 27th the drakes of four pairs, swimming in a close group together, were all making love to the ducks. Each performed to the female whom he favoured at the moment. When rebuffed he promptly repeated the action before another female. Any one seemed to do. The following is an account of what he did. Swimming purposefully towards her, he puffed out the feathers of his crown and cheeks so that his black head and white cheek spots seemed swollen like a small balloon on top of his sleek, white neck. The neck was stretched forwards and the head thrust down. Occasionally his chin and beak dipped into the water. When he came close to the female he suddenly, with a sharp movement, raised his head erect, and exposed his snow-white breast. Stretching his neck to its uttermost length and turning his face skywards, he then opened his beak and uttered a harsh, virile cry. Immediately afterwards the neck snapped abruptly backwards, as if it were broken, until the back of his head touched his rump. After a pause he jerked his head and neck quickly forward again to their normal position. Thus composed once more, he studied the effect of his performance on his audience.

That day the effect was nil. None of the ducks were interested. They swam on without moving a muscle or

49

turning a feather, other than was needed for that customary occupation. For that matter, the drakes themselves seemed rather half-hearted, for in between spasms of violent exhibitionism they floated about calmly and dived for food. They appeared rather absent-minded lovers. I did not notice any of them perform the final act of the full Golden-eye display, which should be as follows. After the bird's neck has been cricked back into place at the close of the convulsions already described he should spring forwards and upwards, kicking the water into a splash behind him and revealing his bright orange legs. That extreme bid for favour often wins him his prize. The duck then lets her head and neck fall upon the water, whilst her relaxed, limp body drifts upon its surface as if she had collapsed in a dead faint. The drake can then do as he wills with her.

But the year was still young. Spring was only on its way. March was apparently too early for that sort of thing. Although in the following days I often saw the drakes throwing their necks backwards and forwards in a passionate frenzy of desire, none of the ducks, so far as I could observe, showed the slightest tendency to swoon.

CHAPTER FIVE

APRIL

I.

IF MARCH came in like a lamb, it went out like a lion. A few days before the end of the month the weather changed. For more than a fortnight warm, sunlit days had succeeded each other with almost monotonous regularity. The last lingering patches of snow dissolved. On the afternoons of the 24th and 25th I actually sun-bathed. It seemed almost too good to be true—and it proved definitely too good to last. On March 28th the sun withdrew behind thick clouds, the temperature dropped many degrees and the weather returned to a more seasonable mood. For more than a week it remained cold, wet and gusty.

One morning at the beginning of April such a gale of wind blew that I could not set out in my canoe at all. On another morning the breeze was so strong that on my return journey from the creek I was blown out of my course and had to abandon the canoe, leaving it tied to a tree some way down river. On yet another morning a thick mist lay over the water and I got lost. Starting complacently into the fog, I felt sure that I could easily find the opposite shore. A slight wind gave a bias to the direction of the canoe, which I thought that I could correct by judicious strokes of the paddle.

After five minutes' progress the familiar notes of a Song Sparrow came to me through the enveloping mist. Triumphantly I set my course by the song, steering straight at it. I made a bet with myself that the bird was sitting on a particular tree, where one often perched close to the shore of Brewery Creek. As I drew near the voice the shadowy outline of the river bank formed in the mist ahead, topped by the silhouette of an imposing building. This was surprising, for no such edifice existed in the creek. On closer inspection it turned out to be the French Embassy, lying a quarter-of-a-mile downstream from Earnscliffe—on the same side of the river!

I altered course and plunged back into the mist. This time my aim was truer. The next Song Sparrow that I heard was, sure enough, an inhabitant of the creek.

One day, later in the month, the elements played another trick with me. The morning was cold and frosty, with a steady wind blowing across the river from the Quebec to the Ontario shore. I had rather a struggle to get to Brewery Creek, for the going was hard and the canoe bucked and plunged like a steer. By dint of firm paddling, however, I reached my goal, beached the canoe and stepped ashore.

After an hour's bird-watching I embarked for the return journey. To get some initial speed I stuck the blade of my paddle into the mud and pushed. The paddle remained rooted and slipped from my hand. I had not the presence of mind to jump overboard whilst the water was shallow, to recover it. A few seconds later, when I thought of doing this, I was too late. The wind had blown the canoe away from shore and the craft was rocking mischievously in ruffled water out of my depth. As the water was freezing cold, I did not feel inclined for total immersion.

I had not brought a second paddle. This was a foolish and flagrant breach of an elementary rule of intelligent canoeing.

The sensitive, playful craft drifted ever further from land. I sat in it helpless, wondering whether I could do anything to restore my mastery over events—or even to influence them slightly. But this seemed impossible. The canoe, the wind and the water could do as they pleased with me. They could make what sport they liked. The shore which I had left receded rapidly, and the opposite bank was far distant. Between me and it lay a wide expanse of river, tossing with petulant waves. I was adrift in an indifferent, if not unfriendly world. I imagined myself being carried into mid-channel and then borne by the current downstream all day towards Buckingham, Rigaud, Hawkesbury and other towns on the way to Montreal. For a moment my mind dwelt on the broad St. Lawrence, the Strait of Belle Isle and the great Atlantic beyond. But this, I reflected, was stupid. I should never see even Montreal for the famous Lachine rapids—so wild that the fur-traders in their palmy days did not dare to shoot them—would swallow me up en route.

Whilst thus ruminating I realized that the wind was blowing the canoe straight into the middle of the river and towards the opposite shore. Its aim, however, was, from my point of view, defective. The craft was not steering properly for Earnscliffe. Dipping a hand into the water, I started paddling to correct the direction. The current was troublesome as the canoe and I went across, constantly trying to push us out of our way. But the breeze remained steady and friendly. By paddling sometimes with one hand, sometimes with the other and sometimes with both I kept the right course. My fingers grew icy cold and numb, but what did that matter? Within a quarter of an hour of starting I landed safely in Earnscliffe garden.

53

I am aware that no one will believe this story, but it happens to be true.

2.

April 5th was a freezing day. Ice formed again along the edges of the river and blinding snow flurries blew across the land. Next day the weather improved and for a while it hovered uncertainly between being good and bad. The buds took advantage of any hours of warmth. Soon they burst and the trees were covered with infant leaves. The first wild flowers appeared on the banks of the creek—a few small Dandelions and a patch of Strawberries whose petals look like little bits of white paper neatly cut out and glued on to their stalks.

But the weather did not make a permanent recovery. On the contrary, it soon had another severe relapse. A sharp frost bound the earth on the morning of the 15th and covered the quiet little bays in the creek with fresh ice. This cold spell continued for ten days. Then the temperature rose suddenly to 50°, but with the new mood came rain. For close on four weeks afterwards rain hardly ever ceased pelting down. The temperature was variable, but a chill wind usually blew and the sky was almost permanently laden with dark rain-clouds. So much rain has never been concentrated on Ottawa in a few weeks before.

These vagaries of the weather had a marked effect on bird migration. When the fine, warm days of March ended and were followed by a period of changeable temperatures the movement did not cease, but it slowed down. When these conditions were in turn succeeded by a severe, cold spell migration first dropped to almost nothing and then for a while ceased altogether.

54

Photo by W. V. Crich, F.R.P.S.

KILLDEER PLOVER
"They build no structure to hold their eggs, but merely select a slight hollow in the ground."

The timing of the first spring migration is largely determined by temperature. The following figures illustrate the point. In the dozen warm, sunlit days in the second half of March, fifteen new species arrived in the creek. In the rather longer period of mixed weather—partly mild, partly cold—which followed, another fifteen species came. In the succeeding ten frosty days only three new migrants appeared and in the next ten days of rain and cold winds the figure fell to nought.

The fact is that the good weather which came in the middle of March was about a month earlier than usual. Spring was prematurely born. Amongst other consequences the earliest bird migrants came ahead of their time. They were taken in by the spell of warmth. Many species who do not usually arrive in the neighbourhood of Ottawa until the second half of April were already there in the last week of March.

Then the weather deteriorated. In Ottawa and elsewhere it reverted to more customary temperatures and the later wave of migrants felt no inducement to leave the sunny south and make the long journey north. They waited until their normal time in May. A long gap in migration occurred.

The list of new arrivals in the creek in March was therefore unusually long and that for April unusually short. The April record reads as follows. On the 1st of the month two Buffle-head ducks alighted off-shore. On the 3rd a Slate-coloured Junco arrived. Next day a Pigeon Hawk was hunting in the region. On the 6th a small party of Lesser Scaup, a Ring-billed Gull, a Savannah Sparrow and a Downy Woodpecker appeared upon the scene. On the 7th some Purple Finches and a Tree Sparrow joined the

55

throng and on the 8th came a brace of Black Duck, a brace of Ring-necked Duck and a gaggle of Canada Geese. On the following morning some Red-breasted Mergansers were on the water. On the 10th a few Field Sparrows and a Mallard drake visited the creek, followed the next day by a pair of Wood Duck. A Tree Swallow flew in on the 14th. On the 19th a Barn Swallow arrived. On the 22nd an Old-squaw duck was swimming with the other ducks and two mornings later a couple of Spotted Sandpipers landed on the shore. After that the rain storms started and no new species appeared for another ten days.

3.

Not all these birds were migrants. Some Downy Wood-peckers, for example, stay in Ottawa all the year round, although their numbers increase at migration times. In all seasons they are models of industry, seldom seeming to rest so long as daylight lasts from their labour of chiselling into tree trunks to extract noxious insects. These activities have excellent results on the health of the trees as well as on that of the birds. Downy Woodpeckers are the smallest North American Woodpeckers. Their piebald, black and white plumage adorned with a splash of red on the males' heads is almost identical with that of their larger relative, the Hairy Woodpecker.

The Pigeon Hawk who visited the creek may also have been a resident in the district, for occasionally members of the species stay through the winter. This small falcon measures less than a foot long, but the spread of its sharp-pointed wings is more than twice that length. Occasionally one came to the creek to indulge in one of its favourite pas-times, chasing Blackbirds.

56

The other birds mentioned above were definitely migrants. Some had made comparatively short trips of only a few hundred miles and others were accomplishing immense journeys covering thousands of miles. Some had reached their journey's end when they arrived in the Ottawa region, but others halted there for only a brief stay on their way further north.

Amongst passerine birds the Slate-coloured Juncos belonged to the latter class. They are members of the same avian order as the numerous tribes of Sparrows. Their pale, pinkish bills, sharply contrasting dark upper parts and light lower parts, and the broad white outer edges to the fans of their tails are unlike the markings of any other small bird. In winter they congregate in suitable areas throughout the United States and southern Canada, but with the return of Spring they transport themselves wholesale to the northern States and beyond, with a strong preference for Alaska, the Canadian far north and Labrador. Many travel to the edge of the Barren lands before settling down to breed. Several stayed in the creek for the greater part of April before flying on.

The Tree Sparrows did not tarry so long. They are prettily marked birds, as Sparrows go. Their grey heads have bold chestnut stripes, on each side of their chests is a rusty brown patch and on their wings are two white bars. But their most distinctive mark is the dusky spot in the centre of their clean, light breasts. They too favour the further north for nesting and remained in the creek only for the middle fortnight of April.

Field Sparrows are rare visitors in Ottawa. One morning a few lodged for a while in a group of small trees on the creek bank. I never saw them again, but their reddish heads and back, spotless breasts and especially their light pink bills were unmistakeable.

Purple Finches are not always easily distinguishable from other streaked Sparrows. The strong wash of rosy-red on the plumage of adult males is recognizable enough, but this attractive decoration is lacking in the females and in immature birds of both sexes. However, the female's large bill is a clue to its real identity and enabled me to recognize the couple who visited the creek one morning on their way to the northern coniferous forests, where they would find mates.

Of the new Sparrows only the Savannah Sparrows settled in Ottawa for the summer. I shall write of them later. The Tree Swallows likewise came to stay. They had already travelled further than any of the Sparrows, for in winter they enjoy the sunshine of Mexico, Cuba, and the southern United States. Some continue their spring migration as far as Alaska in the west and Labrador in the east, but generally they shun the far north.

They are the most companionable of the April migrants, both to themselves and to mankind. I write "April migrants", for normally they come into that group and I happened to see none in Brewery Creek until April 14th. Actually they had arrived earlier. When the weather turns warm prematurely they migrate sooner and sometimes suffer heavy casualties from cold spells which follow. This year they were amongst the birds deceived by the spring-like spell of weather in March. A Tree Swallow appeared in my garden at Earnscliffe on March 30th and on the following day a flock of about twenty, evidently new arrivals, were flying round excitedly in drizzling rain.

The male's glossy blue-black head, neck and back, sooty

black wings and tail and immaculate white chin, breast and belly are pleasing. The female's adornment is only slightly duller. But even more charming than the birds' appearance is their character. Their graceful liveliness in the air, their habit of perching fearlessly close by you, and their constant twittering chatter make them particularly friendly creatures. In the second half of April they came in large numbers to the creek, where squadrons of them soared and swooped over the water as they hawked for flies.

The other species of Swallow which arrived in April had made an even longer journey than its cousin. Barn Swallows resort to Southern California and Florida, Central America and South America, even going as far as Chile and Argentina, for the winter. In summer they settle anywhere from Mexico north to Alaska, the Hudson Bay regions and Labrador. So not only the sky but also the continent is the limit of their vast migrations. The Barn Swallow is the beauty of Canadian Swallows. Its graceful, stream-lined figure with glossy, steel-blue crown and back, chestnut forehead and chin, pinkish underparts and deeply forked, white-spotted tail make it everything that a Swallow should be.

Some of the most extensive bird migrations are accomplished by wild fowl, the greatest of them involving flights of several thousand miles. Of these I shall write in a later section.

4.

Although the colder weather which marked April slowed down the arrival of new species, it did not cause those who had already arrived to withdraw. Only the Killdeers disappeared for a few days. The party of sociable Golden-eye, one or two Mergansers and numerous Herring

Gulls stayed on the water. On land, Crows, Starlings, Song Sparrows and Robins remained plentiful, whilst a Tree Sparrow, a Flicker or two, the pair of Phoebes and some Meadowlarks were usually somewhere in sight. Blackbirds increased greatly in numbers. In the first few days of April a veritable invasion of Bronzed Grackles, Red-winged Blackbirds, Rusty Blackbirds and Cowbirds occurred.

Red-winged Blackbirds especially crowded the trees along the water's edge, filling the bare branches as if with dark leaves. I could hear their noise half-a-mile away. Blackbird society is one of those democracies in which liberty of speech has declined into licence to screech, where everyone is an orator and no one an audience. The assembly in the creek all yelled at once. Their conversation was as deafening as the babel in a monkey-house in a Zoo. Much of this was sheer garrulousness. But part of the outcry was, to a Blackbird's way of thinking—or rather feeling, for birds do not think much—the winsome language of love. The hens had arrived and the cocks had caught the mood of the moment and were busy making proposals of marriage. Fortunately most of them soon drifted away to breeding grounds elsewhere. But for some days their raucous din was the predominant sound in the creek, drowning even the music of the Song Sparrows.

This was not entirely due to talkativeness on the part of the Blackbirds. It derived also from a quieter mood amongst the Sparrows. By now they had ceased to greet the dawn with their chorus of loud song. The fact was that they had progressed to another stage in the yearly cycle of their lives. The boundaries of their respective territories were established and mutually recognized. The hens had arrived and been duly attracted. So singing became less important.

The birds were otherwise engaged. Pairing was taking place. Song plays only a secondary part in the male Song Sparrow's technique in courtship and love-making. Mrs. Margaret Nice—whose devoted study of Song Sparrows through many years at her home in Columbus, Ohio, has made her the classic authority on the species—writes that the males "sing almost constantly until joined by a mate, when singing abruptly drops to almost zero". Later she adds, "The arrival of a male on his nesting grounds . . . is a conspicuous thing, for he himself sings his loudest. . . . The arrival of a female is the converse. . . . Indeed, I often say to myself on nearing a territory where silence reigns over-night, 'such and such a male must be either dead or married', and upon careful search I find either two birds or none."[1]

So the decline in Song Sparrows' singing at the beginning of April was evidence that they were in undisputed possession of their homes, had selected their mates and embarked on domestic life. Occasionally I caught a glimpse of their courtship. The male of each species of bird has its own particular method of wooing. A cock Song Sparrow draws his mate's attention to himself by forceful means. Swooping down suddenly upon her from above, he collides or nearly collides with her and immediately flies away, singing loudly. This bravado pleases her and in due course induces her to encourage greater familiarity. Eventually she is in a mood for copulation and indicates it in the frankest possible manner. Whilst alternately stretching and fluttering first one wing and then the

[1] Margaret Morse Nice, *Studies of the Life History of Song Sparrows.* The Linnaean Society of New York.

other, she sticks her tail straight up in the air and so uncovers her posterior. The male readily avails himself of the invitation thus lewdly extended.

I watched these proceedings in the second week of April. By the middle of the month the hens had started making nests. They flew with wisps of building material held in their beaks. Before the end of the month the first set of nests must have been built and some of the first clutches of eggs laid. I did not look for them. They lie hidden in the long grass and it is easier for clumsy feet to destroy than for keen eyes to see them. In any case, there would be plenty of time later for watching nests, since Song Sparrows are prolific producers of nests and eggs. Most pairs rear three and some even four families in a season.

5.

The general laws of migration, pairing, nesting and rearing young families regulate the lives of most birds, but there is no uniformity in their detailed application. On the contrary, almost infinite variety distinguishes the practices of different species. Thus Song Sparrows usually have three and sometimes four broods in a year, whereas most species are content to produce one or at most two. A difference like this is partly responsible for other differences. The necessity for Song Sparrows to be on their breeding ground long enough to hatch and bring up so many young families helps to explain, no doubt, their early arrival in spring. Less fecund birds need not be in such a hurry. They can delay their migration longer. So the time-tables of birds' lives vary. Some arrive on their breeding grounds, mate, build nests and lay eggs before others so much as put in an appearance.

For example, the Savannah Sparrows in Brewery Creek were two or three weeks behind the Song Sparrows. The latter had selected their territories and begun pairing before the first Savannah Sparrow set foot in the place. I saw one, a solitary male, on April 6th. He had only arrived that morning, yet was already perched on top of a grassy hillock staking out his claim to territory. His title deeds also were a song. Its theme was the same as the Song Sparrow's, but the voice and music were very different. They had none of the brazen, ringing tones of the other bird. The Savannah Sparrow's effort was modest, consisting of a few *pianissimo* phrases which ended with a louder little trill. Yet to other cock Savannah Sparrows—if any had been there to hear—it would presumably have sounded as a resounding challenge.

The gentleness of the performance was in keeping with the character of the bird. The Savannah Sparrow seems in every way as unpretentious as its song. Its striped plumage of quiet browns is unassuming, in spite of yellow "eyebrows". Nor does the bird fly with boisterous self-assurance through the air and alight near the top of a tree to announce its presence noisily to the world. It keeps near the ground, creeping surreptitiously amongst the long grasses. When it takes wing it usually flies for only a short distance and does not rise more than a few inches above the wild-flower tops. It does not often perch in trees at all, but proclaims its proprietorship of territory from a convenient stone, or tussock or stem of a weed protruding above the rank grasses. From such a humble vantage point it makes its important little declaration to the world, tilting up its head, opening its beak and pouring forth its song as lustily as it can—which, as I have already indicated, is not saying much.

It is a rather confiding, trustful bird, allowing one to approach near before it interrupts its singing and flies away.

A few days after the arrival of the first cock Savannah Sparrow a second appeared and took up a neighbouring territory. Both could be seen and heard any morning after that, advertising their respective properties. For some days this couple were the sole holders of Savannah Sparrow rights in the area. Then more males arrived.

So far as I could ascertain no hens came until the 21st. That morning a considerable agitation disturbed the Savannah Sparrow colony. During the previous night a fresh wave of migration of the birds had reached Brewery Creek. It included, I think, both males and females, for their behaviour seemed to indicate that a new crisis had arisen in their affairs. In the first place, the song of the males had distinctly changed its tune. It had grown harsher in tone and into it at short intervals came an unpleasant sounding "Buzz . . . buzz . . . buzz". Mr. Forbush[1] says that this note is employed when two birds are "quarrelling". The change was undoubtedly mainly due to the fact that so many males had now arrived that competition amongst them for territory was keen; but perhaps some contests were not for the ownership of territory but for the possession of wives.

In the second place the birds were restless and kept chasing each other. Most of the chases were of one cock by another, each trying to keep a rival out of his selected territory. These were similar to the Song Sparrow's formalized contest which I had watched almost a month earlier and have already described. One bird would flutter away

[1] E. H. Forbush, *The Birds of Massachusetts and other New England States.* Massachusetts Department of Agriculture.

64

before the other, fast enough to elude his clutches but not
so fast as to avoid him altogether.

Savannah Sparrow society thus seemed to reach towards
the end of April the same situation as Song Sparrow society
had reached at the end of March. Neither the exact bounds
of the various territories nor the definite rights of particular males over particular females had yet been established.
A double process of fighting and flirting had to be accomplished before these matters were fixed for the new breeding
season. The consequent agitation in the colony continued
for several days. Then everything seemed orderly and
quiet, so no doubt the period of transition and adjustment
was over and the Savannah Sparrows settled down contentedly to married life.

The Song Sparrow country and the Savannah Sparrow
country were neighbouring but distinct. I never saw a
Savannah Sparrow in the wide area where the Song Sparrows were nesting and only once or twice met a Song Sparrow in the region which the Savannah Sparrows appro-
priated to themselves. This was not due so much to the
belligerent nature of Song Sparrows—who are inclined to
drive away other species of their own size and even a size
or two larger—as to the taste of the two species for different
types of territory. Song Sparrows prefer rough ground
plentifully sprinkled with shrubs and occasional trees whilst
Savannah Sparrows favour open fields or meadowland.

Areas of these two kinds lie contiguous to each other
near the point of land where the creek meets the river. I
could walk for two hundred yards over ground covered
with rank grass, bushes and trees and pass continuously from
the territory of one Song Sparrow to another. Each
property covered about half an acre. No Savannah Sparrow

was to be seen or heard there. Then I stepped from a line of young trees into open, meadow-like country stretching for another hundred yards or more along the riverbank. Song Sparrows were absent from it, but Savannah Sparrows were common. Before the war the place was being developed as a park, but work on it had been stopped. A half-finished, weed-covered road curved across an area of rough grass, with a curbstone running along its edge. The cock Savannah Sparrows used this curb as a singing ground. As I strolled along the road and passed from the territory of one bird to the next, each proprietor in turn sang his declaration of ownership to me. I called the place Savannah Sparrow Row.

6.

Other birds were also starting domestic life. Well before the end of April male Robins could be seen defending their territories from each other and female Robins were constructing nests. Red-winged Blackbirds and Bronzed Grackles were similarly employed. A pair of Tree Swallows took up their habitations in a nesting box nailed to a telegraph pole, whilst Starlings were busy popping in and out of tree-holes, carrying bits of grass to furnish their homes.

More decorative than any of these were a pair of Northern Flickers. Flickers are rather large birds belonging to the Woodpecker family. Their plumage is striking and gay. In most respects the sexes are alike, with a slate-grey crown, a red bar across the nape, a black gorget, a fawn-coloured back and wings streaked with black, light underparts richly speckled with black spots, a white rump and bright yellow shafts to the wing- and tail-feathers. The whole under-surfaces of the wings and tails are also bright

66

yellow and have earned the bird the name Golden-winged Woodpecker. The only obvious distinction in marking between the sexes is a black "moustache" stretching from the side of the male's beak across his cheeks, an adornment which the female lacks.

These attractive birds have a loud, merry call. I often heard it in mid-April issuing from a sumach thicket on the creek bank. Following the sound, I was sure to find one or both Flickers crouching against the sumach stems, greedily pecking at clusters of hairy red fruit which at that season are amongst their favourite foods.

The joyous spring notes of the male's voice are not his only love call. Another is the loud tattoo which he beats with his bill on resonant bits of wood or metal. The bird in the creek often took his stance on the roof of the saw-mill and drummed a bold rat-a-tat-tat on its tin-covered chimney. This lusty declaration of his passion was long sustained and oft-repeated. Sometimes his mate sat nearby to listen. They were rarely far apart and evidently greatly enjoyed each other's company. When one flew with characteristic, undulating, Woodpeckerish swoops across an open space, the other usually followed a few moments afterwards. The first was the female and the second the male. He was wooing her. Their progress was constantly marked by his merry cries of endearment. He was very much in love. In due course he got his way and they became betrothed.

I have already referred to the black moustache which distinguished him from his mate. This moustache of the cock Flicker was the subject some time ago of a celebrated experiment. Those conducting it were seeking knowledge on one of the many little problems which intrigue scientific ornithologists. How do male and female birds of a species recognize each other? For us human beings the marks of recognition between them are generally differences in plumage. But for the birds themselves other distinctions may exist, either more important or supplementary to these. We should not make the mistake of assuming that what influences us necessarily influences birds in any sphere of conduct. Human beings and birds are entirely different creatures, governed in many things by different laws.

It is in fact established that for many birds the posture and movements of individuals are at least as important aids to sex recognition as are distinctions of plumage. The interplay of these various elements in the case of Flickers was interestingly illustrated by the experiments to which I have referred.

A pair of Flickers had settled down to domestic life. Their partnership was in its early stages, but the supreme intimacy had begun between them. At that point the experimenters caught the "moustacheless" female, attached a false moustache to her face and released her again.

The male bird appeared, approached her from behind and mounted her. This indicated that her posture attracted him and conveyed to him that she was his mate. At that moment, however, she looked round and he caught sight of her moustache. Immediately he adopted an attitude of aggressive masculine display, attacking her and driving her away. The poor female could not understand this sudden change of mood, this cruel loss of temper in her partner. She kept trying to return to him. But each time he treated her as a rival male invading his territory. For two and a half hours he kept chasing her off their premises, with every sign of violent affront and jealousy.

68

Then the authors of the experiment recaptured her, removed the moustache and set her free again. When next she flew to her mate he greeted her with warm affection.

So the moustache or lack of it in a Flicker is a decisive means of establishing its sex in the eyes of its own kind. Even a false moustache can have such a powerful effect on the mind or emotions of a bird that, for a long time at least, it more than counterbalances the influence of all the other little indications of posture or behaviour which reveal the true sex of the disguised creature.

When I think of this incident in the life of Flickers I am reminded of a story which Leonard Brockington, the noble orator and charming raconteur, tells. Once upon a time a man walked up to a complete stranger and said, "You'd be the dead spit of my sister, if it weren't for the moustache."

"What's that you're saying?" asked the stranger, puzzled.

"You'd be the dead spit of my sister," repeated the first man, "if it weren't for the moustache."

"You idiot," retorted the other, "I haven't got a moustache."

"I know," answered the first, "But my sister has."

7.

By the beginning of April the Phoebes had abandoned any intention that they may have entertained of making their nest on a rafter under the mill. They decided to build instead on a roof-beam in the little shed close by. When I approached the place on April 1st both birds flew hurriedly out of the shed, one after the other. I did not on that occasion enter it, for fear of frightening them in the early stages of their enterprise and causing them to desert.

A week later the hen was busy building. In the family economy of Phoebes (and of many other species) the female is generally the nest builder. One morning I peered into the shed to see how she was getting on. She was away. I entered and saw that she had started work on the untidy remains of the earlier nest. Already a new layer of moss and grass had been added to its top. Whilst I stood inspecting the structure from below (it was beyond my reach) she flew into the shed. Not expecting an intruder, she hurried straight towards the nest with some wisps of grass held in her beak. Then she noticed me, swerved quickly away from the nest, flew once round the inside of the shed uttering wild alarm calls and darted out through the doorway. When I emerged she was sitting anxiously in a small tree close to the entrance.

That day she must have worked hard, for when I visited the shed again next morning the untidy pile of nest had grown considerably higher. I withdrew and stood hidden behind a bush for half-an-hour, watching her on the job. Her mate was also in the vicinity, but he took no part whatever in the nest building. Neither that morning nor at any other time did I see him lift a feather to help her. He sat on a bough somewhere more or less in the neighbourhood, no doubt doing sentry duty. Sometimes he was so far away that he did not seem to be performing it very conscientiously. However, that would probably be an unfair conclusion to draw, for wherever he was he could command a wide view of the region and spy the approach of likely enemies. In any case he was within hearing of a call from his spouse. His work required no particular energy. Occasionally he shifted his position from one tree to another and sometimes he made a swift, fluttering sortie into the air

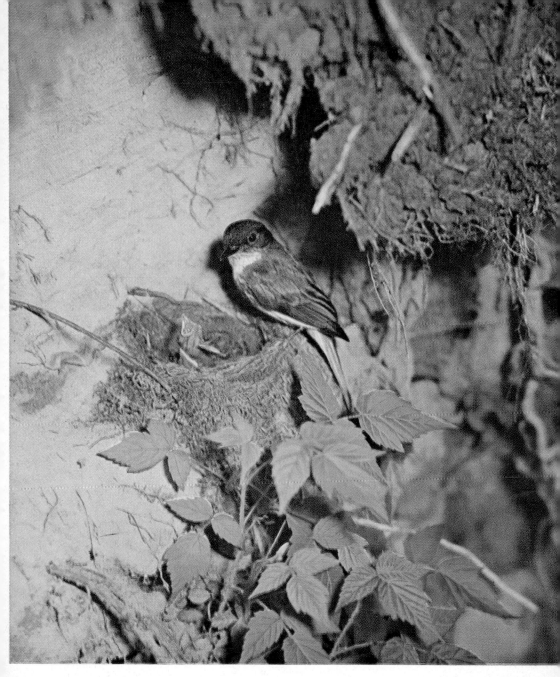

Photo by W. V. Crich, F.R.P.S.

PHOEBE
"The female is always the nest builder."

to catch a passing fly. Otherwise his was a passive, lazy role demanding no manual labour. The hen bore that part of the task.

She remained busily at work all the time that I watched, flying continuously in and out of the shed. Every few minutes she arrived with a fresh load of building materials carried in her bill, disappeared into the shed and remained there for a while. No doubt she went straight to the nest, unloaded the material and wove it into the growing structure. Then she would come flying out again, with the air of one exceedingly occupied and having no time to waste. Almost invariably she alighted first on a twig near the door and glanced round to make sure that no unwelcome eyes were watching her. Afterwards she flew quickly and purposefully to one of the "quarries" where she collected her building material. She visited several of these. I could see her tugging at bits and pieces of dead grass or weeds on the ground, loosening them from the matted tangle of old growth which had lain crushed beneath the snow all winter. When she had disengaged the required strands she flew back to the shed. Sometimes she made the journey in one direct flight, but at other times she hesitated for a cautious, momentary look-round at each of several points on a regular route from the quarries to the nest. She was indefatigable in her labours.

Two mornings later she was still making periodic visits to the shed, but they were less regular and frequent. Nor did she now carry anything in her beak. Probably she had finished building and merely went every now and then to cast an eye on her handiwork. Perhaps she sought to make little improvements in its structure. If this was her aim, she did not, at any rate from the aesthetic point of view of a human being, achieve much. The nest never looked anything but an untidy and unsightly heap of rubbish.

For ten days both birds hung about the neighbourhood, passing the time companionably before the hen should retire to incubate her eggs. During this period she was laying them. I am not certain on what date she produced the first, for I had no means of climbing to her nest. But the following chain of facts indicates that it must have been about the 20th. Phoebes (like other birds) usually lay one egg each day until the set is complete, and they do not start sitting until the whole clutch is laid. I afterwards ascertained that this Phoebe laid five eggs and started incubating them on either the 25th or the 26th. Those dates are several days ahead of the usual Phoebe schedule, for the mother bird does not normally commence laying so far north as Ottawa until the end of the month.

After she commenced sitting I visited the shed every morning and saw her enthroned in its shadowy interior, half hidden on top of her little stack. Hour after hour and day after day she demonstrated the remarkable patience of a parent bird performing the tedious task of hatching young. The father was usually perched somewhere in the sunshine outside, not far away. Every now and then he exclaimed with a complacent air, "Phoebe . . . phoebe."

8.

A few other birds were equally precocious. Amongst them were the Killdeers, who remained the only shore birds in the creek until some Spotted Sandpipers arrived in the last week of April.

Two or three pairs of Killdeers were well established before the middle of the month. The species are early nesters. They are also cunning nesters—if they can be called "nesters" at all. They build no structure to hold their eggs, but merely select a slight hollow in the ground, increasing it perhaps by the pressure of their bodies, and deposit in it their eggs. Occasionally they line this simple home with a few pebbles or stalks, but as often as not they leave the place as they found it. The drab ground colour and dark streaks and speckles of the pear-shaped eggs give them excellent camouflage. It is difficult to pick them out from their surroundings.

I never found a Killdeer's eggs. But in the second week of April and frequently in succeeding weeks parent birds betrayed that I was not far from their eggs or their chicks. Sometimes they merely ran or flew nervously over the ground, uttering alarm calls with monotonous iteration. At other times, probably when I was dangerously near their treasures, their action was more elaborate and complex. Then they treated me to the famous performance in which birds attract you away from the nests by dragging themselves over the ground with fluttering wings. They are popularly supposed to be pretending to be wounded. But this explanation seems to me questionable. Let me first describe the Killdeer's action and then comment upon it.

On two occasion in April I witnessed it on the shore of the creek. On the first occasion, the 10th of the month, only one bird was concerned. Previously any Killdeers about the place had flown away with protesting cries at my approach. This time, however, the bird made no attempt to fly. It maintained a continuous piping, eloquent of extreme agitation, but stayed deliberately on the ground at no great distance from me. First it crouched close to the earth, as if sitting on a nest. After a few moments it started

73

jerking its body up and down, alternately sitting, standing and sitting again several times in rapid succession. Its back was turned towards me, but it held its head sideways and eyed me intently. For quite a while, without moving from the spot, it continued these violent motions of its body. All the time it kept uttering insistent calls. In fact, by voice and movement it was trying hard to attract my attention.

When I took no notice it rose, ran a dozen paces forwards, then crouched again and repeated the performance. It still gazed at me, almost appealingly. After a while, when I obstinately maintained an apparent indifference, it began to vary its body movements. They became wilder and more abandoned. Sinking its body to the ground, the bird half-opened its wings and held them away from its back in a bedraggled, drooping fashion, at the same time depressing its tail and spreading the tail-feathers fanwise. In this position its bright, orange-brown rump and the tail's decorative white edge were fully revealed. Occasionally it fluttered a wing or flirted its tail. The bird appeared to be in difficulty, as if it were hurt and helpless. This was, indeed, the celebrated action sometimes described as a bird acting a broken wing, feigning being wounded. But to me it looked more like a particularly brazen piece of courtship display. I shall have more to say about that presently.

The Killdeer never remained still for more than a few moments at a time. It kept ringing the changes between these different posturings in what could only be described as a desperate attempt to catch my attention. When at length I gave it the satisfaction of following it, it still did not fly away, but retreated over the ground ahead of me, stopping every now and then to repeat its agitations and tempt me further.

On the second occasion when I watched any sustained effort of this sort, ten days later, two Killdeers were involved. When I arrived on the shore one bird was there. At my approach it betrayed the customary excited alarm. First it ran several paces away from me. Then it squatted on the ground with its hindquarters tilted upwards and its breast buried in the earth. It wriggled its breast in the sandy soil, as if settling into a nest or trying to deepen the hollow of a nest. All the time it kept calling loudly. When I moved towards it it rose, ran forward a few yards, then sank to the ground again and repeated the performance. Once more the facts that it drew attention to itself by its outcry, that it deliberately allowed me each time to approach quite close before moving on and that it never sought to escape me by taking wing—as would have been so easy— indicated without a doubt that it was endeavouring to attract me, to draw me after it, to lead me away from some place where it did not wish me to be. This place was of course its nest.

Most of this time the bird added no other frills to its performance. But once it fell into the "broken wing" attitude. It crouched, hunched its body, drooped its wings and spread its tail. Then it walked, almost staggered, in this position with the tips of its tail feathers dragging over the ground. Again I was struck by its sensuous appearance, reminiscent of a bird's sexual display.

Shortly afterwards a second Killdeer flew on to the scene and landed near the first. Probably this was its mate, for the first bird showed no resentment at the newcomer's arrival. On the contrary, the two seemed united by a friendly understanding, by a bond of partnership. More-over, the inclination of the first bird to indulge in something like sexual posturing seemed to be immediately and greatly stimulated by the arrival of the second. It "displayed" violently, opening its wings wider, quivering and fluttering them, fanning its tail and even shaking its rump in what appeared to be an excess of naughty desire. These agitations of its body continued for several seconds and were repeated thrice in separate spasms.

The other bird made no response that I could detect. It stood motionless for a while, eyeing me. Then it ran a yard or two away from me, calling gently. The first Killdeer reverted likewise to the duty of decoying me. The pair went forward in a series of rushes and halts, more or less in parallel lines, sometimes converging, sometimes diverging, but never actually meeting or crossing each other's paths. The first occasionally squatted on the ground and made as if settling on a nest. The second added no such enticement to its attempt to lure me away. But both were evidently in alliance in their plot to draw me on.

I had seen similar behaviour many years before, on the shore of the Moray Firth in the north of Scotland. The performer on that occasion was a Ring Plover, a bird distinct from but related to the American Killdeer. I described the incident with the Ring Plover in a lecture which I gave afterwards. As my observations on that occasion illustrate the remarkable, inherited similarity in the behaviour of two cousinly species who inhabit different sides of the Atlantic Ocean and have probably not met since the days of some common ancestor centuries ago, I include them here. I said:

In May family life is beginning and one cannot help occasionally disturbing it. For instance, let me tell you about a Ring Plover family that I watched one

Whitsuntide. There are some pebbly patches of ground above the sandy beach and at the edge of the moorland where Oyster-catchers and Ring Plovers nest. One afternoon I came without warning upon a little Ring Plover family. The young amongst them cannot have been many hours old. There was scarcely more to them than a pair of swiftly running legs with a ball of fluff on top.

When I disturbed them I was promptly treated to a fascinating performance . . . As soon as I came on the scene the mother Ring Plover ran a few paces from where she had been sitting with her chicks, then turned and whistled to them. They started to run away in the opposite direction to that which she had taken. She gave a second whistle and they halted. After a few moments she whistled again and the chicks ran on once more. They stopped again when next she whistled and started to move at her following whistle. Thus she controlled and gradually guided them into concealment amongst some long grass.

Her first task accomplished, she turned deliberately to undertake her second. Having hidden her infants, she wished to try to draw me away from the danger zone. Turning her back on me, she drooped both her wings, spread her tail feathers in a fan and began to drag her body lamely over the ground in the opposite direction to that where her chicks crouched concealed. After proceeding about ten yards she stood up and looked at me. I had not moved. She hastened back to her starting point and again, with drooping wings and fanned tail, drew her body slowly away from me over the same ten yards. Then she looked round at me again. Still I had not moved. She returned hurriedly and repeated the same performance. She repeated it four times.

No doubt you have seen various birds go through similar antics. They are popularly explained by the idea that the bird is "feigning a broken wing". But surely this description has nothing to do with the facts. The mistake that many people make in studying bird life is that they try to interpret bird behaviour through the human mind instead of through the bird mind. If you try to think what was going on in the bird mind of this Ring Plover, you will reject the broken wing theory. Why should a Ring Plover know anything about a broken wing? And why, even if it did have the misfortune to do so, should the little bird know or feel that a broken-winged creature might be attractive to a strange human being? One must search elsewhere for an explanation of the Ring Plover's remarkable and deliberate performance.

What was the bird endeavouring to do? It was trying to attract me, in order to draw me away from the place where its young were hidden. The sense that it must be attractive and draw me after it had command of the little creature. A bird's experiences are very limited, but there is another occasion when the idea of attraction dominates its life. That is in the courting season, when a bird goes through the elaborate performance known as "display" in order to attract its mate. And what struck me most about the Ring Plover's performance that afternoon was the similarity between its motions when "feigning a broken wing" and the motions that some birds go through in "display". For all I know, the two sets of motions are the same in Ring Plovers. I do not know, as I have never watched them in the mating season. But certainly the drooping of the half-stretched wings, the fanning of the tail so that the white band along the feather tips was prominently shown, and the crouching, seductive

78

retreat over the ground appeared like a repetition or imitation of "display".

Can it be that the Ring Plover, filled with the idea of attracting some strange being, instinctively repeats a performance similar to that which it is accustomed to use when attraction of its own kind is necessary in courtship? I suggest that there may be something in this. A great deal of careful watching of different birds would be necessary before you reached even tentative conclusions. One must not judge by superficial appearances; they must be tested over and over again. But I think that the theory is worth serious examination.

Strong objections can certainly be raised to it. . . . It may be argued, for example, that the "display" action is only associated with powerful sexual stimulus, and that this is entirely lacking in the "broken wing" situation. On the other hand, in the latter situation the mother bird's maternal instinct is deeply aroused and so the association is not so remote as might appear. Again, the critic may say that though it is true that in the case of the Ring Plover the "broken wing" action appears to be somewhat similar to the "display" action, in most birds the two actions are not recognizably alike. I do not know how far research might reveal any similarity between the two actions in birds other than Ring Plovers. But even if it yielded little of this, that does not necessarily mean that we should abandon my theory. It is conceivable that the difference between one action and the other has grown up in the course of long evolution, that the original "display" action used in the "broken wing" situation has gradually been modified and some of its details exaggerated in the course of centuries, until the origin of the whole action is no longer obvious. It would not be unnatural or unusual that this modification should have gone much further in the case of some birds than in the case of others, the Ring Plover being an exception in which for one reason or another very little modification at all had taken place.

It would be possible to indulge in a great deal of fanciful speculation on this topic, but it would be idle to do so without further evidence on which to base one's discussion. I merely throw out the theory for what it is worth and as an amusing object for observation.

Probably there are many flaws in this argument. It does not pretend to be more than the untutored theorizing of an amateur. I am aware that more experienced observers have advanced another explanation of a bird's strange action when disturbed at its nest. They suggest that its contortions are brought on by a sort of paralysis, a desire but inability to fly, produced by fright. I wonder. I have not had time for more than the most infrequent bird-watching since seeing the Ring Plover and so have had no opportunity to make further researches into the subject. But the behaviour of the Brewery Creek Killdeers reminded me so exactly of that earlier Ring Plover occasion that I have reproduced the description here. The conduct of the pair of Killdeers which I have recorded above seems to lend support to the idea that a connection may exist between birds' "display" and "decoy" action. Let me make a few additional comments on their combined antics.

They were without doubt endeavouring to decoy me away from the nest. The first bird that I saw (almost certainly the female) tried two particular stratagems to accomplish this. First, as she retreated before me she squatted every now and then, apparently pretending to sit on a nest. She seemed to invent a series of false nests for the purpose of bamboozling me as to the whereabouts of the real one. If this was her intention, it was cleverly executed. She was a consummate actress. Her attitude each time was exactly what it would have been if she were sinking down on her nest to brood eggs. The performance seemed to be cunningly thought out, yet probably the bird had given it no thought whatever. The whole action was most likely instinctive, a more or less automatic reaction to her emotion when disturbed on eggs. As Dr. Julian Huxley says, "Birds have kept instinct as the mainstay of their behaviour whilst mammals have gradually perfected intelligence and the capacity for learning by experience."

It is possible that the true explanation of her conduct was not that she was mechanically pretending to sit on a series of nests. This attitude itself may sometimes be a part of the normal courtship behaviour of one Killdeer trying to attract another. I do not know. Certainly the spreading of their wings and fanning of their tails is a characteristic part of their sexual display, but I have neither seen nor heard of this additional refinement in their particular case. Such conduct does occur, however, in the "display" of some other plovers, like the English Green Plover. A Green Plover seeking to attract its mate sometimes squats on the ground and wriggles its breast into the earth, as if to make a hollow for a nest. Action suggestive of nest-making is typical also of some passerine and other birds during courtship. Before they have reached the nest building stage, one of a pair will occasionally give a piece of grass or other nesting material to its partner as part of the invitation, the inducement to mate. If "nest-making" action is also sometimes employed by Killdeers when courting, then the behaviour of the Killdeer trying to draw me away from her nest supports further the idea of a sexual origin of "decoy" action.

When this device failed to lure me away the bird resorted to its second stratagem, which was more violent and more definitely connected with courtship display. This was the drooping of her wings and spreading of her tail—the conduct which is usually described as feigning a broken wing. The connection between this and actual sexual display seemed to be more firmly proved by the bird's behaviour, shortly afterwards, when her mate arrived. As I have described, her display action then suddenly became even wilder and more abandoned. Why? Did the appearance of her mate confuse her mind? Did her motives then get mixed? Her display to me was prompted by the emotion of fear, lest I should find her eggs. It was an automatic, rather cold-blooded exhibition aimed at attracting my attention (but certainly not my embraces!) so as to draw me away. Then her mate arrived. Did his presence partly change her emotion to desire, making her display warm-blooded, with the aim of attracting him to her own actual person? This may be the explanation of the sudden increase in the vigour of her action. If so, her mate's indifference to her attempt at seduction and his concentration on the object of luring me away from their nest restored her conduct to what was appropriate, and indeed most necessary, in the circumstances. She returned to a single-minded effort at the milder form of seduction—the seduction of me from the neighbourhood.

9.

The wildfowl swimming and diving in the creek lent it an air of being "far from the madding crowd", remote from the hurly-burly of city life, a place of natural, undisturbed wildness. Yet they were within a minute's flight of the Parliament Buildings of the nation's capital.

Many new wild duck appeared in April. Huge flocks of them were migrating. A study of the various species' airways through the skies is fascinating. Each has its regular route, or set of routes, which it follows unerringly on the northward journey in spring and in reverse when it comes south again in autumn. Some fly up the Atlantic coast and others hug the Pacific coast. Most of these are ocean-going birds. Huge flocks of them can be seen passing any given point, hour after hour continuously. Other species, including some sea-duck, travel by inland waterways, flying along the great river valleys, "portaging" so to speak, from river system to river system and resting periodically on wayside lakes, until at last they reach their distant nesting grounds.

The Ottawa River fills a section of the route for many species and Brewery Creek provides a placid inlet beside it where duck can conveniently halt for a few days or a few weeks on their way. April is the busiest month for their spring migration. During it I saw ten different kinds of wild duck and one species of wild goose. Others doubtless passed by when I did not happen to be watching. Many additional species dropped in at the creek on their return journeys in the fall, as I shall record later.

In the early days of April one or two American Mergansers and a party of American Golden-eye were usually on the water. They had arrived, as the reader knows, in March. Neither species makes a far-reaching migration. At any rate, their flights do not compare with those of many others. Generally speaking, both species winter in the central and northern United States and southern Canada and spend the summer in southern and central Canada.

The first newcomers to the creek in April were some Buffle-heads. They are related to Golden-eye, whom they resemble to some extent in size, plumage and habits. But as migrants they are more ambitious. After wintering in the southern and far-western States, they transport themselves mostly to western and north-western Canada and Alaska to breed.

Amongst the next wildfowl to appear were two moderate travellers. Mallards and Black Duck are so well-known that descriptions of their appearance are unnecessary. The former spend the winter almost anywhere in the United States and nest almost anywhere in the northern States, Canada and Alaska south of a line stretching roughly from Montreal via Winnipeg to Fairbanks. Black Duck winter over most of the eastern States and breed mostly in eastern Canada and Labrador.

At about the same time several of the greater travellers arrived. I shall not weary the reader with geographical details of their migrations. In extent they are more or less intermediate between the flight of a few hundred miles made, for example, by American Mergansers and that of four thousand miles and more accomplished by a later visitor to the creek, the Old-squaw duck.

Amongst these middling travellers were a pair of Ring-necked Duck. They too are related to Golden-eye and are in some respects similar in appearance. But they seemed as shy of their cousins and other wildfowl as they were of me, for during the few days of their stay they rarely left a quiet, secluded, shallow corner of the creek to join the lively parties of birds swimming and diving elsewhere on the open water. This was a characteristic show of reserve by birds who normally prefer marshy places where society is limited.

84

Next came some Red-breasted Mergansers. They are smaller than their American cousins, but the distinction in size is not obvious when the two birds are apart. Other distinguishing features are more reliable. The untidy looking, double-pointed crest on the Red-breasted Merganser drake's dark head and his white collar and red-banded chest are distinct. Both species share the long body, snakey head and slender, red, saw-toothed bill which are the unmistakable marks of Mergansers.

Wood Duck also appeared a few times. The drake is the best looking of all North American wildfowl. Indeed, his flashing, ruby-red eyes, full crested head and many-coloured plumage would win him a high prize in a beauty competition amongst ducks all over the world. Blue, green, purple, white, black, bronze, brown and chestnut all figure prominently in his intricately patterned dress, which is all the finer because of its smooth, irridescent quality.

The female is more modestly clad, yet she too has more colour than any other member of her sex in Canadian duck society. I hoped that a pair of these engaging creatures would nest in the neighbourhood of the creek. Once or twice they seemed to be prospecting for a site in the woods. Like a few other duck, they do not lay their eggs on the ground but in a cavity in the trunk or branch of a tree. This may sometimes be as high as fifty or sixty feet above the ground. In due course the ducklings appear at the entrance, take their courage in both wings and jump to earth. Unfortunately the Wood Duck who visited the creek passed on, perhaps because no tree on its shores had a hole spacious enough to tempt them.

Early in April a few Lesser Scaup appeared for a day and in the second half of the month half-a-dozen pairs stayed in the creek for almost a fortnight. In appearance they have some features in common with Golden-eye and Ring-necked Ducks. They are best distinguished by the white patch above the beak on the female's face, the grey back of the male and the white speculum revealed on the wings of both sexes when they fly.

Their journeys on migration bring them into the class of the greatest travellers. In winter they reside in the Central American Republics, the Caribbean Islands and the "Deep South" of the United States. When the urge to nest awakes in them in spring they take wing and fly up the length of the North American continent to the Canadian prairies, the Mackenzie valley and Alaska.

One day towards the end of the month their party in the creek was joined by an even more adventurous traveller. Seeing a strange, small, dumpy duck amongst the Scaups, I turned my field-glasses on to it and recognized the white and brown plumage of a female Old-squaw. She only stayed one day, for she still had far to go. Having spent the winter on the Atlantic seaboard of New England, she was now hastening to the Arctic. Old-squaws build their nests on the tundra of the remote north, anywhere from the Bering Sea to Hudson Strait. Nor do they all stay on the mainland. Some cross the ocean to the Aleutians, others to the Arctic Islands and yet others to Greenland and Iceland. Those with the greatest "wanderlust" inhabit the furthest shores of Ellismere Island and Peary Land, below latitude 80°, the last bits of solid earth facing the North Pole.

10.

As I have already observed, the earliest migrant duck to arrive in April were some Buffle-heads. On April 1st two

WOOD DUCK
"The drake is the best looking of all North American wildfowl."

females of the species were swimming together close to shore. Their small size and the white face-patches relieving their otherwise dull brown colouring were unmistakable.

For a week these spinsters remained in the creek, unsought and unwooed by drakes. Usually they were both present, but sometimes one or the other had disappeared. I always hoped that she had found a mate. But no, later the same day or the next morning she would return and resume the vigil with her sister. I began to feel sorry for them. They swam about quietly, appearing meek, mild and neglected. They kept themselves to themselves, never venturing near the little flock of American Golden-eye who were always swimming and diving in a sportive crowd elsewhere.

Then, on April 8th, things changed. The morning was beautiful and windless. Bright sunshine sparkled down on a sheet of water as serene and polished as a mirror. Reflected in it was a perfect upside-down image of the surrounding landscape.

Wildfowl were plentiful. This was the morning when a pair of Ring-necked Duck made their first appearance. Some Black Duck also alighted near by. A company of Golden-eye, a mixture of black-and-white males and brown females, were fishing in the open water where the creek and the river meet.

Beyond this group I saw two birds who seemed to show rather more white than the male Golden-eye. Turning my field-glasses on them I found to my delight that they were a couple of Buffle-head drakes. Their pure white breasts, flanks and necks were similar to those of the Golden-eye, but they lacked the white cheek spot. Instead the greater part of the back of their heads, reaching forward to the eyes, was white, in sharp contrast to the rest of their dark crowns and faces. It was an odd, bold decoration, all the more striking because of the inordinate size of their heads. The word "Buffle-head" is in fact a contraction of "Buffalo-head", which was the original name of these birds. They acquired it because the drakes' large, round, fluffy heads, appearing out of proportion to the rest of their bodies, were reminiscent of those of buffalo.

The Buffle-head drakes were swimming in leisurely and stately fashion on the calm water. They had a swaggering air, as if they knew that in the sunlight they were a handsome pair of bucks. A couple of Regency dandies strolling along the Mall could not have looked more natty.

I felt sure that if only a rendezvous could be arranged between them and the two females it would be, as the advertisements say, "something of advantage" to both parties. But the little ducks were nowhere near these devastating males. Their usual haunt was further up the creek, probably out of sight from where the drakes were swimming. I hastened to the place to see if they were present. Sure enough, one was there, though the other had disappeared. The solitary female was floating disconsolately above an image of herself, ignorant of the gallant, consoling companionship only two hundred yards away.

I felt a strong urge to achieve an introduction between them, but the situation seemed hopeless. This was an occasion when I regretted that birds have a poorly developed sense of smell. Surely those fine males sent some perfume, or at least some masculine odour, wafting across the water. But wildfowl, like other birds, act by sight and hearing, not by smell.

For an hour or more the situation remained unchanged. At one moment the duck, startled by something, rose from the water and flew hurriedly across part of the creek, uttering her "guk, guk, guk" alarm note as she went. My hopes rose with her. But either the drakes did not hear her call or else it was all Greek to them. They made no response. She did not catch sight of them and they did not catch sight of her. After circling round once or twice she alighted back in her original place.

Then a fortunate thing happened. A man in a boat appeared at the far edge of the creek, rowing towards the drakes. They saw him and took fright. Leaping from the water, they flew fast and straight in the direction of the duck. She was floating not far from shore and I happened to be sitting nearby. I got an excellent, close-up view of the drakes as they approached and flew before my eyes. They were not more than ten feet up in the air and passed directly over the duck. But they seemed not to notice her, for they did not swerve or hesitate for a moment in their flight. Soon they disappeared beyond a point of land further up the creek—and the duck remained unconcernedly where she was.

This was very disappointing. My hopes had risen for a second time, only to be dashed.

But I was too hasty in reaching conclusions. The drakes had not been so blind as I feared. Half-a-minute afterwards they reappeared, flying straight and purposefully back towards the duck. They had spotted her after all and been intrigued by her presence. But they had not felt it prudent to interrupt at once their retreat from the man in the rowing-boat. For the moment their fear of men was stronger than their love of ducks. Now, however, having had time to calm down and collect such wits as they possessed, they had decided to fall to the temptation of joining her.

They circled low above her and then splashed into the water at her side. Both were wildly excited. They swam quickly round and round her, with their head feathers puffed out and their heads jerking rapidly up and down on telescopic necks. This was their particular style in courtship display. They certainly did not believe in wasting time. The duck, however, made no perceptible response, seeming entirely unmoved. She showed neither delight nor annoyance, neither attraction nor aversion, but accepted her visitors and their demonstration of enthusiasm as a simple matter of course.

After a while the drakes' first emotional excitement subsided. Their spasm of automatic love-making died. They ceased their antics. Though they felt no less happy, they expressed the feeling in quieter ways. Their introduction over, they swam calmly beside the duck as if they were three long-established friends.

Then the man in the boat, who all this time had been rowing steadily across the creek, approached them. The trio felt disturbed and eyed him nervously. Of a sudden they rose gracefully from the water, flew low and fast down the estuary, swerved out over the river and disappeared from view.

When I was paddling back to Earnscliffe half-an-hour later I saw them again, swimming together companionably in the middle of the river. At my appearance they immediately took wing. As they sped in a wide half-circle over the water they changed positions from time to time. Sometimes the two drakes led and the little duck seemed to be pursuing them. At other times she caught them up, passed them and took the lead, so that they seemed to be chasing her. It was a pretty piece of manoeuvring. Eventually they re-entered the creek and alighted simultaneously with a splash on its glassy waters near the party of Golden-eye.

In due course, no doubt, the duck selected one of the drakes for her mate and spent the summer happily with him and their ducklings.

II.

Most other wild duck were also selecting mates as they moved north towards their breeding grounds. The Ring-necked Duck and the Wood Duck seemed to have paired already. Each drake had his duck and the two appeared invariably together like an inseparable married couple.

In other cases the conjugal relationship seemed to be only in process of establishment. That situation prevailed, for example, amongst the Golden-eye. In the early days of April their numbers increased until eight males and eight females were swimming and diving in a group together. But particular males did not yet appear to be attached to particular females. The drakes were still bent on love-making. Even in windy weather, when the surface of the water was ruffled into choppy waves, they made frequent advances to the ducks. When a suit was rejected, however, the drake concerned seemed to have no compunction about offering himself to another duck. These approaches were almost always rejected. Only once did I see a duck look like making any response, but she did not carry the affair very far. It was as if her spirit were willing but the flesh was still weak—and once more a drake was disappointed.

The Golden-eye stayed until April 9th. After that they disappeared, moving no doubt to some lake where the business of bringing families into the world could be performed in all seriousness.

The flock of a dozen Lesser Scaups who arrived later in the month and stayed for two weeks was also divided equally between ducks and drakes. But amongst them I noticed no signs of courtship display. This may have occurred, and definite partnerships have been established, before the birds started on their great journey. Although the group kept more or less together, certain pairs tended to swim *tête-à-tête*. Once matters went further. Without any apparent warning, a drake swam deliberately to a duck on the water, mounted her back and remained sitting on top of her for several seconds. Presumably he mated with her there and then. The act was accomplished in spite of the fact that the creek at the time was badly wrinkled with rough waves. Wildfowl almost invariably copulate on water rather than on dry land.

12.

Sometimes the weather got really tough. A stiff wind blew and "white horses" charged across the grey, tossing water. Then the creek seemed less like a wild lake and more like a stormy ocean. At those times its dominant spirits were not the wild duck but the sea gulls.

By the beginning of April many Herring Gulls had gathered on the river. Occasionally one or two Ring-billed Gulls were with them. These were smaller birds and although they too were good fliers, they had not the appearance of effortless mastery of the air which the larger Gulls possessed. The Herring Gulls' superb powers of flight came alive when half a gale was blowing. The more viciously the wind roared, the better pleased they seemed to be. They rose into the sky and remained aloft in a veritable storm, sometimes beating their wings strongly yet nonchalantly against it, making slow but steady progress in the teeth of the wind, and at other times resigning themselves to its force and gliding and wheeling spaciously wherever the gale chose to drive them. It was beautiful to watch them soaring against a background of dark, storm-tattered clouds, screaming wildly as they went. Their mournful cries pierced the howling wind and was like the voice of the sea. In imagination I could hear the crash of breakers on a stormy beach and smell the tang of salt spray in the air.

As the days passed, however, the Gulls went with them. By the end of the month their numbers had considerably decreased. Their minds too were turning to more tender things. They flew away to the lakes north and west of Ottawa, where they are accustomed to nest. Perhaps some travelled along the Ottawa River and down the St. Lawrence to join colonies of their kind on rocky islands in the real sea, where they could produce a new generation of Herring Gulls.

13.

On the day of the meeting of the Buffle-head duck with her two wooers I saw another memorable sight. My ears advised me of it before my eyes noticed it. From overhead came the most thrilling music in the bird world—the honking of wild geese. Looking up, I saw about sixty Common Canada Geese flying over the creek.

They were travelling in the famous arrow-head formation which they usually adopt on migration. In front flew an old gander who knew the way and could guide the flock by the straightest route to their destination. Behind him the other birds were spaced more or less regularly in two long, diverging, streamer-like files. Their wing-beats were strong, leisurely and graceful. Their long black necks were outstretched, like those of Swans. Their white cheeks and throats were clearly visible in the sunlight. The birds' great size added to their majesty. A Canada Goose's wing-span measures anything between five and six-and-a-half feet, and its weight can develop to about fourteen pounds. In the list of Canadian waterfowl only Swans are larger than Common Canada Geese.

As the flock flew onward each long streamer of birds seemed to ripple, to undulate slightly. This motion is an optical illusion, due to the fact that the wing-beats of the Geese are not in perfect unison. Their timing varies. The beauty of the flocks, formation and motions was matched by that of its voices. The leader and his followers frequently exchanged calls and filled the air with clear, resonant wild goose conversation.

They flew at no great height across the mouth of the creek, no doubt making for breeding grounds in the region of Hudson Bay. It is said that Canada Geese, unlike wild duck and most other birds, usually mate for life. Their marriage is a contract entered into and faithfully preserved "until death do us part". It is even claimed that the partnership, in effect, remains binding beyond death and that when either member of it dies the survivor does not pair again.

The courtship of Canada Geese cannot, of course, be watched anywhere so far south as Brewery Creek. But I quote the following account of it written by the great John James Audubon, partly because it is apposite in this section of my book and partly because it shows (what is not generally recognized) that Audubon could be as brilliant and dramatic in describing birds with his pen as he was in portraying them with his brush. In *The Birds of America* he wrote:

It is extremely amusing to witness the courtship of the Canada Goose in all its stages; and let me assure you, reader, that although a gander does not strut before his beloved with the pomposity of a turkey, or the grace of a dove, his ways are quite as agreeable to the female of his choice. I can imagine before me one who has just accomplished the defeat of another male after a struggle of half-an-hour or more. He advances gallantly toward the object of his contention, his head scarcely raised an inch from the ground, his bill open to its full stretch, his fleshy tongue elevated, his eyes darting fiery glances, and as he moves he hisses loudly, while the emotion which he experiences causes his quills to shake and his feathers to rustle. Now he is close to her who in his eyes is all loveliness; his neck bending gracefully in all directions, passes all around her, and occasionally touches her body; and as she congratulates him on his victory, and acknowledges his affection, they move their necks in a hundred curious ways. At this moment fierce jealousy urges the defeated gander to renew his efforts to obtain his love; he advances apace, his eye glowing with the fire of rage; he shakes his broad wings, ruffles up his whole plumage, and as he rushes on the foe hisses with the intensity of anger. The whole flock seems to stand amazed, and opening up a space, the birds gather round to view the combat. The bold bird who has been caressing his mate scarcely deigns to take notice of his foe, but seems to send a scornful glance toward him. He of the mortified feelings, however, raises his body, half opens his sinewy wings, and with a powerful blow, sends forth his defiance. The affront cannot be borne in the presence of so large a company, nor indeed is there much disposition to bear it in any circumstances; the blow is returned with vigor, the aggressor reels for a moment, but he soon recovers, and now the combat rages. Were the weapons more deadly, feats of chivalry would now be performed; as it is, thrust and blow succeed each other like the strokes of hammers driven by sturdy forgers. But now, the mated gander has caught hold of his antagonist's head with his bill; no bulldog can cling faster to his victim; he squeezes him with all the energy of rage, lashes him with his powerful wings and at length drives him away, spreads out his pinions, runs with joy to his mate, and fills the air with cries of exultation.

CHAPTER SIX

MAY

I.

THE WEATHER in May, like that in April, was by no means all that it might be. Occasionally the month remembered that it should look like the beginning of summer, and produced a few hours of sunshine. But it soon forgot itself and indulged again in fits of cold wind and dreary rain. We were paying with a vengeance for that premature burst of spring in March. If the Clerk of the Weather were trying to correct his earlier mistake and restore the year to its normal seasons, he showed excess of zeal. He overdid the job badly and swung things too far in the opposite direction. After being a few weeks ahead of his usual schedule he slowed things up so much that he fell two or three weeks behind the proper time table. Day after day, from the 1st of the month until the 31st, with few exceptions, we had rain, rain, rain.

However, Nature gradually unfolded herself. Wild Strawberries continued to flower in beautiful white and green masses. In some places Dandelions gilded wide areas of ground and in others bunches of Violets and Ground Ivy dressed it in purple. When the Dandelions lost their yellow flowers and were topped by airy grey "clocks" their place in the colour scheme was taken by Buttercups. Canada Anemones too began to lift their nodding heads and open their pale blossoms. White Dogwood, lavender Speedwell and pink Spring Beauty all bloomed at the same time.

97

By the middle of the month most of the trees were well covered with leaves. It became harder to detect small passerine birds amongst the foliage. This difficulty was greater than usual because the later wave of migration was delayed by the inhospitable weather. When the Warblers, for example, arrived, the green veil of leaves between them in the tree-tops and an observer on the ground was thicker than is customary for that auspicious event.

Nevertheless May was easily the most important month for spring migration. Whereas I had seen sixteen species of migrants in the creek in March and a further eighteen in April, in May I saw no fewer than fifty-three additional birds. Two or three of these, like the Hairy Woodpecker and the Black-capped Chickadee, may have been all-the-year-round residents in the Ottawa district whom I had not happened to see in the creek before. But the others were certainly newcomers. Some stayed for the remainder of the spring and summer, mating, nesting and rearing their young amongst the creek's grasses, shrubs and trees. Others were hastening through on their way further north and only loitered for a day or two beside the Ottawa River.

First I shall give a list of all the newcomers in May in the general order of their appearance, with a few comments on each of them, and then describe more fully the way of life of some of those who stayed as summer residents.

The forerunner of the swarms of May migrants was that charming little creature, the Ruby-crowned Kinglet. Early on the morning of the 3rd a flock of them appeared with the first rays of sunshine following several cloudy days. Except for the tiny Hummingbirds and two species of Wrens, the Kinglets are the smallest birds to be seen in Canada. There are two distinct species, the Ruby-crowned and the Golden-crowned. Each measures about four inches long, nearly half of which consists of tail. They are pretty birds, dressed soberly enough as far as their bodies are concerned, with olive-green backs, light underparts and dusky wings crossed by pale bars. On their heads, however, they wear brilliantly coloured caps. That of the Ruby-crowned Kinglet is scarlet and that of the Golden-crowned is yellow on the female and orange on the male. They are lively, restless birds, never remaining still on a bough for more than a few seconds. At one moment they perch upright and at the next hang upside down, pecking at insects on the twigs. The flock of Ruby-crowns stayed for only one day and then passed onwards to the coniferous forests where they nest. None of their Golden-crowned cousins looked in at the creek this spring, but they appeared on their return journey in the autumn.

On the same day two new Sparrows arrived. One was the White-throated Sparrow. Its spotless white chin and throat, black and white headstripes and yellow patch in front of each eye were conspicuous. The bird did not treat me that morning to its most distinguished feature, its song. That clear, wistful, sweet melody is commonly interpreted in New England by the words, "Old Sam Peabody, Peabody, Peabody" and has earned it there the nickname of the Peabody Bird. But in Canada the bird is understood to be singing in prosperous seasons "Sweet, sweet Canada, Canada, Canada" and in times of depression "Hard times, Canada, Canada, Canada"—an utterance which has won it the enviable title of Canada Bird.

My attention was drawn to the second Sparrow by its voice. From a poplar tree I heard the "Chip, chip, chip, chip, chip . . ." of a Chipping Sparrow. When I walked to the tree I saw the dull-coloured, small-sized Sparrow opening its beak wide, as if to send forth a glorious song, and only succeeding in producing this monotonous, rapid, tuneless contribution to Nature's sounds. Other Chipping Sparrows had already been in the Ottawa region for three weeks or more, but this was the first and only time that it appeared in the creek, at any rate whilst I was there as audience.

On May 6th an American Sparrow Hawk appeared and perched on top of the tall chimney-stack. The little Falcon, no larger than a Robin, sat preening its pretty blue, chestnut, black and white feathers until the rude noises of a motor-boat entering the creek disturbed it. With a fierce look at the intruder, it spread its wings and flew away.

Then the Warblers began to come. This is one of the events for which all bird-watchers wait with keen anticipation. It is symbolic of the arrival of spring. In Canada the event is particularly welcome not only because of what it symbolizes but also because of the gay variety of the Warblers themselves.

An ornithologically-minded visitor from Britain, like myself, receives many surprises in Canada. The first is the almost universal difference between the birds of the two countries. Even when they belong to the same families they almost invariably bear some significant distinction from each other. Thus of the 160 species which I observed in Brewery Creek less than a dozen resembled exactly in form and colouring their relatives on the other side of the Atlantic Ocean. English and Canadian birds are two entirely separate nations of animals.

Another surprise for a visitor from Britain is the brilliant plumage of the Warblers. In Britain we have about a dozen common species, but with the exception of the yellow Wood Warbler they are rather plainly coloured. The fact is that they belong to a different family from the forty-odd Canadian Warblers, most of whom wear gay, many-hued dresses. These make them appear like bright flowers fluttering amongst the woodland foliage.

The Warbler vanguard usually reaches Ottawa early in May. For about three weeks afterwards the tree-tops are alive with large numbers of different species of these birds. As the earlier species move onwards their place is taken by later kinds. These in turn stay for only a few days and then travel on. A few species, however, stay through the summer and nest in Ottawa and its neighbourhood. I shall treat the Warblers whom I saw in the creek as a group, describing briefly the principal distinguishing marks of their plumages. Afterwards I shall return to the other creek birds.

The first Warblers whom I saw were some Myrtle Warblers, who arrived on May 8th—V-E Day. The other species came on various dates until the 24th, when one of the last to migrate, the Black-poll Warblers, appeared. The descriptions below are taken almost word for word from Mr. Roger Tory Peterson's useful *A Field Guide to the Birds*. For simplicity I give only the spring plumages of the more splendidly coloured bird, the cock, of each pair.

The Myrtle Warbler's plumage is blue-grey above and white below, with a heavy inverted black "U" on the breast and sides, a patch of yellow on the crown, two more on its sides and a bright yellow rump. The Yellow Warbler is all yellow, with fine chestnut-red streaks on its breast. The Black and White Warbler is striped lengthwise from head to tail with black and white, making one think instinctively

of the markings of a Zebra. Wilson's Warbler is entirely
yellow except for a black cap on its head. The Chestnut-
sided Warbler is, on the other hand, most easily distinguished
by its yellow crown as well as the chestnut band on each
flank between olive, yellow-banded wings and a white
breast. The Tennessee Warbler is more modestly marked
than the others, sporting a grey head, olive-green back and
white underparts. It is chiefly distinguished by a conspicuous white stripe over each eye. The Bay-breasted Warbler
is a dark-looking Warbler with a chestnut throat, upper
breast and sides and a large pale-buff spot on each side of its
neck. The American Redstart is mostly black, relieved by
bright salmon patches on the wings and tail and by a white
belly. The Canada Warbler is plain grey above and bright
yellow below and wears a necklace of short black stripes
below its throat. The Cape May Warbler has a black crown,
a chestnut cheek-patch, yellow underparts thinly striped
with black and a yellow rump. The Nashville Warbler has
a grey head, white eye-ring, olive-green back and yellow
throat and underparts. The Black-poll Warbler is a striped
grey bird with a solidly black head and white cheeks.

This is far from being a complete list of all the Warblers
who might be seen in the creek in May. I was particularly
busy in my office that month and my morning trips across
the river were short. As a result I missed several species.
Certainly every kind of Warbler which visits Rockcliffe
Park also visits Brewery Creek, for the natural conditions
of the two places are similar. Mr. Hoyes Lloyd, who is
now President of the American Ornithologists' Union,
showed me his list of Warblers seen in his garden and its
neighbourhood near Mackay Lake. Incidentally, I enjoyed
his company on a bird-watching expedition. In the first

CANADA GOOSE

"Their marriage is a contract entered into . . . 'until death do us part'."

place, when he came to the creek one morning the canoe upset off-shore and we were both thrown into the river. We floundered around for a while waist-deep in cold water. That sort of experience creates a bond between men. In the second place, he has an unsurpassed knowledge of the birds of Canada in general and of Ottawa in particular. His information is authoritative and reliable. The following is the list of Warblers seen by him in Rockcliffe Park this spring, with the date of arrival of each species. It must be remembered that owing to poor weather the dates incline to be rather later than usual.

May 5th. Myrtle Warbler.
May 9th. Black and White Warbler.
May 10th. Black-throated Blue Warbler.
May 13th. Black-throated Green Warbler.
May 15th. Yellow Warbler.
           Chestnut-sided Warbler.
           Oven-bird.
May 19th. Nashville Warbler.
           Blackburnian Warbler.
May 20th. Tennessee Warbler.
           Parula Warbler.
           Magnolia Warbler.
           Cape May Warbler.
           Bay-breasted Warbler.
           Canada Warbler.
May 21st. American Redstart.
May 22nd. Mourning Warbler.
           Maryland Yellowthroat.
May 24th. Black-poll Warbler.

Thus I saw in the creek in May one bird which Mr. Lloyd did not see in Rockcliffe, a Wilson's Warbler.[1] On

[1] He saw one later, in the first days of June.

the other hand he saw eight species which I missed. However, when the birds returned south in September and October every individual in his list visited the creek, plus a Palm Warbler and some Water-Thrushes. I shall write of these in a later chapter.

Warblers are smaller than Sparrows. They have trim figures and slender beaks. Most of them are birds of the tree-tops, where they flit actively and elegantly to and fro as they search the leaves and branches for the insects on which they thrive. The Spaniards call them *Mariposas*—butterflies. Their beauty and grace are a constant delight.

So much for the Warblers on their spring migration. Let us now return to the other May arrivals in Brewery Creek.

Two days after the appearance of the first Myrtle Warblers an ocean-going bird arrived. Next day two more species of sea birds came. This nautical trio were a flock of Bonaparte's Gulls, a Glaucous Gull and some Double-crested Cormorants. It was as if a party of sailors came swimming into the estuary. They gave a salty touch to the scene. The fresh water seemed to acquire a tang of briney and to become an arm of the sea. In imagination I felt the ground heave beneath my feet like the deck of a ship and I found myself whistling a sea-shanty:

"What shall we do with a drunken sailor?
What shall we do with a drunken sailor?
What shall we do with a drunken sailor
    Early in the morning?"

Not that any of the birds looked inebriated. On the contrary, they were models of decorum. The Cormorants appeared particularly sober. Standing on woodpiles jutting from the water, dressed in priestly black from head to foot and holding out their wings to dry—like the arms of orators declaiming—they looked like temperance fanatics preaching the virtues of an abstemious life. To revert from the human to the avian world, they appeared in that attitude like heraldic birds, staying so still that they seemed inanimate creatures carved in dark wood. But presently they grew tired of the pose, came to life, leapt into the water and began swimming and diving after fish. That morning five of them breakfasted in the creek.

The Bonaparte's Gulls made a pretty entrance on the scene. Some Herring Gulls and two or three Ring-billed Gulls were in the air. Then from a distance a dozen strange gulls came flying up the river. They were smaller birds than the others and their flight was lighter and more playful. Keeping in a flock together, they rose and fell in the air, sometimes altering their course erratically, as if moved by sudden whims. They fluttered a lot, their wings flashing like the sails of yachts buffeted in a wind. Suddenly they swooped down and alighted in a row on a log-boom moored in the water. Then I saw distinctly their black heads. Not all of them wore these jet hoods, for a few were immature birds with only a black spot behind each eye on otherwise white heads.

They were on their way to a nesting colony further north, probably beside some lake or muskeg in the northwest. But they were in no particular hurry. For several days small parties of them could be seen in the creek, floating buoyantly on the water, their neat figures held erect as if they paid particular attention to deportment. After a week they disappeared and in the latter half of the month only an occasional immature representative of the species passed by.

Glaucous Gulls appeared twice whilst I was watching. They were unmistakeable, being a size or two larger than Herring Gulls who stood or swam beside them. Also they had no dark tips to their chalky-white wings. Their bigness was impressive yet rather forbidding, as might be the case with any other giant.

In contrast, the next new bird to arrive in the creek was a pigmy—a House Wren. I could write about the astonishing loud voice of this diminutive bird, which made a schoolboy friend of Lord Grey refer to one of its English cousins as "that shattering Wren". Or I could describe its other charming attributes. But this book will become intolerably tedious if I dwell on the characteristics of all the creatures who flit through its pages. In any case everybody knows all about the House Wren.

On the same day an unusual visitor appeared. Standing amongst the gulls was a bird rather larger than a Bonaparte's Gull and smaller than a Ring-billed Gull. Its face was white, its back pearl-grey, its beak light yellow and its feet were black. But the surest mark of its identification was revealed when it flew. Its black wing-tips then appeared unrelieved by any white spots and were cut straight across, "as if they had been dipped in ink".[1] This is the hall-mark of a Kittiwake.

The next arrival, in the middle of the month, was the last of the wild duck to migrate, a Blue-winged Teal. These Teal are delicate, warm-weather birds who abhor any hint of frost in the air. They seem to be as delicate and squeamish about the temperature as are hot-house plants. So they dally in their winter haunts in the sunny marshes of Florida and the bayous of Louisiana, or even the warm

[1] Roger Tory Peterson, *A Field Guide to the Birds.* Houghton, Mifflin & Co.

lakes of Chile and Brazil, until the last possible moment. In the autumn they are amongst the first birds to leave the treacherous north again on their southward journey.

The bird that I saw was a drake. He did not recognize me as a possible enemy sitting on the shore, and flew past within a few feet of my eyes. He appeared to me in precisely the same position as did one of his relatives to Audubon a century ago. If the reader will look at the naturalist's picture of the Blue-winged Teal, he will realize what a vision of beauty I saw. The bird's grey head and neck shot with purplish gloss; its black forehead and chin; its long, crescent-shaped white face-patch; its brown and cinnamon body speckled with black; and its large blue fore-wings and green speculum make a handsome costume. In May these colourings are fresh. They have a bright, brand-new quality. I am told that this is because Blue-winged Teal acquire their breeding plumage late, not long before they migrate, so that their feathering in May is indeed like a party dress being worn for the first time.

This particular drake stayed two days in the creek and then flew elsewhere. Another appeared towards the end of the month. I saw no more until large flocks returned in the autumn, with their party dresses moulting and spoilt.

Whilst the first Blue-winged Teal was in the creek a Greater Scaup duck also appeared. Its markings are similar to those of the Lesser Scaup. It is distinguishable from the latter partly by its larger size. But this can hardly be judged when the birds are not seen together, and the chief recognition mark is the longer white stripe on the Greater Scaup's wings.

It was now the middle of May and migration had reached an immense volume. Almost every morning three, four or more new species arrived in the creek. Some of these were represented by countless individuals. At the same time the established species were being reinforced. I got the impression of a vast movement of creatures, as if great armies were on the march. What was happening in Brewery Creek was being repeated everywhere right across Canada. The bird population of the Dominion was being multiplied many times—increased by millions.

On May 16th the air squadrons of Tree Swallows and occasional Barn Swallows hawking for insects over the water were joined by several Chimney Swifts. They travelled at a high velocity like small, black aerial torpedoes. As they made wide whirlpools of flight around the heavens they combined business with pleasure, for the prolonged, high-pitched twittering which accompanies their hunting is a cry of gladness.

A few days later another kind of Swallow joined these revellers. A Bank Swallow arrived. This bird is more or less plain, with a brown back, dusky chin and white under-parts. I was sorry that the creek did not provide a specimen of the terrain which it requires for nesting. In sandy cliffs beside lakes and rivers a colony of Bank Swallows will dig rows of tunnels, at the far ends of which they make their nests and lay their eggs. Several such Bank Swallow settlements, looking like miniature Pueblo villages, can be seen along the Ottawa and Rideau Rivers. Each bird has an uncanny knack of recognizing its own particular burrow and flying at high speed through its entrance to the chamber within.

In the meantime a host of newcomers had arrived on land. Two of them, the Catbird and the Bobolink, added more to the charm of the music in the creek than to the physical beauty of its inhabitants. Catbirds, both male and female, are sombre-looking creatures, dark grey and black. Nor is the bird's most customary vocal expression a promising introduction to its talent as a singer. Hidden amongst the bushes, it "meows" harshly like a bad-tempered cat. From this sound it gets its name. In other moods, however, it is an accomplished performer with an extensive repertoire. Before I was properly acquainted with its character it deceived me more than once. I would hear a medley of lively, pleasant carols issuing from a small aspen. The tree seemed full of birds, for several different songs came from it. I approached it eagerly to identify the various singers, only to discover that the branches supported a single Catbird.

The explanation is that the Catbird is the northern representative of the Mockingbird, who does not often appear in person across the Canadian border. On the subject of the Catbird's voice I cannot do better than quote Mr. F. Schuyler Mathews, a learned musical critic of bird song. He writes:[1]

> There is a certain lawless freedom to the song of the Catbird which invests it with a character essentially wild. The bird does not appear to entertain any regard for set rhythm; he proceeds with a series of miscellaneous, interrupted sentences which bear no relationship with one another. The fact is, he is an imitator, and possibly does not know himself exactly what he is talking about, or what impression he will embody in "the next line". He can imitate anything from a squeaking cart-wheel to the song of a thrush. He

---

[1] F. Schuyler Mathews, *Field Book of Wild Birds and Their Music*. G. P. Putnam's Sons.

intersperses his melodic phrases with quotations from the highest authorities—Thrush, Song Sparrow, Wren, Oriole and Whip-poor-will! The yowl of the cat is thrown in anywhere, the guttural remarks of the frog are repeated without the slightest deference to good taste or appropriateness, and the harsh squawk of the old hen, or the chirp of the lost chicken is always added in some *mal à propos* manner. . . .

The male Bobolink is more distinguished in plumage than the Catbird, yet its costume is such a patch-work of striking but inconsequential colours that it appears almost clownish. Its head, face, wings, underparts and tail are black. On this ground are imposed odd patches of corn-yellow on the nape of the neck, cream-buff on the back and white on the shoulders, rump and upper tail coverts.

Even its attractive song conveys a suggestion of buffoonery. Mr. Mathews calls the bird "the soloist of comic opera in the fields". I heard it first when a cock bird, on the morning of its arrival, sang from a dandelion stalk protruding from meadow grasses. I was struck by the pleasant originality and individuality of the effort. Mr. Mathews describes it thus:

> The Bobolink is indeed a great singer, but the latter part of his song is a species of musical fireworks. He begins bravely enough with a number of well-sustained tones, but presently he accelerates his time, loses track of his motive, and goes to pieces in a burst of musical scintillations. It is a mad, reckless song-fantasia, an outbreak of pent-up irrepressible glee. The difficulty in either describing or putting upon paper such music is insurmountable.

One of its notes in particular I shall long remember; a

sweet, tinkling, metallic sound like the stroke of a cow-bell wafted down an Alpine valley.

Another arrival in mid-May was the Baltimore Oriole, in truth one of the loveliest of North American birds. It has a neat figure and glorious plumage. The male bird's head, face and throat are black. Its back and wings are also largely black, but the latter are boldly striped with white. Its underparts and rump are fiery orange and its tail is half black and half orange. The female is also finely feathered, though her style is more subdued than that of her sire. She is mostly olive above and yellow below. They are a pair of beauties worthy of each other.

The legend of the origin of their name is pleasing. It is said that when George Calvert, the first Lord Baltimore who in the seventeenth century promoted settlement in Maryland and Delaware, visited Virginia he was attracted by a strange, gay Oriole inhabiting its woods. The bird so delighted him that he adopted the colours of its plumage—orange and black—for his coat-of-arms. This may or may not explain truly the origin of his family emblem. It is certain however that when Linnaeus later saw some skins of these Orioles he named them Baltimore Orioles because they wore his lordship's colours.

As their bodies are "easy to look at", so are their voices easy to listen to. They frequently utter a melodious whistle so clear and loud that it can be heard from a great distance. Their song is short and fragmentary, but pure and rich in tone. One day I watched a cock Baltimore Oriole and a cock Red-winged Blackbird sitting on branches on neighbouring trees. The Oriole was brilliant both to see and to hear. At short intervals it sang. Each time the Blackbird answered with a self-satisfied screech. He seemed to fancy himself as a rival of the other, and to be showing off his feathers and producing his atrocious noise in competition with the Oriole. This only goes to show how shamefully defective an eye for beauty and an ear for music the Red-winged Blackbird has.

Other birds who arrived at about the same time were the White-crowned Sparrow and the Veery or Wilson's Thrush. The broad, black and white head stripes and spot-less, pearly-grey breast of the former make it one of the handsomest of the multitudinous tribe of Sparrows. The Veery is, in contrast, the most modestly marked of the Thrushes. Uniformly tawny-brown above, it has few spots on its light breast. It is a quiet-behaved, gentlemanly bird. Often it flits silently and self-effacingly amongst the under-brush in a wood, and its song—which has the fine quality of most Thrush songs—has an air of sadness and mystery.

On the same day a Hairy Woodpecker came to the creek. Though this individual bird may have been a sum-mer visitor, representatives of the species stay in Ottawa throughout the year. I have seen one in my garden at the end of December flying from tree to tree, calling cheerfully and hammering with its beak on the wood, indifferent to the fact that every bough and twig was covered with white hoar-frost. The bird is like a large edition of the Downy Woodpecker, the spotted and checkered black-and-white markings of the two being almost exact replicas of each other.

Next came two gaily feathered birds. The first was an American Goldfinch. It had visited the creek earlier, in April, and is an all-the-year-round resident in Ottawa. But its previous appearance was less distinguished, for then it still wore its plainer winter plumage.

Now the cock birds had donned their spring and summer splendour. I know a girl, a glimpse of whose sparkling eyes, smiling mouth and lovely face once made a stranger exclaim, "Who is that little flash of joy?" Like her, a male American Goldfinch flying through the air in May is a little flash of joy. Its body is brilliant, with sharply contrasting black and lemon-yellow markings. It wears a black cap, black wings and black tail on an otherwise wholly yellow body. The female is more subdued in colouring, her wings being merely blackish and the rest of her body olive-green. But neither bird could be called subdued in behaviour. When feeding they move quickly from bush to bush or weed to weed. No creature in the animal world makes eating appear such a restless, hectic occupation. In flight they sing scraps of their song, which has a spontaneous, care-free, gay character. Some of its phrases sound like tinkling glass. When writing of the reasons for bird song I remarked that in some species singing really is an expression of pure pleasure. The Goldfinches' song is an example of this. Similar to that of the Canary, it adds to the appropriateness of the bird's charming colloquial name, Wild Canary. Several pairs arrived in the creek on the same day and some of them stayed all summer.

The other gay bird was the Rose-breasted Grosbeak. With all due respect, the female of the species is at all times a drab looking hussy. But the male in spring is a dandy. His large, pale beak is ugly, but otherwise he has fine quality. His head, throat, back, wings and tail are sable except for a few white streaks on the wings. In sharp distinction his lower parts are flawlessly white. On his chest, however, dividing the area of black from the area of white is a large, triangular rose-red patch. Such boldness of design is almost incredible. My first sight of the bird was when two males perched close together in one tree. Hardly trusting my eyes when I caught sight of the red bosom of the first bird, I looked at the second. Seeing that it too had this rich adornment, I knew that the vision must be true.

It gives me no pleasure to mention that the next bird which I saw was a House Sparrow. All we mortal creatures have our faults as well as our virtues, but the House Sparrow seems to be unduly endowed with the former. It is an infernal nuisance—so noisy, messy and destructive. One aggravating thing about it is that its shortcomings are associated in American parlance with England. It is not indigenous to North America, being, like the Starling, an importation from Europe, and unfortunately an alternative name for it is the English Sparrow. I shall not expand on the subject. Mr. Taverner has summed up the situation in a sentence. He writes, "Without doubt the introduction of the English Sparrow into America was a mistake."

Shortly after the middle of May several new shore birds arrived. They were passage migrants who stayed at most only a few days in the creek before moving on to whatever summer resorts they favoured. I have a soft spot in my heart for these waders. They are associated in general with wild, free ocean beaches and in particular, for me, with the shores of the Moray Firth, where I was born and have my true home.

The first of these newcomers was a Common or Ruddy Turnstone. This bird is supposed to be an unusual visitor to Ottawa. But I think it is probably a regular, brief visitor each year and that observers do not happen to notice it as often as they might. It is not a becoming creature. Its body is rather heavily built and its head is fixed to its shoulders with no apparent neck. Though its orange legs are handsome, the black, white and russet-red markings of its body seem to have been thrown on anyhow, with no eye for design. However, when the bird takes wing these streaks and splotches, which seemed so aimlessly placed, are shown to compose a complicated and attractive pattern covering the whole back of the bird. This plumage gives it prudent camouflage as it strolls about searching for food amongst the flotsam and jetsam cast upon the shore. Its habit of poking its bill under stones, bits of wood and seaweed and turning them over to expose the crustaceans on which it feeds underneath gained it its name.

On the same day as the earliest Turnstone a Black-bellied Plover also arrived. It had not yet, however, acquired the said black belly. That feature was only in process of formation. In their breeding plumage both sexes of the species are solid black from the level of their eyes down their lower faces, necks, breasts and underparts as far as their thighs. Above they are largely grey and brown, beautifully mottled with black. In their winter plumage this upper pattern is preserved, but the black of their lower parts disappears as completely as the darkness of night flees at the arrival of day. Its place is taken by white feathering. The black returns late in spring. In the first bird that I saw the dark plumage was beginning to reappear. It shaded the space between the bird's legs and had started to creep upwards towards its breast. In another representative of the species which arrived in the creek several days later no sign whatever of the black breeding plumage appeared, the bird's face, throat, breast and abdomen being still entirely white.

One morning a merry little party of Least Sandpipers were running over the mud and wading in the shallowest water. These lively pigmies of the shore are only about the size of Sparrows, though their longer legs and bills give them an air of rather greater importance. They have equals in size, figure and plumage in Semipalmated Sandpipers, but these otherwise almost perfect twins can be distinguished at close quarters through field-glasses by the rather reddish brown plumage and yellowish or greenish legs of the former in comparison with the grey or sandy brown plumage and blackish legs of the latter. A quartette of tiny Sandpipers scurrying over the shore on the following morning may have included both species, but they flew away without giving me an opportunity to study at close quarters their coats and nether limbs.

Within the next few days two other birds who might be classed as shore birds, though of a different nature, flew over the creek. The first was an American Bittern and the second a Black-crowned Night Heron. Though two days later I heard an invisible Bittern making its famous "pile-driving" noise, I did not catch more than this glimpse of either bird in May. Later in the year they were more frequent visitors to the shore and I shall reserve an account of them for another chapter.

Other waders did not arrive until almost the end of the month, but I may as well mention them now in order to treat the group as a whole. One morning a Semipalmated Plover was feeding at the water's edge. At my first casual glance, when its back was turned towards me, I took it for a Killdeer. Then I noticed that it was smaller than a Spotted Sandpiper close by, whereas a Killdeer would have been considerably larger. Turning my field-glasses on it,

I saw that it had only one black band across its breast instead of the Killdeer's two. It stayed for only a few hours in the creek and was gone before evening.

The handsomest visiting wader was a Red-backed Sandpiper, which remained for two days on the precincts. It was not frightened of me or my canoe and let me approach quite close by water and by land. I got perfect, close-up views of it as it stalked across the sand and mud, frequently plunging its long beak into the ground to catch tempting morsels of food. The pattern of its plumage was beautiful in both form and colours. Its red crown had long black stripes; its rufous back was speckled with black and white; its face, neck, breast and flanks were white, with fine grey and black streaks; and its abdomen was black. This was the adornment of a bird whose head, neck and body had good and shapely proportions, enhanced by tallish, dark legs and a longish, black, down-curving bill.

Another handsome migrant, which first appeared in the middle of the month, was a Common Loon. This bird, which is at home on either fresh or salt water, has two notable attributes. The first is its voice. Its mournful, far-carrying wail and its long, loud, rippling "laugh" both have haunting beauty. Some people would object to such an approving comment. They feel disturbed, even frightened, by the note of despair in a Loon's weird call. At night especially it has a sadness and mystery, an eeriness and other-worldliness which make it sound like the cry not so much of a living bird as of a lost soul. But to me it expresses all the lovely wildness of northern Canadian lakes and forests.

On two occasions when the water was calm in the creek a Loon came and showed off its second remarkable attribute, its striking plumage. Nature arranges many bold, original designs in the shapes and colours of flowers and birds. None is more successful than the markings of the Common Loon. The effect is not gained by rich colours, but rather by simplicity. No pigments except black and white are used. The result is most comely. It is like a dress made by a superlative dress-maker for a smart lady who is in mourning.

The Loon's own figure is partly responsible for the effect. It could be described as a "good bird to dress". Its body is large, measuring almost three feet from the tip of its bill to the end of its tail. Its back is gracefully arched, the base of its neck has a curve reminiscent of a Swan's, the long neck is thick and strong and supports a large, snakey head from which protrudes a stout, dagger-like bill. This bill is shining black. The head and neck are a rich, glossy, velvety black with purplish reflections. Across the throat stretches a row of small white stripes. The same *motif* is repeated lower down, once on each side of the neck. The edges of the breast are striped with black and white and the back and flanks have a black and white checker pattern. The underparts are pure white. In this whole design the only spots of colour are the red irides of the eyes. The costume is simple and yet magnificent.

One morning I got a surprise. As I stood in the shade of some trees looking up at a nest, I saw out of the corner of one eye a flock of large birds flying in close, irregular formation into the creek. My view of them was partly obstructed by the trees and I ran into an open space to see them better. Perhaps they caught sight of me or perhaps something else frightened them. When they were about to settle on the water they changed their minds, accelerated

COMMON LOON
"Its striking plumage."

their slowing wing-beats, wheeled round and flew out of the creek to the river. There I lost sight of them.

I had seen enough, however, to excite me. At first I thought the birds were a kind of duck. Although they seemed rather large for duck, they seemed too small for geese. Yet when I got my glasses on them their membership of the goose family was undoubted. I saw from their black heads, necks and breasts that they were American Brant Geese.

About an hour later I confirmed this when returning across the river to Earnscliffe. The geese rose from the water ahead of me—a flock of about sixty birds. Flying in a ragged, confused crowd whilst manoeuvring for position, they formed a thrilling mass of wild wings. Then they found their direction and went in formation straight up the river towards the Chaudière Falls and Lake Deschênes. Dropping within two or three feet of the water's surface, they moved off close together low over the calm river. It was a beautiful sight. A day or two later a couple of injured Brant Geese, too hurt to fly away, were found on Lake Deschênes.

This was something of an event, for very few records of Brant Geese on the Ottawa River exist. An occasional bird, seen at intervals of many years, has always been regarded as an accidental wanderer. The regular line of spring and autumn migration for these geese lies hundreds of miles to the east of Ottawa. Was this flock a mere eccentric party or the blazer of some new trail from their winter quarters to their breeding grounds in the north?

Meanwhile on land Kingbirds had arrived. They never stayed still for long, but were for ever in the air, fluttering their wings and spreading their tails like the large Flycatchers which they are, hawking for their insect prey.

Then Cedar Waxwings came. They are amongst the best-looking of the smaller birds. There is something exotic, a suggestion of the foreigner, about them. The dusky line across their faces, their soft, subtle colourings with here and there a touch of finery, their sleek, silky feathers and erect crests, as if they were miniature cockatoos, have a tropical air.

At the same time came three Vireos—Warbling and Red-eyed Vireos to stay and a Philadelphia Vireo for only a fleeting visit. Two new representatives of the Flycatcher family also arrived, the Least Flycatcher and the Eastern Wood Peewee. I could count on hearing their voices and seeing them sitting upright on their respective branches at any time in a certain part of the wood. One day two Black-capped Chickadees paid a call on them . . . But I must not weary the reader with accounts of all these birds.

Early in the last week of May a Black-billed Cuckoo visited the creek. First I heard its voice at a distance. Gradually the sound came nearer as the bird flew from tree to tree, until finally it perched on a low branch twenty yards from me. It was in full view on my eye-level—so close that I saw distinctly not only the details of its sleek, slender body, its olive-brown and white plumage and its dark bill, but also the bright red circle of naked skin round each eye. As it settled there it began to sing, softly and tentatively at first but then confidently and loud. Its voice was pleasant, consisting of a liquid, rippling, throaty sound which seemed to rise upwards from deep in its chest. Indeed, I could see the effort necessary to produce it. As the Cuckoo sang its vocal muscles made a vibrant, up-and-down movement and its throat swelled until the bird seemed afflicted with goitre.

This Black-billed Cuckoo remained in the creek for several days, but then found a mate and a nesting place elsewhere. Afterwards it was only an occasional visitor.

On the day of its first appearance a Brown Thrasher also came to a thicket on the creek bank. Its figure is similar to that of the Cuckoo, for it too has a sleek head, a slender, down-curving bill, a slim body and a long, elegant tail. Its colour is mostly reddish brown with heavy dark streaks on its white breast. Its yellow eyes lend it an air of fierceness, but its song is sweet. It belongs to the Mockingbird family and often tries to out-Catbird the Catbird.

Last and quite definitely least—by physical standards—of the May immigrants came the Ruby-throated Hummingbird. The smallest Canadian bird, it measures about 3¾ inches long, half of which consists of bill and tail. But the bird is least only in size. In beauty and character it is amongst the most fascinating of creatures.

Hummingbirds reached Ottawa soon after the middle of the month, but I did not notice any in the creek until the 27th. Then I saw one perched on a bough of a Willow tree. The tiny bird, about the size of a large moth, is usually in such a constant quiver of motion that I was surprised to see it sitting motionless. Behind it shone the light of the rising sun and so I only saw it in black silhouette. Its figure was trim. Its most striking feature was the long, delicate stiletto of a beak with which it pierces flowers to their honeyed hearts.

Several times in the following days I saw a Hummingbird whizz past, like an overgrown bee. Sometimes I met one over the middle of the river, flying from one shore to the other. I should not have been surprised to see any other bird there, but could not help feeling astonished when I

saw this tiny creature making a considerable journey over
water. It was like seeing an aeroplane flying the Atlantic.
But of course my surprise was absurd. Ruby-throated
Hummingbirds are tremendous fliers. Their flight muscles
are unusually large in relation to their size and even their
shortest journeys are executed with conspicuous energy and
dash. Their migrations are amongst the miracles of bird
travel. They winter in Central America, and in the Gulf
States and nest anywhere from the middle United States
northwards as far as the shores of Hudson Bay. A journey
of a thousand miles is therefore nothing to them. Nor do
they always travel overland where they can stop and rest
when tired. Thousands of them cross vast stretches of
ocean, hurling themselves 500 miles across the Gulf of
Mexico from Yucatan and Central America. After that
they doubtless find it child's play to cross the Ottawa River
from Ontario to Quebec.

They have the anatomy of birds, the movements of
flying insects and the colours of flowers. Their plumage is
gem-like. True, it is not so spectacular as an enthusiastic
early settler in New England averred when he wrote that
"for colour she is as glorious as the Raine-bow".[1] But it has
the brilliance of a jewel. One day I watched a bird as it
raided the nectar in hundreds of flowers on a Wild Honey-
suckle tree. It darted impetuously yet easily and gracefully
from blossom to blossom. In front of each it paused unmoving, except for its almost invisible, whirring wings,
whilst it inserted its pin-like beak amongst the petals to
suck honey. During those moments of feeding the bird
remained so steady in one spot of air that I got as excellent
a view of the plumage as if it had been perched motionless

[1] William Wood, 1634, *New England's Prospect.*

on a branch. Sunlight illuminated the sweet creature. It was a female and so lacked the glowing ruby gorget of its mate. Instead its throat, like its breast, was white. But the head, back and middle tail feathers were golden bronze-green. They glinted like polished metal. Nay, they gleamed and glistened and at some angles glittered like a bright green flame. Perfection is rare in this world, but the beauty of a Ruby-throated Hummingbird is perfect.

2.

As I have already observed, long before many of these May migrants arrived the resident birds and earlier immigrants were already nesting. Now their affairs reached yet another stage. In the tree holes inhabited by Starlings eggs hatched and chicks grew rapidly. By the middle of the month greyish-brown fledglings with lean faces and fluffy feathers left the nests and perched in trees or stood on the ground yelling for food. The parents were kept busy searching for insects to stuff down their throats. The squawking in these Starling nurseries was a hideous noise and soon the new generation became deplorably numerous.

Bronzed Grackles were equally advanced. They had built nests and laid eggs before the beginning of May. I first realized this when I saw a pair of them pursuing a Crow through the sky. The sight soon became common. The two Grackles would fly above their enemy and each in turn swoop down on it, almost strike it and then swerve up again to prepare for another attack. They were like dive-bombers in action. The Crow is an egg-thief and they were chasing it away from the neighbourhood of their nest. When doing so they should be troubled by guilty consciences, for they themselves steal the eggs of smaller birds.

Infant Grackles began to leave their nests and wander uncertainly in the outer world at about the same time as the young Starlings.

Meadowlarks were others whose love-making and home-building started early. On May 2nd I disturbed a couple flirting in the grass. They took wing hurriedly and made off like conspirators. Afterwards I sometimes saw one perched on top of a small tree, showing off its charming yellow and black breast and singing its sweet, short song in evident proclamation of territory. But I doubt whether the pair nested successfully in the creek. The grass in the most likely area was soon cut for hay and I did not often see a Meadowlark after that. Probably they decided to go elsewhere, where the lush grass grew undisturbed by a scythe.

Red-winged Blackbirds also were occupied with domestic duties. Numbers of them were always perched in the trees at the edge of the creek, especially where willows and maples stood in the flood waters which, in this rainy season, swamped the lower areas. The Blackbirds maintained a perpetual harsh din. Almost all wore the black uniforms and red epaulettes of males. Few brown, striped females appeared. The self-assertive cocks were proclaiming their ownership of territory, proprietorship of wives and guardianship of youngsters whilst the quiet, demure hens stayed out of sight sitting on eggs. Long before the end of the month fledgling Red-winged Blackbirds were exercising their infant legs and wings on the willow branches.

In contrast to the dutiful, invisible mother Blackbirds the female Cowbirds were only too much in evidence. They flaunted themselves on many a bough, shamefully free from family responsibilities. As they flew about they whistled and flirted, like loose women on a street as distinct from pious mothers in a home. Solicitation in broad daylight was their accepted custom and they were always attended by willing males. It was sad to see the goings-on of so many in a neighbourhood filled with nests of smaller, passerine birds—their prospective victims. If a bird Parliament could pass and enforce a law against public solicitation in avian society, the danger to other birds would be greatly reduced. But no such legislation exists and the Cowbirds pursue their rakes' and harlots' progress with impunity.

They too have their "territories". It is curious how this fundamental condition of bird existence in the breeding season applies, with adaptation, even to them. Each hen Cowbird arrogates to herself an area of ground containing a suitable number of other birds' nests, say about thirty. She keeps a watch on these and chooses which one she shall use as a foster-home each time that she is ready to lay an egg.

Different pairs of the same species of birds reached the same stages of nesting activity at different times. One morning in mid-May, for example, I saw two male Robins engaged in a dispute about the boundaries of their territories, a female Robin carrying nesting material into bushes where she was building and another female sitting on a nest already containing eggs, all within a comparatively short distance of each other.

Before the end of May most of the migrants who arrived during that month had likewise settled down to the paramount duty of begetting young. It would be confusing and exhausting, to the reader even more than to the author, if I attempted to write a comprehensive series of nest-histories of all the species summering in the creek. Instead I shall select a few representative species, chosen at random, and describe what I saw of their lives during May, June and July. In earlier chapters I have already started the stories of some of these. Others now begin. The species are the Song Sparrow, Northern Flicker, Phoebe, Yellow Warbler, Catbird, Baltimore Oriole and Spotted Sandpiper. Occasionally incidents in the family life of other species, like the Savannah Sparrow and the Veery, are added. I wish that I could include one or more wild duck, but none nested in the creek. They visited it only in the course of their northward migration in spring and their return journey in autumn. Between the end of May and the middle of August no wild fowl stayed in Brewery Creek.

3.

I did not find a Song Sparrow's nest until almost the end of May. On the 27th a hen bird suddenly fluttered from the earth near my feet and, looking down, I saw the nest half hidden in a clump of Dandelions. It was a neat structure. From above, its rim looked like a bracelet of brown, intertwined dead grasses and weeds thrown amongst the yellow flowers and green leaves. Its strong, upright circle of wall stood unbuttressed. The nest lay casually there, like a cup accidently left on the ground. In it were five eggs, their colour greenish-white speckled with light and dark brown spots.

When I returned next morning five eggs were still the grand total. The mother Sparrow had evidently stopped laying. I could not tell how long she had been sitting, but the process of incubation was well under-way.

Each day after that I visited the nest. Whenever I appeared the parent birds went through the same performance. The hen was sitting in the nest, concealed by Dande-

RUBY-THROATED HUMMINGBIRD
"Its figure was trim."

lion leaves and long grasses. The cock was keeping guard over her, close by. As soon as I came near he uttered a warning to his mate.

"Tik, tik, tik," he called.

As I approached closer he repeated the exclamation two or three times. But she sat tight, trusting that the wild flowers and rough grass would hide her from my view. Not till I was within a pace or two did she move. Then she slipped hurriedly but quietly from the nest, flew a short way low over the ground and rose to a neighbouring bush.

The cock meanwhile had taken up his position on a bough overlooking the nest, where he could keep an eye on its precious contents. The respective parts played by the two birds illustrated their division of labour during the incubation period. The female sits patiently on her eggs and the male keeps constant guard over her and them.

As I looked into the nest to see whether any chicks had yet hatched, he could not contain his anxiety. At regular, short intervals he uttered a subdued alarm note. After a few moments I left. Not long afterwards the mother returned to the nest and the father fell silent again.

When May passed into June she was still sitting on her unhatched quintuplets.

4.

The pair of Northern Flickers continued to haunt the creek. Some time early in May they must have started to prepare their home. Flickers usually nest in a hole in a tree or a fence-post. Often they dig out their own nest in a rotten tree trunk. For some time I was not sure where the Brewery Creek Flickers chose to reside this summer and did not make much effort to find out. When they are establishing a home Flickers have difficulties and enemies enough to contend against, without the additional worry of guarding against an inquisitive ornithologist. Starlings, for example, are only too apt to eject them from their holes and commandeer the places for themselves.

Moreover, I had an excellent opportunity to watch a pair of Flickers who built their nest in my garden within easy view of my study window. So I did not need to go elsewhere to observe the process. Let me give an account of their experiences, which may well reproduce those of the pair in the creek.

The Earnscliffe birds had been flying and flirting in the garden for some weeks. On the morning of May 21st I discovered them making their nest. It was in the trunk of a dead birch tree, about fifteen feet from the ground. First I noticed the male, conspicuously moustached, clinging to the tree and methodically tapping the wood with his powerful beak a few inches below a round, sizeable hole in the trunk. Then he hopped up a step or two, poked his head into the hole and, after a few moments hesitation, half-disappeared into it. Only his tail, rump and legs remained visible outside. When he pulled himself out again his long beak was stuffed with wooden chips. Jerking his head sideways, he threw them away. I saw that the wood at the edge of the hole was fresh-coloured, indicating that it was newly exposed to the light of day. The Flicker was evidently engaged in excavating its home.

It poked its head and fore-body into the hole again and emerged once more with a beakful of chips. As before, with a toss of the head it threw them in the air. Several times it repeated the performance, evidently cleaning out the inside of the nest.

After a while the female flew to the tree and alighted beside her mate. He promptly cast himself from the trunk and left. She hopped into the position which he had occupied and continued, with precisely the same actions, his work of cleaning out the nest. This was obviously a change of shifts between the nest-builders.

At intervals during the day I watched the progress of their work. The male was usually on the job, but now he had changed his occupation. He was no longer engaged in clearing chips from the nest, but in enlarging the cavity itself. Clinging with his strong feet to the bark below the hole, he pushed as much of his body as possible into the hole and hammered with his bill at its inside. The angle of those portions of his anatomy left outside showed that he was attacking the floor. They stuck up in the air at such a sharp angle that he was balanced almost upside-down. Meanwhile the vibrations of his abdomen indicated how rapid and powerful were his beak blows. At more or less regular intervals he emerged for a rest. Each time he stayed in the hole for about a quarter-of-a-minute and his rests lasted for about the same period. His changes of position were accomplished without any alteration of the placing of his feet, which acted as a lever for the movement of his whole body.

As the day wore on his steady progress was marked by the ever smaller fraction of him protruding from the hole when he worked inside. In the morning his rump and tail had both stuck out. In the afternoon only his tail showed. By then he had shifted his foothold to somewhere just below the hole on its inside wall. In the evening only the tip of his tail protruded. He was digging deep.

On a second occasion that day I saw him relieved by the female. As soon as she perched on the tree he flew away.

129

as before. She at once moved to the hole and inspected it, first peering curiously into it, then half-disappearing inside and staying there for a while. But she did no work and soon flew away. It was just a housewife's visit to view the amenities of her prospective home.

Male and female Flickers both help in the construction of their nests. But this female at least did not appear to do more than light work, such as the removal of superfluous wood-chips. So far as I could see, the male alone engaged in the heavy labour of enlarging the hole by boring and hammering.

When I went out soon after six o'clock next morning the male bird was already on the job and he stayed on it until early in the afternoon. His labour was truly Herculean. Once more he had changed its nature. Whereas on the previous day he was busy deepening the cavity inside the tree, now he was broadening it. He still clung with his claws to the outside of the trunk, but less of him disappeared when he was at work on the interior. The position of his body was also different. Whereas yesterday he had been tilted upside-down whilst his beak struck at the nest floor, today he remained more or less upright whilst he chiselled at its back wall.

The force which he put into his blows was tremendous. His whole strength was concentrated behind them. His widely splayed toes held the wood in an immoveable grip, his tail was pressed on the bark to add to the firmness of his hold, his abdomen leaned against the trunk to give greater purchase to his body and every muscle that could contribute anything was mobilized to support the battering-ram of his beak.

He worked more quickly than on the previous day, for

his upright position made movement freer. He could pop
his head and shoulders in and out of the hole more easily.
Each bout of battering inside the hole now lasted less than
ten seconds and his periods of rest in between were reduced
to less than five seconds. This made him appear to be
working in a hurry, as if he were racing against time.

The entrance to the nest was little larger in circum-
ference than the girth of his body. Consequently his feathers
got fluffed-up and untidy as he poked in and out. At the
end of a few hours' hard labour he looked thoroughly
scruffy. But at that time personal appearance meant
nothing to him. He was engrossed in his task. So intent
was he on it that few things disturbed him. He treated
with indifference even the occasional, noisy passing of a
truck along the drive immediately beneath the tree.

Sometimes he stopped chiselling and again started
removing the accumulation of chips from inside the nest,
throwing them away with the characteristic toss of his
head. They fell to the ground below. The lawn and drive-
way there became white with them. They represented a
truly remarkable amount of carpentry.

That afternoon a gale of wind blew up and the Flicker
suspended his efforts. Neither he nor his mate appeared
for the rest of the day. But at dawn the next morning, in
spite of a continuation of the storm, he was at work again.
He clung close to the tree to get as much shelter as possible
from the wind whilst pursuing his excavations. All that
morning he laboured without ceasing. By lunch-time the
nest was so deep that when he was upside-down inside it
only the extreme tip of his tail showed. After lunch he
was standing right inside the hole and when he stooped to
chisel he completely disappeared from view. But every now

and then he stopped work and peered out of the hole, like Punch in a Punch-and-Judy box.

I had not seen the female for two days. When I went out the next morning, however, she was sitting inside the nest. In the shadowy interior I could discern her beak and moustacheless cheeks. As I approached, her whole face poked out. Suspicious of me, she emerged and flew away to a nearby telephone pole, where her mate joined her.

Later in the morning she was back in the nest. Every few moments her face appeared at the entrance with a beak full of wood-chips, which she tossed out with a vigorous shake of the head. Whenever I looked towards the birch tree during the next few hours she was still engaged on this occupation. The spacious nest hole must have been half full of "sawdust" and emptying it with a bird's beak was as slow and tedious work as emptying a bucket of water with a thimble.

Once the male came to the nest. But he did not enter it, only perching in front of it, looking at his mate and then flying away. His massive carpentry was evidently completed. The digging-out of the Flicker apartment was finished. Nothing remained to be done except to tidy it inside and prepare it for a clutch of eggs. That was the female's duty. She was the expert in interior arrangements. She would lay the eggs and do most of the incubation and her maternal instinct told her what was required.

At last the whole task was completed. The nest was ready for occupation. It was deep and wide and roomy. Its floor was covered with several layers of well-packed wood chips, to give firm yet comfortable support to eggs and, later, chicks.

That evening the expectant mother was thoroughly

settled in the nest. Now and then her face peered from its entrance as she surveyed the prospect in the outside world.

She might well look, for developments had taken a sinister turn. Throughout the previous four days, during the patient, laborious building of the nest, no other bird had come near that birch tree. But now an intruder had arrived. On a bough not far from the hole stood a Starling, covetously eyeing the nest. The Flicker inside it felt troubled by her visitor. Once she flew out and attacked the Starling, forcing it to beat a retreat.

Later in the evening the situation took a turn for the worse. Two Starlings and a House Sparrow all appeared on the scene and stood gazing at the hole from various branches round it. The Flicker in the nest stared back at them with a defiant "I'm the King of the Castle" sort of gaze. But I did not like the look of things. The trio of visitors reminded me of vultures gathered for a kill.

When I went to the tree early next morning I saw a bird inside the nest industriously throwing out wood-chips. It was a Starling. Neither Flicker was anywhere in sight. So the *coup d'état* had been accomplished. A pair of Starlings were in unchallenged occupation of the nest and it was to hold the pale-blue eggs of these unattractive immigrants instead of the white eggs of the beautiful, native Northern Flickers.

5.

At the end of the last chapter we left the Phoebes playing their respective parts as mother and father during the incubation period. Their eggs were laid in a nest in the shed beside the old saw-mill. The hen bird had already been sitting a few days, whilst the male kept guard from a convenient tree near by.

133

This state of affairs continued for the first ten days of May. Whenever I visited the shed a bird was sitting on the nest. Generally it was the female, but occasionally it may have been the male. The light in the shed was poor and I could not distinguish between them. Usually, however, the male was conscientiously doing sentry duty outside. But once or twice when he was not visible there I suspected that the bird on the nest was he, relieving his spouse whilst she was away feeding. Although the male Phoebe apparently takes little or no part in building the nest, he does every now and then share in keeping their eggs warm.

The eggs must have been near hatching, for the normal period of incubation of a Phoebe's clutch is about fourteen days. Then tragedy intervened. When I entered the shed on the morning of May 11th I saw a sorrowful sight. The nest beam was empty except for a few *distrait* wisps of grass. On the earth floor below lay the broken nest. There too were five smashed eggs, containing the remains of almost fully formed chicks.

This piece of senseless and wanton destruction could only have been perpetrated by a human being. No egg-stealing bird or other similar enemy would have broken the nest so completely and left the eggs and their contents strewn upon the ground.

I searched for the bereaved parents, but could not find them. For a day or two I thought that disappointment had made them desert the creek to try their luck elsewhere. But no, they were not to be deterred by vandalism. They had probably nested and reared their families in this particular corner of this particular creek for a few seasons and would not easily be discouraged from doing so again.

Two mornings after the tragedy I saw them both hawking for flies from bushes near the shed. In the fol-

Photo by W. V. Crich, F.R.P.S.

SKUNKS
"Perhaps it had a young family in the neighbourhood."

lowing days one or the other or both of them were always
to be seen in the neighbourhood. They shifted their customary perching places, however, a dozen yards further
along the bank, beside the old mill itself. I decided that
they must be building a new nest under the mill.

Sure enough, on the 28th, I found it in an inaccessible
part of the woodwork under the floor, where the building
was supported by tall piles driven into the sloping ground.
It was another untidy specimen of Phoebe architecture
constructed of mud and moss, dead leaves and bits of grass.
On top of this unsightly edifice, like a queen on a ruined
throne, sat the mother Phoebe. She eyed me uncertainly
as I climbed into a position where I could get a reasonably
good view of her. But she did not fly away, showing a
stubborn refusal to budge which indicated that she was
once more sitting on a full set of eggs.

Not far away sat the male, calling gently but nervously.
The pair had started all over again the business of raising
a family.

6.

Of all the birds who summered in the creek I came to
like the Yellow Warblers best. In character they are
friendly, lively and charming. They seem unafraid and
trustful, not flying away at one's approach but remaining
boldly visible and unconcerned even when you are within a
few feet of them. This is partly due to their occupation
with other affairs. They rarely stay still for a moment, but
flit from bough to bough and tree to tree with something
of the vivacity of butterflies. Often they express their
emotions in song—a loud, melodious, sparkling string of
notes and phrases. The bird is a virtuoso with a pleasant
variety of music.

It is no fool. On occasions it shows a surprising streak of sagacity. For example, Cowbirds often try to make it their victim. But frequently, as I have already written, it outwits the parasite. When it finds a Cowbird's egg amongst its own it abandons that nest, builds a new one on top of it and lays a fresh clutch of eggs. Occasionally an obstinate Cowbird lays a second egg in this second nest. Not to be beaten, the Yellow Warbler promptly deserts that nest also and builds a third on top of it. Cases are known where a Yellow Warbler had to build a fourth and even a fifth nest before its Cowbird tormentor acknowledged defeat.

Above all, the Yellow Warbler has true beauty. It is endowed with the trim figure and neat movements of most Warblers. Its plumage is not so guady as are some of theirs, but that is one reason why it is more lovely. The Yellow Warbler is an example of the truth that simplicity is more beautiful than grandeur. Other Warblers boast brilliant patches and juxtapositions of various colours. Some of them look like bright scraps of patch-work. The Yellow Warbler, on the other hand, gets its effect by dressing largely in one colour, being almost wholly yellow from the crown of its head to the tip of its tail. The shade of yellow varies in different parts of the body. It is greenish on the back and brownish on the tail. The cock bird is particularly handsome. His yellow is brighter and purer than that of his mate, and his throat and breast are finely streaked with pale chestnut.

These charming creatures first arrived beside the creek on May 16th, a sunny morning which seemed all the sunnier for their gay colour and cheerful songs. Only a few came then, but within two or three days they were plentiful. Soon they were chasing each other and flirting with joyous abandon. The air was filled with their calls and fragments of song. Wherever I looked small yellow bodies darted amongst the trees, some of them flying into bushes and saplings with tell-tale wisps of grass or other nesting material held in their beaks. They had not lost much time in pursuing the main purpose of their sojourn to the creek.

I watched one pair especially. The hen bird did most of the nest building, though her mate helped occasionally. She took four days to finish the work and was sitting cozily in the completed nest on May 29th. It was built in a briar patch, being securely attached to some crossing stems about two feet from the ground. It was a strong and pretty piece of work made of fine grasses, vegetable fibres and plant-down tightly woven together. Outside, its shape was determined by the angles of the stalks to which it was bound. Inside, it was round like the interior of a small ball with the top-quarter cut off. That is to say, its rim turned over and inwards so as to prevent, in due course, the young birds from tumbling out.

A bird's skill in nest-building is wholly instinctive. No parent has an opportunity to teach its offspring the delicate art of construction. Ability to build is inherited. Nor does a bird learn by experience, by trial and error. Qualified observers who have studied the matter report that a young bird's first attempt at nest-making is usually as good as its more mature efforts.

My Yellow Warbler laid her first egg on May 30th, a second egg the next day and a third on the day following. This practice of laying one egg on each of several successive days until the clutch is complete, and of not starting incubating any of them until then, is the usual, though not invariable, habit with most species. Generally a Yellow Warbler lays four eggs and sometimes five. This bird however, contented herself with three. On the third day she settled down earnestly to the business of hatching them.

7.

On the same day as the first Yellow Warblers arrived the first Catbird also came to the creek. Many others followed in the next few days. The commonest summer residents in the place were Starlings, Bronzed Grackles, Red-winged Blackbirds, Song Sparrows, Yellow Warblers and Catbirds.

As soon as they arrived the male Catbirds began to establish their territories. Catbirds have a reputation as rather shy, retiring, even secretive birds, and they did assume this character later in the year. For a while after their arrival, however, they were anything but secretive. Far from withdrawing into the deep undergrowth, the males seemed to choose deliberately a prominent stance, well exposed to public view, from which to announce their occupancy of the surrounding area. Nor, as I have indicated earlier, did they declare themselves modestly or shyly. Their melodious voices poured forth a merry medley of loud songs. No herald reading a Royal Proclamation to the accompaniment of trumpet blasts could have chosen a position or made a noise more calculated to draw attention to himself.

However, whilst the males were so conducting themselves their mates maintained the family reputation for shunning the limelight. The females were elusive. When I searched carefully, however, I could see them in thick shrubberies, gathering nesting material and flitting silently with it to the branches chosen as building sites. Once again, the female does most of the construction, although some males, according to their individual whims and natures, occasionally assist.

138

I did not actually discover a Catbird's nest until the beginning of the following month. They are usually built in such thick-growing places that one cannot easily approach them without disturbing and perhaps driving their builders away. But the birds' behaviour, as well as the early dates in June when I found nests already containing full sets of eggs, made it plain that in the last week of May they were busy making nests and laying eggs. The Catbirds, like the Yellow Warblers, lost no time in getting ahead with the main business of the summer.

8.

Baltimore Orioles first appeared in the creek a few days after the Yellow Warblers and Catbirds. A considerable wave of them must then have arrived, for suddenly the trees seemed well populated with these beautiful creatures. On all sides their gorgeous colours and rich voices could be seen and heard. One or two females came with the earliest males, and others soon followed. The males immediately began to prepare for domestic life. Two days after their first appearance I saw one viciously drive another off his territory. Perhaps matters proceeded before the end of May to the length of females building nests. But I did not find any of these cunningly woven and extraordinary structures until the early days of June and so shall reserve and account of them until the next chapter.

9.

As I have already recorded, the first Spotted Sandpiper arrived in the creek towards the end of April. To be exact, two birds appeared on the shore on April 24th. They may have been a pair or they may both have belonged to the same sex. Male and female Spotted Sandpipers are so similar in appearance that, short of killing and dissecting them, one cannot easily tell the one from the other. They are pretty creatures, of medium size by Sandpiper standards, with greyish-brown heads and backs and white underparts freckled with black spots. They do not go in for the dramatic, even freakish features—like elongated bills and lanky legs—which some shore birds favour. Their bills are moderately long, their legs are not stilts and every other part of their anatomy also has conventional proportions.

For a few days the first two arrivals were the only representatives of their kind. I often saw them running over the ground and making short reconnaissance flights. They appeared very much at home, as if they had lived all their lives in Brewery Creek and never gone to winter in Louisiana, the Caribbean Islands or South America.

They often "bobbed" in characteristic Spotted Sandpiper fashion. After running on quickly moving feet along the shore, they would suddenly halt, hold their bodies still and their heads erect for a moment, and then bow two or three times. This movement was made by a quick downwards and then upwards inclination of the whole body, turning on the axis of their thighs. No one can tell what may have been the origin in the dim past of this courteous gesture. It seems now to serve no useful purpose, but to be in the nature of a nervous habit.

Several more Spotted Sandpipers arrived in the last few days of April and during the night of May 1st. Next morning the population of Sandpipers was considerable and their behaviour indicated a new kind of liveliness. The earlier comers may all have been of one sex, for until that morning I saw no sign of anything which could be called courtship. Now, however, wooing had commenced. The birds called constantly to each other, their gay, care-free whistling filling the air. It had the light, joyous quality of the "tra-la-la's" of young people who have just fallen in love.

Even more indicative of their amorous mood was the conduct of some of the birds. They were "displaying". An uninitiated observer might have assumed that these were male Sandpipers, but that assumption would probably have been wrong. In the relevant section of Mr. Arthur Cleveland Bent's monumental and invaluable, though still uncompleted, work on the Life Histories of North American Birds it is written that "the courtship of the Spotted Sandpiper has not been observed very intimately," that "some of the published reports on the subject show a discrepancy in details" and that one such report described a bird indulging in aggressive courtship display who proved afterwards, on dissection, to be a female. This, remarks the writer, "casts doubt on all records of courtship based on sight identification and raises the question as to the respective roles played by the sexes in the home life of the species."

That was written in 1929. Since then a few more displaying birds have been shot and dissected and in every case have been identified as females. It therefore seems to be well-established that the Spotted Sandpiper is one of those surprising, unorthodox species in which the female, not the male, takes the initiative and plays the aggressive part in love-making. I shall assume that this was always the case amongst the birds in Brewery Creek.

Let me describe the antics of a typical representative of these forward Sandpiper dames. She postured in front of a male in a pompous, fantastic attitude calculated to attract his attention. Raising herself to her full height, she stood stiffly erect with her chest puffed out, her wings held away from her sides half-opened as if to invite an embrace, and her eyes gazing longingly at her companion. In this awkward position she advanced swaggeringly towards him. He was irritated or embarrassed by her attentions and flew away and alighted further along the shore. She pursued him. Landing beside him, she arranged herself again in her ridiculous attitude and strutted eagerly towards him. He was no more sympathetic on this occasion and again took wing. Once more, however, she followed him, alighted where he alighted, puffed out her chest, half-opened her wings and made up to him. It was as if she wished to say, "I'll walk beside thee through the passing years." But he was resolved not to be pestered and this time flew right away.

I watched two or three other females posing similarly before eligible bachelors. The males were usually indifferent. When they seemed less reluctant to be wooed the females passed to more inviting gestures. They strolled about with their heads stuck forwards, the fore-parts of their bodies lowered towards the ground and their hindquarters tilted in the air. I saw one bird crouching on the ground with a "come hither" sort of look.

Love-making amongst the Spotted Sandpipers continued through May. Several times I inadvertently interrupted their clandestine meetings and flirtations in the rough grassland above the shore. When disturbed they would leap skywards, uttering alarm calls. But so possessed were they by the urge to mate that they quickly recovered their philandering mood and began to move through the air in a graceful, charming way which is part of their love flight. They did not then fly purposefully with sharp, decisive wing beats, as is their wont. They seemed to hesitate in the air, almost to hang suspended there, as if practising "slow-flying". Their wings were held in two stiff arcs and fluttered, or even quivered, weakly instead of striking the air strongly. Whilst thus slowly propelling themselves the birds stuck out their chests and held their heads erect, flying only a few feet above the earth. The performance reminded me of the latter part of the love flight of an English Skylark, when the lark descends from its high, song-filled climb and prepares to alight again on the ground.

One day in the middle of the month I saw another aspect of their courtship, of which I have seen no published record. Many Spotted Sandpipers were gallivanting on the shore. I watched two displaying mutually to each other. Having neither the inclination nor the instrument necessary to catch them and dissect them to determine their respective sexes, I could not tell whether they were rival females or a female and her lover. Each approached the other aggressively in the usual full display attitude. Their bodies were held stiffly erect, their necks craned to their full height, their chests stuck out proudly and their wings held away from their sides. After a while one of them relaxed somewhat, closing its wings at its sides and reducing the puffiness of its chest. It still, however, held itself smartly erect, as if measuring its height against that of the other Sandpiper. The couple were now close to each other. Only two inches separated their heads as they stared challengingly at each other and almost crossed bills, as a pair of duellists might cross swords. Then they started circling slowly round each other, gazing intently at each other all

143

the time. Suddenly one pounced at the other. I do not
know what happened next, for unfortunately the movement carried them out of my sight behind a hillock. I
dared not move for fear of frightening them and inter-
rupting their scuffling or love-making, whichever it was. I
hoped that they would move into view again, so that I
could determine the purpose of their meeting. But they
did not. It was tantalizing.

Some days later I saw another example of this conduct.
Two Spotted Sandpipers were locked together in either an
embrace or a struggle on the shore. When I first caught
sight of them I thought that one had mounted the other
and that they were in the act of mating. One was on top
of the other and was beating the air excitedly with its
wings, as some birds do when keeping their balance in the
ecstatic moment of pairing. But when I turned my field-
glasses on them the situation appeared different. The upper
bird seemed to be gripping the neck of the lower bird in its
beak. The two were struggling doughtily and the wings
of both were flapping wildly. It may be that this was a love
scene, that a male bird was trying to mount a female and
that she resented and was resisting this too eager attempt
to consummate their marriage. But subsequent developments seemed to contradict this theory. The lower Sandpiper successfully broke loose from the other's grip. The
couple then faced each other threateningly, with their
bodies erect, their chests puffed out and their wings held
stiffly away from their sides in the attitude of aggressive
courtship display. For a few moments they posed so. Then
both leapt into the air, fluttering upwards about two feet,
keeping close together and facing each other all the time.
It seemed impossible that they should not collide, especially

as each appeared to be seeking a favourable opportunity to grapple with the other. This action they repeated twice in quick succession. Afterwards they settled on the ground again, glowering at each other. At least, that appeared to be their demeanour. The situation seemed tense and charged with mutual hostility. This time neither of them assumed the upright, stiff display attitude. Instead both lowered their necks and thrust forwards their heads with their beaks pointing at each other, again like the weapons of duellists. Walking rapidly round each other they completed three small circles. Throughout this manoeuvre neither took its eyes off the other for a moment. Suddenly one of them saw an opening. It darted swiftly at its opponent, they closed and the wing-flapping and fighting commenced once more. The combat continued violently for a while, when unfortunately I again missed seeing the final issue. The area over which they fought was uneven and their scuffling soon carried them out of my sight behind rising ground. When they reappeared one was running away from the other. Soon the chase became too hot for it. Spreading its wings, it flew away, with the other flying after it. The only possible explanation seemed to be that the victor in a vicious battle was pursuing the vanquished from the field.

A few minutes later two Sandpipers flew in and alighted on the battleground. Whether they were the same couple, a different couple or one of the earlier protagonists with a new one I could not tell. But they promptly repeated a similar performance to that which I have just described.

During part at any rate of these brawls other Spotted Sandpipers stood in the vicinity, witnessing the sport. Occasionally a few milder chases of one Sandpiper by another occurred. These little affairs were not attended by any fighting and, superficially at least, had the appearance more of amorous than of bellicose pursuits. If this be correct, the male always seemed reluctant to yield to the female. In the cases which I observed she always apparently chased him in vain. But I could not be sure of this, for the flight usually ended by the two birds disappearing behind rocks, rising ground or long grass, and anything may have happened out of my sight.

As for the significance of the regular combats, having refrained from capturing and carving up for purposes of biological research any pair of protagonists, I can only propound the theory which seems most plausible. The combatants were probably both females whose paths, for one reason or another, crossed in the process of courting. Possessed immediately by the fierce passion of jealousy, they fell mercilessly on each other, each resolved to scratch the other's feathers out and do her any other possible injury.

I understand that such conduct is not unknown amongst the females of some other animals—for example, human beings. In this species, however, the males show a similar tendency. But that is another story.

It is possible that, if both actors in these Sandpiper incidents were indeed females, the significance of their struggle was greater. As I have said, during parts at any rate of their engagements other Sandpipers were spectators. Can one or more of these have been males before whom the rival females were deliberately showing off? Were the females doing battle for the right to claim a mate? We know that the males of some species—such as Ruffs and Prairie Chickens—stage not dissimilar competitions in front of desired members of the other sex. In those contests he who shows superior prowess wins the prize. Perhaps public tourneys of that kind, in which females play the active, belligerent part, have a place in the life of Spotted Sandpipers. Probably, however, this is too fanciful a suggestion and the simpler explanation is the true one. I wish that I had enjoyed enough leisure to find the correct answer to the conundrum. I must leave its discovery to some future chronicler of the life history of these attractive birds. I hope that an Ottawa naturalist may undertake the task, for it can be pursued with comparative ease and in perfect conditions along the shores of Brewery Creek.

Whatever is the exact explanation, and however reluctant the males may have appeared, pairing amongst the Sandpipers was successfully and efficiently accomplished. Several nests were constructed in the latter part of May. They were difficult to find, for they merged perfectly into the surrounding terrain. But on the last day of the month I discovered one. It was on the ground, as is almost always the case with Waders. I should not have noticed it if I had not seen a Spotted Sandpiper, taken by surprise at my approach, fly off it. It was nothing more than a slight scoop in the earth surrounded by a low rim made of a few strands of grass neatly woven together. So shallow was it that it was more like a saucer than a cup lying amidst rough grass on high ground about fifty yards from the water's edge.

In it were four eggs. They were pear-shaped and so symmetrically arranged, with their narrow ends pointing to the centre, that they made a pattern like a four-leafed clover. Their light buff colour sprinkled with black and chocolate-brown spots and scratches gave them perfect camouflage.

CHAPTER SEVEN

JUNE

I.

THE WEATHER and the landscape became steadily more summery in June. The foliage on the trees and shrubs grew thicker and darker. The grass became lush, standing waist-high where it was not cut. Many wild plants along the creek banks developed lustily. Some spread in tangled masses, like the Vetches and the Raspberries, whilst others sprang to lone heights, like the Great Mulleins. A few remained green and unflowering right through June, but most produced their blossoms sooner or later during the month.

At its beginning Wild Strawberry blossoms still sprinkled the ground here and there. Blue and white Violets grew in beautiful profusion beneath the woodland trees. In open spaces hundreds of Buttercups added their bright, bucolic touch to the scene. In contrast to their robust comeliness, the pale petals of Canada Anemones had a frail, wan look. Closer to the soil Ground Ivy grew as thick as a carpet.

As the days passed a great variety of other wild flowers opened their faces to the sun and by the end of the month they patterned the earth with spots and splashes and masses of colour. Red and White Clover, Daisy Fleabane, Chicory, Rough Bedstraw, Bladder Campion, Ox-eye Daisy, Hop Clover, Cinquefoil, Blue Iris, Sweet Clover, Purple Flowering Raspberry, Common Chickweed, Convolvulus, Purple

148

Vetch, Toadflax or Butter-and-Eggs and many other plants all blossomed. The place was an unkempt garden of wild flowers.

The shrubs too were blossoming. For some time Black Chokecherry boughs had bent with sprays of flowers, and every Dogwood stem had produced its blooms. Then the Wild Honeysuckles covered themselves with showers of exquisite pink-and-white blossoms. Even the grass appeared to flower. From many a blade-point the single, Cyclops eye of Blue-eyed Grass gazed prettily.

This prolific outburst of new flowers coincided with a sharp decline in the arrival of new birds. The terrific momentum of spring migration was spent. Millions of birds who a few weeks earlier had been in the United States, Central America or South America were now in Canada. Their huge journeys were over. They were scattered in their customary summer quarters all the way from the Atlantic coast to the Pacific and from the 49th Parallel to the Arctic Islands.

However, I did see a few new birds in Brewery Creek in June. On the 2nd, for example, a Pheasant strutted through the wood. No doubt it had been in the vicinity before, but its visits had not happened to coincide with mine. This handsome game-bird is not indigenous to Canada or anywhere else on the American continent. It was imported, in the east from Europe and in the west from Asia, long ago and has flourished in its adopted country. Indeed, one of the ornithological surprises of Ottawa is the fact that many Pheasants stay there all through the winter. They could not do this by their own unaided efforts, but live largely on the charity of human friends who throw food for them on the snow.

149

On June 2nd also half-a-dozen Semipalmated Sand-pipers scurried across a log-raft moored to the shore. Their darker legs distinguished them from Least Sandpipers, which in almost every other respect are their doubles.

On the same day a Purple Martin and two Nighthawks appeared in the sky. As is so often the case with birds, the male Martin is more beautiful than the female. Blue-black all over, larger than the other Swallows but stream-lined like them and blessed with magnificent powers of flight, he is a fine creature.

The Nighthawk is a well-known haunter of the sky at dusk. During the brighter part of the day it usually sleeps. Any bed is good enough—the rough ground, a rock, a bough of a tree or the top of a fence post all suit it equally well. One afternoon on the shore a Nighthawk rose suddenly from the earth at my feet, where it had been snoozing. When disturbed by my approach it no doubt felt confident that its sooty-black plumage irregularly spotted and marbled with buff would afford perfect pro-tection against my eyes. It was right; I did not notice it. Only when I happened to walk exactly in its direction and my next step would have crushed it did it take wing.

Nighthawks are not of necessity night birds. They are as accomplished fliers and hunters in broad daylight as in the evening shadows. Their long wings, finely curved and cutting the air like scimitars, and their spare bodies and forked tails are striking. In sunlight a large white spot in the centre of each wing is conspicuous. The birds are swift fliers, but they pursue an erratic, zig-zag course and some-times throw themselves about the heavens with wild, joy-ful and noisy abandon. Their harsh screams shatter the dusk silence. As they skim through the air their large

Photo by W. V. Crich, F.R.P.S.

FLICKER
"The head of a young bird stuck out of the nest."

mouths, which literally extend from ear to ear, gape wide
and form devilish traps for the insects on which they feed.

Another bird whom I first saw in the creek that month
was the Northern Water-Thrush. Already, however, when
I set eyes on it in a rather inaccessible and swampy corner
of the wood it had been settled for some time. At least one
pair owned a nest hidden in a cavity of ground or amongst
the roots of a fallen tree deep in the undergrowth. They
are elegant and attractive birds. Although called Thrushes,
they are in fact Warblers. They are larger than most
Warblers but smaller than all Thrushes, with the figure of
a Warbler and the markings of a Thrush. Their dress is
dark olive above and yellowish below, with a breast splashed
by fine, sooty-olive streaks and a dark line running through
each eye below a long, delicately curved, buff-coloured
"eyebrow". Their appearance is sleek, dapper and pretty.
Their movements are in keeping with this character. They
walk jauntily and briskly, every now and then jerking their
tails like a Spotted Sandpiper. But they are shy and show
themselves as little as possible amongst the woodland
foliage. I only caught glimpses of them by patiently
stalking them by their loud, pleasant, warbling song.

Throughout June, whilst bird society on land was
crowded and hectically busy, the water was empty of wildfowl. Only thrice did a visitor briefly appear. On two of
these occasions it was a Golden-eye drake. On the third the
visitor was a newcomer to the creek, a Hooded Merganser
duck. Her small size and thin crest distinguished her from
other Mergansers. I was surprised to see her, for she should
have been sitting on eggs or brooding young. Perhaps she
usually was and had merely come to the creek for a change
of occupation whilst a Wood Duck temporarily looked after

her family. Hooded Mergansers, like Wood Ducks, nest in cavities in trees. Sometimes the two species come into conflict over the possession of a suitable site. Usually they put the issue to the test of battle and the Wood Duck wins. But occasionally the matter is settled amicably by the two ducks laying their eggs in the same nest and taking turns to incubate the double set.

I only saw the little Merganser once. She stayed a short while and then flew away uttering her characteristic cry, "Croo, croo, croo".

2.

On the banks of the river and creek bird life had reached its climax of activity.

At the end of May we left the mother Song Sparrow sitting patiently on five eggs in a nest amongst Dandelion leaves whilst her mate kept watch in the surrounding trees. This promising situation continued unchanged until June 3rd.

Then four chicks hatched. No sign of the egg-shells from which they emerged appeared in the nest or anywhere near it. The parents had disposed of this tell-tale evidence of their nursery. Amongst the youngsters, however, lay the fifth egg. It was addled and remained a useless encumbrance in the nest until the end of the family's story.

Not even the wildest sentimentalist could call the chicks pretty. They were tiny, naked creatures with orange skins and a few black tufts of down. Some of their minute features were well formed. Their legs, feet and claws, for example, were perfect models in miniature. Otherwise the youngsters were ugly. They were pot-bellied, their wings were fleshy stumps, their necks were scrawny and their large heads and beaks were out of proportion to the rest of their bodies. Their eyes bulged blindly behind closed, red eyelids. Altogether they looked like caricatures of birds.

They seemed uncomfortable in the nest, for they struggled together as if each wished to secure a better position. Perhaps this was Nature's device for making them exercise their limbs and develop their strength, as a human baby does when it instinctively waves its arms and kicks its legs in the air. Every now and then they lifted their pathetic faces and opened wide their beaks in a dumb appeal for food.

I visited them most mornings. Sometimes a parent flew to the nest with its bill stuffed with green grubs. The youngsters gorged on these delicacies and grew quickly. Their nakedness became slightly more covered with down, their bodies began to attain a better proportion with their heads, and sheaths enclosing feathers pierced their skins like pin-points. On the fifth day their eyes started to open. For almost a week all went well.

But on the seventh day I found the nest empty. The four lively chicks and the one addled egg had all gone. A voracious enemy had made a clean sweep of them. Nothing indicated its identity, but it had done its fell work thoroughly.

The mother bird sat on a bough overlooking the nest, calling lamentably.

This was my first, but by no means my last, experience of the hard struggle for existence which Song Sparrows wage.

3.

During the last few days of May I watched a Wilson's Thrush or Veery building her nest. She performed the job with quiet efficiency. I first discovered her at this occupation on the morning of the 28th, when I noticed her slipping silently into a low clump of foliage with a long strand of dead grass trailing in her beak. I happened to be standing close by, but she did not notice me. Peering amongst the leaves, I saw her weaving the latest addition into a flimsy, rudimentary nest which so far contained only a few grass threads. The structure was almost as open as a spider's web, though it was already cup-shaped and its material was naturally stronger and coarser.

Glancing up, the bird saw me and flew away. I moved behind a tree, where I could continue to observe her. She soon returned and set to work again. She showed zeal and energy, continually flying between the nesting place and some bushes close by, where she had evidently found a good supply of suitable building material.

Light rain began to fall and I went away. Soon the shower increased in force and became a storm. All day a heavy downpour continued, in the evening a thunderstorm shook the earth and throughout the night a gale of wind blew. When flashes of lightning illumined the scene I saw trees wildly tossing their branches, like raving lunatics waving their arms.

When I visited the creek next morning I felt sure that I should find the frail beginning of a nest destroyed. But no, the industrious Veery's work had prospered. Her nest had grown substantially and looked almost complete. It rested eighteen inches from the ground, bound to the stem of a sapling Elm tree and supported by a crossing of stalks of wild plants. Some large dock leaves helped to conceal it. It was built of strong grasses and weeds, rather loosely woven, with high walls and a deep cup.

That morning I did not see the Veery herself and the weather on the following day was too wild for me to visit the creek. Wind and rain combined to make a most unpleasant impression on the river, making it seem like a miniature sea whipped by a hurricane. The next morning, May 31st, was not much better, but by lunchtime the elements had calmed down enough for me to launch the canoe and voyage to the creek.

Again I did not see the Veery, but her nest was intact and in it was one glossy, blue-green egg.

When I looked the next morning, expecting to see a second egg, none was there. The egg of the day before had disappeared. The nest was untouched and commodious, but empty. I could not tell whether its content had been taken by a human or an avian enemy and I wondered whether the Veery would desert.

She persevered, however. On the following morning a new egg lay in the nest.

I visited the place again that evening and the single egg was still there. But a struggle had taken place. Stuck to the shell of the egg was a Veery's breast feather. The nest itself was dented on one side and more feathers were ominously attached to its edge. A crushed dock leaf leaned against the nest and the dock stalks below had been trampled upon and broken. A bloody battle must have occurred. What sort of foe had attacked the Veery in her home? Clearly it was not a human being. I suspected a cat which I had once or twice seen slinking through the long grass.

Next day the battered nest with its solitary, pretty, blue-green egg was unrepaired and looked forlorn. The egg was

155

stone cold, so the Veery had deserted. I kept my eyes open for her in the neighbourhood afterwards, but never saw her again. Whether she had been mortally wounded in the fight and retired to a quiet place to die, or had merely taken an unfavourable view of the prospects of a peaceful, happy life in her first nest and gone to build another elsewhere, I do not know.

4.

Nature is full of such mysteries. There was, for example, the strange case of the three young Phoebes.

When I went on June 1st to pay my respects to the Phoebe under the saw-mill she was sitting perkily as usual on the summit of her nest. For another three weeks she continued so. Sometimes she flew off as I climbed to my observation post six feet away and at other times she sat obstinately there in spite of my inquisitive stares. Whether she left or stayed made no difference to my knowledge of what was happening in the nest. I could not get near enough to peer into it and for long did not know whether it contained eggs or chicks. The period of incubation for Phoebes' eggs is supposed to be about a fortnight, so chicks must have been there during the latter part of these observations.

I first saw them on the 24th. That morning three heads protruded above the rim of the nest. I could see them only in silhouette, but they clearly belonged to downy, shock-headed youngsters with blunter beaks than the slender bills of their elders and betters.

When I visited the place again a few days later they had, so far as I could see, changed very little. They were still clothed in fluffy down and, again, I distinctly saw three chicks. This was a likely number. Customarily a set of

Phoebe's eggs contains anything between three and eight eggs. Possibly this set had consisted of the minimum, or perhaps one or more addled eggs lay in the nest with the healthy infants.

Each time both parent birds perched on some Willow branches near the nest, flirting their tails nervously, fluttering occasionally into the air and frequently making fussy little sounds of maternal and paternal anxiety. They kept their eyes on their family and on me.

When I climbed to my observation post on the 30th the parents flitted about in the neighbouring trees as usual. But in the nest a change seemed to have occurred. Only one chick appeared in it. At least, the object there looked like a young Phoebe with the spikey figure of a bird on which sheaths containing feathers were sprouting. Yet it stayed ominously still, an inert lump lacking the customary small movements of life. For a while I doubted whether it could be a bird at all. But a close examination of its silhouette through field-glasses showed that it was indeed a chick. Its shape, however, clearly accounted for only one, not three.

What had happened? Was the youngster in the nest alive or dead? Was it alone? If so, what had happened to the other two? From even my short distance away I could not discern the answer to these riddles. The strange affair became the Mystery of the Three Young Phoebes. I shall write of it further in the next chapter.

5.

From the moment when the Yellow Warblers built their nest in the briar patch everything went well with them.

As I have already recorded, the mother stopped laying and began sitting on June 1st, having produced three eggs.

They were tiny, ovate objects scarcely more than half-an-inch long. Their ground colour was greyish-white and on it were innumerable brown and blackish spots arranged as if they had been shaken there from a pepper-pot. The eggshell—as I afterwards discovered from an addled egg in another nest—was about as thin and fragile as any substance could be. That they survived being sat upon continuously for eleven days shows how remarkably carefully and lightly a parent bird sits.

The mother incubated them herself with no direct, though plenty of indirect, assistance from her mate. She was invariably sitting when I visited the spot. It would be hard to imagine a prettier sight than this little yellow bird settled on her nest in the mixed sunlight and shadows amongst the briar leaves. Normally she sat buoyantly upright. When I approached, however, she gradually sank lower into the cup of the nest until her whole body was hidden except for the tips of her tail feathers protruding at one end and the point of her beak jutting out at the other. Her bright black eyes were on a level with the nest's edge, just high enough to keep a watch on me. I could detect their keen gaze. I am told by big game hunters that a similar attitude is adopted by a hippopotamus hiding in a pool. Its whole body is submerged under the water until only its eyes and snout are visible. Nature can have few more charming analogies than that between a Yellow Warbler trying to conceal itself in its nest and a hippopotamus trying to conceal itself in its bath.

The Warbler was a courageous sitter, usually staying on her eggs until my face was almost directly on top of the nest. Then she slipped quietly over its edge, flitted quickly and discreetly amongst the briar stems and flew up to a

Photo by W. V. Crich, F.R.P.S.

CATBIRD
"Both parents . . . eyeing me disapprovingly."

branch on a near-by tree. As soon as she was away from the immediate vicinity of the nest she uttered her alarm notes, "Chip . . . chip . . ." Even they showed restraint and self-control. They were spoken in a low voice and seemed expressions of mild disturbance rather than of fear. They were partly addressed to her mate, to warn him of what was happening. If he were at a distance and my arrival had not already attracted his attention, he soon joined her. The pair would then flit about agitatedly in the neighbouring trees until I left.

What a good-looking couple they were! His brilliant yellow body with a chestnut-streaked throat and breast was the brighter and lovelier of the two. But her greenish-yellow colouring, though more subdued, was also pretty. In figure and movement they both had enchanting grace.

I never stayed long at their nest, my purpose merely being to see whether any of the eggs had yet hatched. When I withdrew the hen lost no time in returning to it. As soon as I started to move away from it she started to move towards it. Flitting quickly from branch to branch and stem to stem, with only the slightest hesitation at each stopping place, she quickly reached the nest, hopped over its edge and settled comfortably on the eggs again. On the first day her mate accompanied her back to the nest and fussed around her solicitously for a few moments. When he felt satisfied that she was safely re-established he flew to a tree close by, collected some grubs from its twigs and flew back to feed her. He did this several times, on each occasion making only a short expedition from the nest, gathering food and returning quickly to her.

Once or twice I saw the "incubation patch" on her breast. This exists on many species in the breeding season

159

and is one of Nature's typical functional devices. The feathers in the centre of the breast fall out, so that a considerable patch of skin is laid bare where the bird sits upon her eggs. The feathers along its edge grow as thickly as before and the bird fits neatly over the eggs, like a tea-cosy fitting over a tea-pot. The naked bosom enables the warmth of the bird's body to be communicated directly to the eggs. I sometimes touched an egg to feel its temperature. Even when a bird had been off it for a considerable time it retained a distinct warmth.

Matters continued thus at the Yellow Warbler's nest until June 12th. Then things began to happen. Early that morning a tiny chick sprawled prostrate between the two remaining eggs. For a while it showed no sign of life and I thought that perhaps it was dead. Then it stirred feebly.

When I returned to the nest that evening all three youngsters had hatched. The tidy mother had removed every fragment of eggshell from their home.

Here let me digress for a short while to write of some other Yellow Warblers' nests. For a few days I had been watching one in another part of the creek. When I first discovered it, on June 9th, it contained five eggs. The first chick hatched on the morning of the 11th, two more appeared that evening and a fourth hatched on the following day. The fifth egg was unfertile and remained in the nest until the chicks had flown.

On the 13th I found a third Yellow Warbler's nest. Two eggs and three chicks were in it. The infants were so minute that I felt certain they had only emerged from their shells on the previous day. In other words in the three nests which I happened to be watching no fewer than ten young Yellow Warblers hatched between the morning of June

11th and the morning of the 13th. At least a dozen of this species' nests existed on the banks of Brewery Creek. In the whole of Canada thousands of them must have been built, each containing three, four or five eggs. Assuming that most of them were at about the same stage of development, the increase in the Yellow Warbler population of the Dominion in those two days must have been gigantic.

To return to the first Yellow Warbler's nest, the newly hatched chicks were so small that it was hard to believe that a spark of life could burn in them. No wonder the eggs had been so tiny, if that was all that they could produce! Except for a few tufts of down as light as gossamer the babies were naked. Their bodies, including their feet and claws, were orange-coloured, except for the eye-lids which were dark reddish-brown and their beaks which were yellow. Like the infant Song Sparrows, they were exceedingly ugly. Their heads were too large for their bodies, their bulging eyes were blind, their skins were wrinkled and their limbs so weak that they seemed sickly. Their rapid breathing inflated and deflated their whole bodies, as if they consisted of nothing but bellows. They all sprawled helplessly in uncomfortable attitudes in the bottom of the nest. Never for a moment did they stay still, but were always changing positions in an apparent effort to get more comfortable. Every now and then they craned their skinny necks, raised their heads and gaped for food, revealing orange-coloured mouths.

They grew quickly. Within two days they were already distinctly larger and stronger. Their skin colour darkened to a browny-red and the tufts of down became thicker, though still not thick enough to conceal or protect their nakedness. Presumably because of this bareness and their liability to catch cold, the mother continued to brood them, crouching over them, as far as I could see, as constantly and closely as if they were still eggs.

On the third or fourth day quills containing feathers began to grow on them. Now they lay more comfortably in the nest and were less restless. I suppose they had grown accustomed to their quarters and learned by experience a few positions in which they could recline easily and pleasantly. They seemed to spend most of their time sleeping, but this may have been an illusion due to the fact that their eyes were not yet open. Certainly none of them had lost the habit of raising their heads periodically and opening their beaks to demand food. Both parents helped to feed them, each in turn coming to the edge of the nest, perching there, bending over and ramming caterpillars down their offsprings' throats.

After that the youngsters changed rapidly. By the fifth day the bulk of their bodies had grown so large that their heads no longer seemed out of proportion to the rest. Their eyes, still blind, hardly bulged abnormally. Their beaks were well formed, efficient instruments. The quills on their wings were big and the beginnings of feathers began to sprout along their backs. Otherwise they were still naked, for their down was never more than the skimpiest negligée.

Next day their dark eyes opened. The most dramatic transformation, however, was the change on their bodies. The chicks were entirely covered with feathers. A few wisps of down still protruded through this new, spick and span plumage, but otherwise they appeared suddenly fully fledged. It seemed incredible that on one day they should be almost naked creatures, sporting only a few sets of quills like mouldy porcupines, and on the next well feathered beings like true birds. The fact is that the feathers appear upon them almost in an instant. The feathering first grows inside quills or sheaths, like petals of a flower growing inside buds. Then the quills fall off and immediately the feathers bloom like flowers.

The youngsters had grown quite bulky. In the nest of which I am writing, inhabited only by triplets, they were not too squashed. But the other two Yellow Warblers' nests, each housing quadruplets, were full to bursting point. They seemed to be overflowing with young birds so closely packed that it was difficult to distinguish which of their heads belonged to which body. These nests were inclined to sink under their burdens and looked the worse for wear. However, apart from sagging crookedly on their supporting branches, they continued successfully to stand the strain. The mothers had been wonderfully cunning architects and builders.

Now the youngsters were well-formed, infant birds. They looked cosy in their nests, but in comparison with their parents were plain. Their plumage was uniformly brown, except for yellow tips to their feathers hinting at the glory to come.

The young birds in the other Yellow Warblers' nests left home earlier than the family whose fortunes I was particularly following. For example, when I arrived in the creek on the morning of the 21st one of these nests was empty, save for an addled egg. This was less than ten full days after the chicks had hatched. I think the four fledglings had left only a few moments earlier. Possibly they had been startled into flight by the sound of a gun-shot fired by a man hunting a rabbit nearby. The two parent Yellow Warblers were troubled. They flitted nervously in the branches overlooking the nest, calling in great agitation to their children, who answered excitedly from various places on lower branches or on the ground. I saw one fledgling hopping cautiously and uncertainly along a bough. It was a pretty, well-groomed little bird with a neat body but no tail. It looked surprised but not dismayed at its first experience of life in the outer world.

I could not make out what the members of the family were calling to each other, but it sounded something like this:—

Father: "You young scamps, what on earth are you doing?"

First Child: "Whoopee!"

Second Child: "Oh boy, my wings actually work."

Mother: "Be careful children. Do please go back to the nursery."

Third Child: "Don't be a spoil-sport Mummy."

Father: "How dare you answer your mother like that! Do as she tells you."

Fourth Child: "It's ridiculous to treat us as if we were still kids."

Mother: "But darlings, how will you live? You can't even feed yourselves yet."

First Child: "You've said it. I'm hungry. Come down and give me a caterpillar."

Second Child: "Crikey! I nearly fell off the tree that time."

Mother: "Oh, my angels! Are you all right?"

All the children: "Whoopee! Whoopee! Whoopee!"

On the same morning two of the four fledglings in the third Yellow Warbler's nest also left. This was less than nine days after they emerged from their eggs. I saw them go. When I approached the nest the mother bird was beside it, feeding her young. She slipped quietly away. Probably startled by me, two youngsters promptly rose, leapt from the nest and half-fluttered, half-fell to the ground. They looked like parachutists jumping from an aeroplane. Their two companions stayed discreetly where they were, but when I went to visit the family next day they also had gone.

The three youngsters in the first nest remained longer. They were still sitting in the nest on the evening of the 22nd. On the morning of the 23rd, however, eleven days after they had hatched, the nest was empty. They were still somewhere near, for the parents were fussing and calling in the trees beside the briar patch.

The superior judgement of this young family in staying longer in the nest was perhaps due to a better up-bringing. Their mother was a remarkably capable little creature. It is true that other Yellow Warbler mothers whom I knew laid more eggs, but in each case one of them was addled. This mother alone hatched all her eggs and then kept a wise authority over her youngsters until they were really ready to fly. Her whole conduct from the moment when she arrived in the creek and started building her nest had been a model of wifely and maternal devotion and efficiency. I felt that it was not only a pleasure but also an honour to know her.

A few days later I saw evidence of a sadder side to Yellow Warbler life. Besides the three nests which I have mentioned above, I observed the later developments in two others. Although Yellow Warblers are favourite victims of Cowbirds, none of these five nests were troubled by a parasite's egg. But not all the Yellow Warbler parents in the creek were so fortunate.

On the 25th I noticed a young Cowbird in an aspen tree. Its drab grey-brown plumage, faintly streaked on the breast, seemed appropriate to its sinister character. The youngster cannot have been long out of the nest, for its half-grown tail was still scarcely air-worthy. I was in a hurry that morning and could not wait to watch it. A pair of Yellow Warblers were industriously searching for insects in the surrounding trees and I suspected that this domestic tragedy had befallen them.

Two days later, in the same place, I saw a young Cowbird being fed by two Yellow Warblers. Doubtless they were the same trio. It was a pitiful sight. The Cowbird was a giant compared with its foster parents, being nearly twice their size. It sat silent on a bough and appeared sleepy, for its eyes kept closing. But it always perked up when one or other of the Yellow Warblers came near. As its beautiful little benefactor hurried towards it the fledgling waited with ill-concealed greed. It raised its wings slightly from its sides, quivered them as if trembling with excitement and opened wide its beak. The Warbler alighted on a twig beside it and fed it. The young Cowbird uttered no sound. Without a "Please" before or a "Thank you" afterwards, or any other exclamation of pleasure or gratitude such as fledglings usually employ, it gulped down the food. Then the foster-parent hastened away to forage for more and the Cowbird snoozed until the second parent appeared. The two Warblers worked very hard to keep their gross changeling fed—but perhaps no harder than if they had three or four of their own true children to nourish.

Next day I saw the young Cowbird hopping adventurously in the high branches of an elm tree. Its tail feathers were now full length and the bird looked more mature. Now and then it called aloud. This was something new for it and indicated an access of self-confidence. After looking round inquisitively and hesitating for a while it

CANADA WARBLER
"Like bright flowers fluttering amongst the woodland foliage."

suddenly took wing. First it made a small circle of flight and perched again on the branch from which it started. This may not have been its first serious trial flight, but it had an air of experiment. The bird seemed quite excited. When next it flew it travelled in a bee-line to a group of bushes forty yards away, alighted ungracefully amongst them and disappeared. I did not see it again.

The young Cowbird was on its own now and its foster-parents were likewise free. I trust that they heaved a sigh of relief and murmured to each other, "Good riddance to bad rubbish."

6.

The pair of Northern Flickers in the creek eventually nested inside the old mill. They entered it through a large knot-hole in a window shutter. This hole doubtless appeared to them like any other hole in a rotten tree or nesting-box, and they regarded the interior of the mill as the inside of a huge tree trunk.

Since the building was locked, bolted and shuttered I could not enter it to find the nest. I often observed one of the parents fly to the knot-hole, alight at its edge and dis-appear through it. Shortly afterwards I saw the bird emerge again. That was all. The rest of this Flicker family's story was hidden from me in the shadowy interior of the mill.

However, I watched some other Flickers who inhabited a Silver-birch tree near Mackay Lake. As existence for the birds beside Brewery Creek and those beside Mackay Lake were no doubt similar, let me continue my narrative of Flickers by describing life in the birch trunk.

The tree had died of old age. In some past storm the

top half of its enfeebled trunk had snapped off. Only its lower twenty feet now stood erect, with the equally decrepit and amputated stumps of half-a-dozen branches jutting from it. Its bark, as silver-white as an old man's hair, was gradually peeling off.

The birch stood in a piece of woodland well populated by forest creatures. Beneath a hickory tree next to it lived a Woodchuck. I sometimes caught sight of this quiet, unassuming animal ambling in and out of its burrow. A Chipmunk too had its home in the neighbourhood, for I often heard a rustling in the grass and saw it scampering by. One day a Squirrel ran up a tree beside me, peered down from a branch and scolded me with a vehemence which would have done credit to a Billingsgate fish-monger. On another occasion a Skunk trotted past. Perhaps it had a young family in the neighbourhood. Fortunately its handsome sable-and-white coat brought my sense of sight into play before I made any move which would have caused it to appeal to my sense of smell. Not far away, on the edge of the lake, a pair of Muskrats built their home. I used to see their eyes and snouts protruding from the water as they swam from shore to fetch fresh weeds to fill their larder.

American Redstarts, White-throated Sparrows, Crested Flycatchers and Veerys all had nests near the old birch tree. Some Song Sparrows were not far away. They had bad luck, for later I saw them making slaves of themselves to feed a fledgling Cowbird. Pheasants picked their way daintily through the underbrush and Crows sailed overhead towards a nearby nest. From the reeds beside the lake came the voices of Swamp Sparrows, Maryland Yellow-throats and Virginia Rails, as well as of commoner creatures like Red-winged Blackbirds. If you rowed a boat quietly round the lake, you could catch glimpses of all these.

One day I noticed a Northern Flicker fly several times to the birch tree. Examining the trunk from the ground, I saw two Flicker holes about twelve feet above me. I climbed to them without difficulty, for the branches formed such convenient rungs that the tree was a natural ladder. I was disappointed, however. Both holes were dummy nests, neither of them penetrating more than a few inches into the wood.

I was about to descend when I heard a strange noise inside the tree. It was a faint but distinct sound which can only be spelt "Zzzzzzzzz", like a high-pitched buzzing of bees. Then I spied another Flicker hole further up the trunk. I tried to reach it, but no branch grew high enough to give access to it. Above me the timber was so rotten that I dared not risk shinning up. I would probably have brought the upper parts of the tree with myself and the Flicker's nest (if any such thing existed) crashing to the ground.

Once more I felt frustrated and prepared to descend. The tantalizing buzzing or hissing continued, increasing in volume. Then I realized that it came from a point inside the tree exactly opposite my head, and that if this were indeed the noise of young Flickers, it was probably too low for the highest hole to be the entrance to their home. Did another hole exist in the tree? Manoeuvring myself cautiously to the other side of the trunk, I saw just above my eye-level a gaping cavity made not by Flickers but by some past accident to the tree. Standing on tiptoe on the only un-rotten bit of branch anywhere near, I was able to squint inside it.

I was greeted immediately by an almost deafening increase in the volume of buzzing, as if a large orchestra of insects had suddenly worked into a crescendo. The hole in the tree was weather-worn, roomy and deep—but not so deep that I could not see the faces of two baby Flickers stretched up appealingly towards me, their large beaks open for food. The youngsters' crowns were bald except for fluffy scraps of down and their bodies were naked except for some well-formed quills. Their heads were still rather too large for their shoulders and their beaks looked grotesque and coarse. These implements had not yet acquired the slender, smooth curve which would later grace them. In fact, the birds were still very young. They were, moreover, exceedingly untutored in the wicked ways of the world, for they seemed to imagine that I was some huge Santa Claus of Flickers come to pour on them bounteous gifts. Their eyes were open, so they should have known better.

Whilst I peered at them the parent birds flew close past the tree, much agitated. I jumped to the ground and hid behind a neighbouring shrub to observe them. The young Flickers fell silent and for five minutes nothing happened. Then the moustacheless mother perched on the summit of the topmost branch, about six feet above the nest. She looked round suspiciously. I think she saw me behind my shrub and was uncertain what to make of me. For a few minutes she waited, undecided. Then she cast herself from the branch and dropped towards the nest, obviously intending to alight at it. But nervousness got the better of her. She hesitated for a fraction of a second in the air before the nesting hole, changed her mind and turned and flew away to another tree.

I retired further, so as to be out of her sight, yet still able to watch the nest. Soon afterwards she returned and alighted just below the nesting hole. Her arrival was welcomed with a chorus of buzzing, clearly audible from where I stood. She promptly half-disappeared into the nest, leaving only her hind-quarters outside to mark her presence. After a few moments she re-emerged, remained perched there, glanced round to make sure that no enemies were watching and then half-disappeared into the nest again. This action she repeated three times, to the continuous accompaniment of the youngsters' excited buzzing. She was feeding them by the well-known process of regurgitation. When she had exhausted the food supply stored in her gullet she flew away. Once more quiet reigned in the silver birch.

Four times in the next hour this performance was repeated by a parent. Sometimes it was the female and sometimes the male. Twice an additional domestic duty was added to that of feeding the youngsters. On these occasions the adult Flicker, when it had finished popping several times half in and half out of the nest to push food down its offsprings' throats, jumped right inside the nest and disappeared completely from view. A few moments later it reappeared and flew away, carrying a small white bundle in its beak. This was a young bird's excrement. The parent was house proud and had an instinctive sense of hygiene. It had been cleaning the nest. Nature enables this duty to be performed easily by providing that the excrement of chicks ejected in their nests is enclosed in a mucous sack or envelope. The parent bird can carry this bundle away and drop it at a distance from the tree.

That was on June 20th. Three days later I visited the nest again and found the young birds fairly fully fledged. Their quills had burst and feathers had sprouted. A beautiful, black-and-brown checker plumage covered their backs.

They had grown more than feathers since my previous visit; they had also grown sophisticated. This time when I climbed the tree and peered at them they did not buzz and open their beaks to be fed. They remained silent and flattened themselves upright against the inside wall of their apartment, giving as good an imitation of bits of dead wood as circumstances would permit. I now counted four of them. When one did ultimately start buzzing faintly, it was with a note.of threat rather than invitation.

Several times during the next few days I visited them. They grew steadily larger, cannier and in every way more mature. Whenever I appeared they stayed quiet and still, as if lifeless. I often watched their parents feeding them and cleaning the nest. In spite of these latter labours the place began to smell unpleasant and before the youngsters flew the odour had become positively nauseating.

By the 27th their plumage had grown similar to that of adult birds. Its black and brown mottling had the freshness of new paint, their wings were yellow-shafted and their eyes dark and bright. They all wore black moustaches, for both sexes favour that adornment until their first autumn moult. The youngsters looked strong and hearty. One in particular was making efforts to climb up the inside wall of the nest to see what lay beyond the entrance hole.

By the next day it had succeeded. I watched from the ground. Every now and then its face appeared above the edge of the hole, like a wistful child's face at a window. It gazed curiously on the outside world and felt attracted by what it saw, for it showed signs of struggling to climb out. The mother and father came regularly to the tree with food. They were always greeted with loud buzzings of excitement and joy. The precocious young bird who looked out at intervals was, however, getting beyond these childish babblings. It had acquired a new, adult voice and took delight in opening its beak wide and giving the clear, challenging, beautiful call of a grown-up Flicker.

Next morning it gazed from the entrance again. Now it was perched higher and showed not only its moustached face but also its breast with a fine black gorget. It called constantly, as if anxious that the other birds and beasts in the district should all hear of its existence. Its position at the opening to the nest was no longer undisputed, for occasionally the face of a second youngster appeared behind it. The first, however, seemed the stronger bird. It would not give up its front seat and the second had to be content with a less satisfactory view of the out-of-doors.

Hitherto when a parent arrived at the tree it always half-disappeared into the nest to feed the youngsters. Now, however, this was unnecessary. As I watched, the mother flew to the hole. Before she alighted four young heads popped out, all buzzing ravenously and gaping their bills for food. She fed them each in turn, first inserting her beak into the mouth of one and ramming food down, then withdrawing to regurgitate the next ration, then pushing her beak down the throat of a second bird to feed it, then withdrawing once more to regurgitate for the third. It was an attractive sight. But when she had fed three of her children she apparently had no provisions left for the fourth. She flew away and the youngsters all disappeared into the nest, like a collapsing, many-headed Jack-in-the-box. In two minutes she returned. Instantly the head of the fourth youngster popped out again and she fed it. The others did not bother to buzz or look out. They were evidently satisfied.

I felt that the moment for the departure of the young Flickers was approaching, so I returned that evening to my observation post. A young bird was perched bolt upright inside the hole, looking out on the world with its customary curiosity. A blazing-hot sun had scorched the earth all day and the bird felt half-roasted. The atmosphere in the nest must have been stiflingly warm and airless. The young Flicker held its beak open all the time, panting for breath. Only occasionally did it summon up energy to advertise its presence by calling loudly into the forest.

Now and then the face of a nest mate appeared at the opening. This second bird also kept its beak open in a fixed gasp. It jostled the first bird from behind, trying to oust it from its favourable position for catching any little breeze that passed. But the first bird would not surrender its advantage, in spite of being pushed about a lot. The other two members of the family inside the tree never appeared. They must have been weaker than their fellows and forced to crouch in hot discomfort at the back of the nest.

Then the first youngster decided to make a bid for freedom. As if on a sudden impulse, it scrambled from the hole, spread its wings and flew away. Its flight was laboured yet sure, but was not a typical adult Flicker's flight. In that the wings first make a series of rapid strokes and then miss a beat or two, with the result that the bird's movement through the air is undulating. My young bird beat his wings rapidly all the time and its flight was even and direct. It flew straight over an area filled with small bushes, above a dense thicket of Stagshorn Sumachs and into a clump of birch trees forty yards away, where it disappeared. Shortly afterwards I heard it calling triumphantly to announce its first happy landing.

That was enough to make one of its young relatives also pluck up courage. This second bird too climbed to the edge of the nesting hole and hurled itself wildly into the air. Its flight was less competent and of shorter duration, for it came to earth somewhere in the Sumach bushes. But I saw it recover itself, scramble on to a low branch, shake its wings, stretch them and continue on its way into the unknown. The other two youngsters remained invisible in the nest.

Next evening—the last day of June—I visited the place again. Once more the head of a young bird stuck out of the nest. Again the day had been hot and sultry and the Flicker showed every sign of distressing warmth. Occasionally it called challengingly to any creatures in the surrounding wood who might be interested. But most of the time it leaned its head against the side of the hole, like a tired puppy in a dog-basket. Its beak was perpetually open and it gasped for breath. Sometimes it caught sight of an ant or fly crawling over the bark near the hole. Then for a moment it woke into life, jerking up its head and flicking out a long, thin tongue—like a snake's tongue—to capture the insect.

In due course its father came to the tree and fed it. It buzzed eagerly and accepted three portions of whatever its parent had to offer. As no second head popped out to be fed, I concluded that this was the only remaining fledgling in the nest and that since my last visit the third youngster had left.

After that it showed reviving energy. Perching upright in the hole, it looked out on the world with keen interest. Nothing missed its sharp eyes. When a squirrel scampered up a tree nearby it stared with surprise. When an aeroplane passed overhead it cocked its head sideways and watched its progress across the sky. Most of the time it gazed far into the wood, following whatever sights and sounds intrigued it. It looked like a play-goer sitting in a box in a theatre, watching intently every detail of the action on the stage. The performance was still proceeding and the audience still sat alert when I left.

As I walked away I chanced upon one of the other young Flickers perched on a stump not far from the nesting tree. It saw me and flew off with the same untutored, direct, slightly clumsy flight as before. Afterwards I heard it calling. From another direction came an answering call from a second emancipated youngster.

When I returned two days later the nest was deserted. Nor did I see or hear any sign of its recent inmates. I climbed the birch tree and examined the nesting hole. It was more spacious than I had suspected. Its floor was about nine inches below the entrance and was a flat surface of loose wood chips. The place was probably already quite roomy when the Flicker parents discovered it, but they must have done some additional carpentry to produce this parquet flooring. The chips continued for a depth of a few inches. Feeling for any addled eggs, I found one sunk in the floor, no doubt kicked through the surface chips by the lively youngsters. It was elliptical in shape, about an inch long, with a white, glossy, semi-transparent shell. I brought it away as a souvenir of the Northern Flickers of Mackay Lake.

7.

Catbirds' nests were common on the banks of the creek. Almost daily I watched four of them. They were typical of their kind, built in bushes or saplings where the foliage was thick. They consisted of bulky masses of dark twigs, dead grass and old leaves. Outwardly their appearance was rough, loose-knit and untidy—so much so that whenever I found a new one I wondered whether it could really be of this year's vintage or was a relic of the previous year which had survived the storms of the intervening seasons. Inside, however, they were neater and more comfortable, being lined with fine twigs and rootlets.

I found my first Catbird's nest on June 3rd. It belonged to the bird whom I had watched gathering building material. In it lay five pretty eggs, ovate in shape, glossy in texture and dark greenish-blue in colour. They were similar to a Veery's eggs, but slightly larger. Nature is not so brilliantly imaginative and resourceful in the colouring of eggs as she is in the adornment of the birds who lay them. Her palette in the former case is much more limited. Is this because she has to be more careful, in the interests of the safety of the eggs? Most adult birds are not a prey to enemies. When they are—whether they be endowed with protective colouring or not—they are blessed with wings. They can exert themselves and attempt to escape by flight. But eggs are not fitted with any means of locomotion. They are forced to remain immobile and docile in the face of the foe—and they have foes in plenty. Gulls, Crows, Grackles and other birds and beasts are egg-stealers and egg-eaters. So Nature cannot with impunity indulge her fancy for gay decorations. Bright reds and yellows, for example, would attract the attention of thieves. The preservation of the various species demands that their eggs should, generally, be protected by something like camouflage. Perhaps it is because colours answering to this description are in short supply that Nature often more or less repeats herself in the markings of eggs.

I could not tell how old the five eggs in the Catbird's nest were. But the set was complete, for the mother was already sitting. Perhaps the father also occasionally sat. In any case he was never far away. When I looked into the nest both parents always hopped about boldly in the immediately surrounding foliage, eyeing me disapprovingly and cursing me with cat-like "meows".

In keeping with this fearlessness was the determination with which the bird brooding the eggs remained sitting on them as I approached. It did not sink from view into the nest, as did the Yellow Warbler, but maintained its upright position even when I was only three or four feet away. I could see the details of its grey and black plumage, and particularly its dark, bright, bead-like eyes staring at me. Only when I came closer did it rise from the eggs, slip over the edge of the nest and fly silently to the next tree. There it joined its mate in voicing protests.

One of the eggs turned out to be infertile and came to nothing. Chicks hatched from the other four on June 10th, a week after I had found them. The clutch must therefore have been already several days old when I first saw it, for the normal period of incubation of Catbird's eggs is about twelve days. In two of the other nests I was able to watch the whole process from the laying of the last egg to the flight of the young birds. The incubation of these eggs took twelve days in one case and thirteen in the other.

As the eggs of the Catbird were almost twice the size of those of the Yellow Warbler, so were the chicks considerably larger. Their colouring was different, the skin being brown and the down black. Otherwise they were the same in nakedness, blindness and ugliness. One youngster gave a special exhibition of a particularly unbecoming

178

feature. It lay upside-down amongst its companions and struggled to right itself. The chick appeared to have swallowed a large round marble which filled its stomach to bursting point. Its skin was stretched to its utmost capacity and I feared that the poor little thing would split in two. But this characteristic is present and normal in any infant chick, for all the internal organs necessary for an adult bird are packed inside, and they naturally make a tight fit in the paunch of a newly-hatched mite.

I need describe only briefly the incidents of the youngsters' growth, for they were similar to those of other species. They grew rapidly, appearing within a few days about double their original size. Their skin darkened until it was almost nigger-black. With long tufts of black down on their heads they looked like small, animated golliwogs. The down was so fine that it did little or nothing to conceal or protect their nakedness. But soon quills began to grow and the slits between their closed eye-lids formed. Their ear-holes were also clearly visible, placed on the sides of their heads below and behind the eyes. The youngsters seemed insatiably hungry, often lifting their heads, stretching their necks and opening wide their beaks. Then the insides of their mouths showed bright yellow.

On the sixth day the mother gave a glorious demonstration of the courage of a parent bird protecting its young. When I arrived she was brooding her family as usual. She slipped quietly over the side of the nest as I approached, but did not fly far away. The father also was somewhere near. I peered closely into the nest. The young birds' eyes had now opened. Their quills were long, almost ready to burst and release the feathers. Their bodies had developed so that their heads no longer seemed too big for the rest of their figures. They were packed together in the nest as tightly as

"Four and twenty Blackbirds
Baked in a pie"

They sat absolutely motionless. One had its head poking upwards, its bill pointing skywards and its eyes unblinking— an instinctive, statuesque act designed to make me believe that it was lifeless.

Suddenly, without any warning, the mother in the next bush started screaming as loudly as she could. It was a frightening, even a blood-curdling wail, such as one might expect to hear murdering the silence in a haunted house. At the same time she flew at me, flapping her wings violently and fluttering round me as if she were going to make a bodily assault upon me. She was trying to terrify me, to fill me with panic, to drive me from the neighbour-hood of her children. I learned to have a profound respect for the devotion and courage of many of these bird mothers. After all, to that Catbird I was a monster more than fifty times her size.

Next morning the youngsters' feathers sprouted and on the following day they looked almost fully fledged. When I visited them on the 21st, eleven days after they had hatched, they were very alert and lively. They filled the nest to over-flowing and one stood upright in it. They eyed me sus-piciously whilst their mother swore at me from the next tree. Suddenly two of them jumped from the nest on to the branch on which it was built, where they stayed balan-cing uncertainly. I withdrew, so as not to disturb or worry them any more.

Next day the nest was empty. The fledglings were somewhere in the surrounding bushes, for the mother bird "meowed" angrily at me.

Catbirds, like other species, suffer many casualties. For example, the contents of one of the other nests which I watched met with disaster. The mother laid only three eggs. One hatched a chick. On the same day the shell of a second was chipped. I could see part of the youngster inside it and returned later in the hope that it would have emerged. But something went wrong. It never hatched. The third egg did not even crack its shell. For a week the mother continued to sit on one chick, one broken egg and one addled egg. Then I found the nest despoiled, robbed and empty.

The families in the other two nests fared better. The eggs were safely laid and successfully hatched, only one out of a total of eight being addled. In due course the fledglings took wing hopefully into the outer world.

8.

One of the most fanciful designers and builders of nests in Canada is the Baltimore Oriole. No bird is more skilful. Its creation is so fine that it might be classified as a work of art rather than one of mere craftsmanship.

Unfortunately I did not observe a bird in the act of building. But I found several completed nests in the creek in the early days of June. I shall describe events at one of these in particular. It was typical of the strange composition and situation of a Baltimore Oriole's summer residence, being suspended from the end of a long, drooping branch of an Elm tree overhanging the creek about thirty feet above the water. A casual observer might have mistaken it for an old string bag which had somehow got caught there.

When the nesting season was over I secured this Oriole nest and examined it. It was a pensile, purse-shaped structure almost eight inches long suspended amongst leaves at the end of the branch. The entrance was through its top. Usually Orioles' nests are bound to the tree by strong vegetable fibres, but this specimen was literally tied on with string. The bird had used a long piece of white string and another bit of green, which were knotted round twigs in four places and looped from twig to twig to provide the nest's support. Joined with them were strands of vegetable fibre and the rest of the bag was neatly woven of this material. Its texture was like a piece of loose yet firm knitting of almost silky fineness. Stuffed in the bottom of the nest was a cushion of grass, cup-shaped where the eggs and chicks had lain. This stuffing made the lower half of the nest-wall thick, but the unlined upper half was so thinly and loosely constructed that it was partly transparent.

This light edifice triumphantly passed severe tests of strength. It had first to support for many days the weight of an adult bird sitting on eggs. Then it accommodated a lively family of growing chicks. But besides this it withstood also the assaults of the elements, of fierce wind and rain. As I have said, my nest was secured (as is invariably the case) to leafy twigs at the tip of an elm branch. This long, drooping branch was sensitive to every puff of wind. In a light breeze it would incline gently, and the nest swayed with it. In a storm the branch tossed violently to and fro and the nest was blown mercilessly this way and that. From their earliest hours young Orioles grow accustomed to sensations which in many human beings would produce awful air-sickness.

BALTIMORE ORIOLE
"He perched on a twig on the edge of the nest."

Half-a-dozen such nests were suspended at different places in two small groups of Elm trees on the bank of the creek. The place became a veritable colony of Baltimore Orioles.

When I found the particular nest of which I am writing the female bird was already sitting on eggs. She was couched deep in the bag of the nest, hidden from view. The male was flitting from branch to branch on the other side of the tree, feeding and advertising his presence not only by his brilliant orange-and-black plumage but also by oft-repeated, melodious calls.

Shortly afterwards he visited her. Flying to their home bough, he perched on a twig at the edge of the nest and peered down into it. In his beak hung a caterpillar. Stooping over until he half-disappeared into the nest, he fed her. Then he flew away to another part of the creek.

After five minutes he returned. This time he landed on a small branch two or three feet above the nest, calling at the same time to his mate to tell her that he was back. Thereupon she emerged from the nest, stood for a few moments beside its entrance, addressed a musical remark to him and then flew across the creek to the opposite bank. She stayed away for about ten minutes, presumably feeding. Throughout her absence he remained on the same branch above the nest, employing the time by making his toilet. He kept stroking his feathers with his beak, scratching his face vigorously with one claw and opening and shaking his wings. From where he was he could keep an eye on the nest.

When the hen-bird came back she first alighted on a bough at a distance and called to announce her return. He immediately left the vicinity of the nest and flew to the

183

opposite side of the trees. Clearly his period of sentry duty was over. She approached the nest by a series of short flights, with cautious pauses in between each to make sure that no unfriendly eyes were looking. Finally she arrived at the nest, jumped into it and settled on her eggs. The bag of the nest shook as she moved about inside making herself comfortable.

On only one other occasion did I see the male feed the female in the nest. Usually she fed herself, leaving home periodically on foraging expeditions which kept her away each time for about ten minutes. Almost invariably she set out on one of these jaunts at a few minutes past eight in the morning. I could have set my watch reasonably accurately by her departure. This may have been pure coincidence, or it may have been an example of the exact regularity of some birds' habits.

The incident described above illustrates the charming working partnership which exists between a male and female Oriole. It was understood between them that whilst she was away he should keep watch over their nest. Sometimes he stationed himself close beside it, but at other times I took some time to find him. He was preening his feathers on some more distant branch from which he could see the home bough.

Neither at this nor at any other Baltimore Oriole's nest that I watched did the male ever enter the nest whilst the female was away. He takes no part in the actual incubation of eggs. Orioles, incidentally, produce only one set of eggs in a season. Although the male had no share in the task of hatching them, he was never far away whilst she was sitting. This was of course partly due to the fact that the whole region of the Elm trees was divided into several territories belonging to different pairs of Orioles and that he had to stay more or less within the bounds of his own property. If he flew beyond it he invaded the territory of a neighbour, who soon appeared and chased him away. Such intrusions were strongly resented and the resultant chases were violent affairs.

However, if the male had felt no responsibility as a husband and father, he could have flown right away. The main motive keeping him in his own tree and its immediate neighbourhood was attachment to his mate. The pair were united by a bond of true affection. As he flew from branch to branch, searching the leaves for succulent caterpillars he would frequently sing his short, cheerful song. It may have been partly a signal to other male Orioles that this was his territory and that trespassers would receive short shift. But its gently uttered notes sounded also like an expression of his own contentment and, at least in part, a message to his mate sitting hidden in her nest that he was near. Baltimore Orioles are examples of birds who constantly employ song during the nesting season as a system of conversational signals between them. Sometimes the male of my pair would interrupt his feeding and fly to the edge of the nest, peer into it and stay beside it for a while. His motive appeared to be solicitude for the hen and anxiety to assure himself that she was safe.

She never called whilst she was in the nest. But whenever she left it or arrived back near it after an expedition she called, thus reporting her movements to him. She took care when she was returning to the nest not to attract hostile attention. Especially at the edge of the nest itself she looked round cautiously to satisfy herself that no enemy was spying as she dropped into it. Friendly or merely harmless eyes did not bother her. She was not troubled, for example, by the presence of other small passerine birds. Sparrows and Warblers hopping and fluttering nearby, as they often did, aroused no agitation in her breast. Sometimes one or two Cedar Waxwings used the surrounding branches as stances from which to hawk for flies. One of these pretty and graceful creatures once followed her to a twig just above her nest and gazed down at it with obvious curiosity. The Oriole dived with complete indifference into the bag.

Thus matters continued from June 10th, when I first saw the nest, until the 21st. On the morning of the 22nd the mother's conduct indicated that her nest was full not of eggs but of chicks. She was absent when I arrived, but soon came flying to the tree with a gay whistle—and a juicy caterpillar hanging in her beak. Alighting on the edge of the nest, she leaned forward into it and remained so poised for some time. When her head reappeared her beak was empty, the caterpillar having been distributed amongst her offspring. She immediately flew across the creek to her favourite hunting ground. In five minutes she returned with another caterpillar, perched at the nest side and fed the youngsters again. No sooner had she finished than she was off once more. A few minutes later she returned a third time with yet more provisions. This time she did not immediately, after feeding her family, depart. Instead she dropped into the nest, which shook as she rummaged around in it. When she jumped out a moment later a small bundle of white substance was held in her beak. Flying off with it, she dropped it some distance away. It was a chick's dung. Like the Northern Flicker, she was a clean housewife who took care to keep her nest from being fouled.

I did not see her mate that morning. In fact I never, to my knowledge, saw him again. In this case the female was wholly responsible for nourishing and bringing-up their children. At feeding times she was kept busy. Every few minutes for considerable stretches of time she came to the nest with a caterpillar, fed the infants and flew away to fetch another victim. Now and then she dropped into the nest to clean it and carry away the refuse.

I could not see the chicks. They lay too deep in the long nest-bag. But after the first two or three days their voices were strong enough for me to hear them. Most of the time they were silent, but whenever she appeared beside the nest they squeaked eagerly and gratefully at the prospect of being fed. They were not yet old enough, however, to distinguish between her and other visitors. Once they set up their hungry clamour when a passing House Sparrow perched above the nest and looked inquisitively into it.

One evening I did catch sight of the young birds, in silhouette. The sun was sinking towards the horizon behind the nest. Light could not penetrate its lower, thicker parts, but the strong sun's rays penetrated and made translucent the more finely wrought upper parts. When the mother Oriole came to the nest and bent down through its entrance to feed the young birds, I saw their shadows, as if through a veil, stretching up to receive the food.

The father's neglect of his family from the moment when the chicks hatched made me conclude at first that cock Baltimore Orioles lose interest at that point and take no part in caring for their young. He visited the nest on the day before the youngsters appeared, but never came to it afterwards. However, my conclusion was wrong. Mother

Orioles are usually assisted by their mates in this as in every other period of family life. The male of every other pair whom I watched shared in feeding the young and cleaning the nest. The two parents took it in turn to bring caterpillars to the nestlings, behaving identically in every respect.

Something unusual must have occurred at the first nest. Perhaps the male happened to be killed on the day when the chicks hatched, leaving his widow to perform all the duties of both parents. But that was not necessarily the explanation. The mother may have been a temperamental creature. An odd streak of maternal jealousy may have made her wish to look after her youngsters entirely by herself, without help from a mere male. In that case she would strongly resent any attempt by her mate to feed their young, and would drive him away. Odd kinks of character exist in individual birds as they do in individual human beings. One day two male Orioles did come to the Elm tree. She flew furiously at them and pursued them to a great distance. They may have been two strange males who supposed that in the absence of her natural protector they could over-step the bounds of her territory with impunity. If so, she quickly showed them their mistake. Alternatively, one of them may have been her one-time mate inadvertently asserting his old right of access to the neighbourhood of their nest. If that was the case, he also learnt a sharp lesson.

Eight days after the youngsters hatched their voices changed in quality. They called continuously from the nest, but it was no longer with an infantile squeaking. They had acquired a more grown-up tone, volume and variety of notes and were yelling for their mother with an insistence which indicated gnawing hunger. They beseeched her to come and feed them. But she did not appear. Perhaps she happened to be away all the time that I watched, or perhaps her absence was due to instinctive design. She may have assumed that the time had come when her fledglings should leave the nest and begin life in the outside world, and for this reason stayed away until ravenous hunger made them scramble from their comfortable cradle into the surrounding foliage.

Whatever the explanation was, next morning they were out of the nest and distributed in different parts of the tree. Their cries for food came from various branches. I do not know how many youngsters were there, for I only caught sight of one of them. Except for the fact that it had no long tail-feathers, it was in size and figure quite a respectable simulacrum of an adult Oriole. In plumage also it had made a fair beginning towards maturity. Whatever its sex (both sexes are alike at that age) it took after its mother rather than its father in the comparative modesty of its colouring. It was adorned, however, with two prominent white bars on each wing and with a yellow breast.

The youngster balanced uncertainly on a branch, calling often. Periodically the mother bird arrived to appease it with a caterpillar. She approached by stages, flitting deliberately from branch to branch with the hapless delicacy dangling from her beak. As she drew near, the cries of the young Oriole rose to a crescendo of impatient excitement and when she finally perched beside it and leaned forward to push the caterpillar down its throat it jibbered and fluttered its wings with delight.

In between visits to this youngster she performed a similar service for her other offsprings. She was a slave to her brood. Motherhood appeared to involve continuous drudgery for her. But birds are emotional creatures and in her heart, no doubt, was a feeling of contentment that her family were growing steadily in strength and beauty.

9.

On June 1st, the day after I discovered it, I visited the Spotted Sandpiper's nest containing four eggs. A bird was sitting and flew off as I approached. It was probably the male. Although the female occasionally takes a turn at incubating their eggs, the greater part of that labour is dutifully performed by him. That is the way of things in matriarchal society.

I found the brown speckled eggs arranged as neatly as on the previous day, with their sharp ends pointed symetrically inwards and their round ends spread out. I withdrew and waited long enough to watch the parent bird return. He alighted in the long grass a dozen yards from the nest, walked surreptitiously the rest of the way and settled down quietly on the clutch.

Next day I visited the place again. As I drew near I watched carefully to see the Sandpiper fly off. But no bird appeared. When I reached the site I had difficulty in finding the nest. At last, however, I recognized the shallow scoop in the ground encircled by a slight, low rampart of dead grass. No eggs were there. All four had disappeared. The day was sunny, warm and dry, yet the nest was soaking wet. It was saturated with a fluid which must have spilled from the eggs. Some thief had discovered them a short while before and eaten them. The empty, yoke-stained nest was a reminder of how fierce is the struggle for existence even where Nature appears to be most innocent and peaceful.

As luck would have it, that same morning I found another Spotted Sandpiper's nest. It lay on the shore, on rising ground safe above high-water mark, amongst a clump of half-grown Evening Primrose plants. Its construction was the same neat but skimpy affair as the other, and in it were three eggs.

When I went to it the next morning I expected to find a fourth egg, for four is the usual number in a Spotted Sandpiper's set. But there were still only three, and three they remained. Nature had cleverly contrived their camouflage. Even though I soon learned exactly where to look for them, I did not quickly pick them out from their background.

During the next three weeks I visited the nest daily. It looked pretty, surrounded by its wild garden of Evening Primroses. As they grew it became more and more concealed. I hoped that the final touch of beauty—the flowering of the plants—might be added before the eggs hatched, but that was not to be.

The parent birds shared the labour of incubation. I could not tell which was the male and which the female, but one—probably the male—had a more thickly spotted breast than the other. It did most of the sitting. Twice, however, I found both birds close to the nest, having no doubt disturbed them at the moment of "the changing of the guard" over their eggs.

Whichever bird was sitting kept a sharp look-out against intruders. In this it was helped by the nest's position on elevated ground. It usually caught sight of me long before I came near. When I was still fifty yards away it would rise from the eggs, with no apparent alarm, and walk quietly away in the opposite direction. During its retreat it used any concealment that the surrounding vegetation or contours of the land offered. Through my field-glasses I could see it picking its way warily amongst the tufts of grass and wild flowers. When it had proceeded several yards it would halt, bob in characteristic Sandpiper fashion, pipe innocently and then spread its wings and fly away to the water's edge. There it would start feeding unconcernedly, as if it had no cares in the world and had come by mere chance to that vicinity.

This act was as successful as it was clever. No one who did not positively know the exact whereabouts of the nest and eggs would have got from the parent any clue to them. A casual passer-by observing the bird would not even have suspected that it had a nest in the neighbourhood. Only by happening to catch a sitting bird unawares and flushing it did I ever find a Sandpiper's nest's location.

For many days I did not see either parent adopt the ruse of violent decoy action, at which Killdeers are such adepts and which I have already described in connection with them. I began to think that it is unknown to Spotted Sandpipers and plays no part in their defensive behaviour. One morning, however, I learned better. I happened to approach the nest from a direction where I was partly screened by a few saplings. Either because of this or because the sitting bird's attention was engaged elsewhere, it did not notice me until I was close to it. Suddenly it saw me, rose hurriedly and began to walk away slowly and quietly as usual. After a few moments, however, it suddenly contorted itself into a strange attitude and started to run. It arched its body sharply, with its neck stretched and head lowered almost to the ground in front and its rump depressed until the tip of its tail almost dragged along the earth behind.

Its wings were half open and drooped at its sides, its body feathers were fluffed out and the tail feathers were spread in a wide fan. In this awkward, bedraggled-looking and thoroughly uncomfortable attitude it ran quickly, with occasional momentary hesitations, across the uneven ground. All the time it cried loudly and plaintively, a sound very different from its customary sweet, musical whistle. I did not on that occasion receive the impression of sensuous movement, such as always struck me in similar circumstances in the case of Killdeers. The Sandpiper merely looked distressed, distracted—indeed, panic-stricken to the point of insanity.

I allowed myself to be led away by the bird, to see what happened. It continued its retreat for a considerable distance, running in a straight line away from the nest. Only when it at length reached the water's edge did it change its posture. Then it relaxed suddenly, as if the performance had been a piece of cold-blooded, calculated play-acting which could be abandoned now that its purpose of luring me to a safe distance had been achieved. It fell into a natural pose, whistled gaily, bobbed its body up and down two or three times and flew across a narrow channel of water to a small island off shore, where it calmly started to feed. Once or twice, however, it reverted momentarily to its grotesque, distraught attitude, as if it were absent-minded and forgot that there was no longer any need for that ruse. Evidently the emotion which had made it instinctively resort to it had not completely subsided. The transition from excitement to calm was not made so easily and suddenly as appeared on the surface.

For a long time after that I observed no repetition of this conduct. Almost invariably the bird saw me coming from a distance and employed the technique of a quiet, cautious, deceitful retreat from its nest. But on a few occasions I saw this Sandpiper and another, which I watched later at its nest, indulge in the more violent action. My observations led me to the following conclusion. A Spotted Sandpiper sitting on its eggs is wary and keeps a constant look-out for possible enemies. I tried a few experiments and am inclined to think that it generally sees a human being as soon as his head appears over its horizon. It moves off its nest either immediately or shortly afterwards. Usually, therefore, it has time to walk unobtrusively away and to avoid betraying the site of its nest. But when it is caught on its nest unawares the situation is different. It fears then that it may have given its secret away and feels instinctively that only drastic action can avert the danger. Moved by an overpowering emotional impulse, it automatically indulges in extreme display action. The resultant exhibitionism knows no limits. By sight and sound it tries desperately to attract attention to itself and so to distract attention from the nest. The Killdeer in its wildest spasms of "decoy" action does not excel the histrionics of the Spotted Sandpiper in a similar situation.

I must confess that this form of display in the Spotted Sandpiper shook my theory that it may have some direct connection with sexual display. In this case the matter was particularly complicated, because of the unusual roles played by the sexes in courtship and the incubation of eggs. In most species the female sits on the nest and therefore engages in "decoy" action. It is possible to compare her postures then with her attitudes during courtship. In the case of Spotted Sandpipers, however, I was not sure which parent I flushed from the nest on any given occasion. Prob-

ably it was generally the male. Whichever it was, the bird's
"decoy" antics had no resemblance whatever to the stiff,
upright attitude of a Spotted Sandpiper, incidentally the
female, in sexual display. Nor did the decoy behaviour
often strike me as having any sensuous element in its make-
up. It seemed too utterly frightened and distraught for
that. I shall have to content myself with these descriptions
of what I observed, and postpone further theorizing.

The Sandpipers continued to sit on their eggs, patiently
and conscientiously, from June 2nd until June 23rd. When
I discovered it on the former date the clutch must have
been new-laid. Ornithologists used to maintain that the
normal period of incubation of Spotted Sandpipers' eggs is
about sixteen days, but in recent years careful watchers have
declared it to be twenty-one. The dates for my Sandpiper
exactly confirm the longer spell. On the morning of the
22nd a parent bird was sitting on the three eggs. On the
morning of the 23rd, however, the nest was empty. Not
even a small fragment of eggshell was apparent. The chicks
had all hatched sometime in the previous twenty-four hours.
Except for the almost imperceptible scoop of the nest itself
no sign remained of the Spotted Sandpipers' three weeks'
intense occupancy of that spot. Quite rightly, Nature does
not like the idea of young Sandpipers sitting defenceless in
their nests on bare, open ground. For their protection she
provides that within a few hours of hatching they shall be
strong enough to run into cover. The youngsters from my
nest had already left their birth-place for ever and, under
the guidance of a parent, were now wandering amongst the
long grasses and wild flowers in the neighbourhood.

I looked forward to finding them and following their
further fortunes.

Even whilst the various summer developments described above were occurring in the creek, autumn sent a few warnings of its approach from afar. Life never stays still for a moment. It is for ever moving out of one phase into another, hurrying inexorably forward. Almost before the birds had settled in the creek and grown accustomed to their summer ways of life, Nature whispered that they must prepare for another change.

By mid-June a few signs and portents began to convey this message. The male Robins and Baltimore Orioles, for example, started to moult. Their plumage grew dowdy. Again, Starlings gathered in small flocks, first in dozens and scores and then in companies of a hundred or more. Here and there amongst the green foliage on the trees a dying, yellow leaf appeared. These were all hints, faint suggestions, that life would not always be lusty and fruitful and gay.

CHAPTER EIGHT

JULY

I.

ALTHOUGH IN JUNE a few early signs of impending decay appeared, the fruitful earth did not take much notice of them. In July it gave its most riotous exhibition of virile splendour and beauty, working itself up to a crescendo of lush living.

Most of the early summer flowers continued to flourish and many new ones also blossomed. Almost every day fresh wild blooms appeared. Yellow Pond Lilies spangled the shallow waters; along the edges of the creek Narrow-leafed and Broad-leafed Arrowheads grew in thick masses like miniature jungles; higher up the shore increasing numbers of Irises unfurled their blue flags amongst their green sword-blades. On the rough meadowland and in open, grassy spaces in the wood Yarrow, Milkweed, Vipers Buglos, Fringed Loosestrife, Great Mullein, Water Horehound, Common St. John's-Wort, Evening Primrose, Swamp Thistle, Purple Loosestrife, Golden-rod, Wild Lettuce, Marsh Skullcap, Silver Weed, Burdock and other flowers added their bright faces to the floral array.

Nor did most of these grow in modest quantities. Some did show a certain restraint. The Great Mulleins, for example, were scattered singly over the ground, each growing in solitary splendour like a tall, richly carved candlestick whose flame was its yellow flowers. But most of the others grew in gay multitudes. In places Chicory bloomed so thickly that it appeared like a continuous blue field; elsewhere Purple Loosestrife covered wide areas of ground, and in other areas Sweet Clover, Goldenrod, Evening Primroses, Swamp Thistles and Chicory were mixed in such broad, high masses that they looked like herbaceous borders. The whole place was like a garden in which untended flowers had run amok.

Animal life was no less prolific. Scores of different insects inhabited the creek. I shall pass in silence over the Mosquitoes and other stinging flies, merely remarking that if anyone feels disposed to make a study of their life histories, Brewery Creek would be as good as any other place as a laboratory for this heroic work.

Many pleasanter small forms of life were equally plentiful. Spiders, beetles and caterpillars were abundant. Amongst the flying insects none were prettier than the Lady Beetles or Lady-birds. Several species summered in the creek. The origin of their charming name belongs to the Middle Ages, when their services to agriculture as pest-killers were rewarded by dedication to the Virgin and bestowal of the title "Beetles of Our Lady".

Moths galore flitted through the woodland shade and many butterflies hovered over the sunlit flowers. The aristocrats amongst the latter were the red and black Viceroys, the brown, yellow and blue Swallowtails and the large, dark-striped, yellow Tiger Swallowtails.

No less beautiful were the Dragon-flies. On hot June days I had watched their larvae resting on floating logs or on the leaves of wild flowers growing from the water. Sometimes I saw a fly split its grotesque waterproof jacket and emerge like a fairy into the sunlight. In July various species of Dragonflies whizzed above the Irises and other shore flowers. The most brilliantly coloured were as red as

SPOTTED SANDPIPER
"Kept a sharp look-out against intruders."

the devil, whilst others had vivid green and yellow patches on their black bodies, and many had glittering, jazz-patterned wings.

Damsel-flies were even more abundant. By the middle of July many hundreds of these small cousins of Dragon-flies sped over the shore and shallow waters. Their long, coloured bodies as thin as crochet-needles, their heads with bulging lantern eyes and their glistening, gauzy, whirring wings had an appearance of fantasy. They were of many colours—bright blue, golden green and jet black. Brilliant blue ones were the commonest. Pairs of Damsel-flies flew tandem-fashion together. The male seized the female by the scruff of the neck, with pincers attached to his hind-quarters, and pulled her behind him. This arrangement is inspired by dire necessity rather than mere convenience. The female has weak legs and when she goes under water to lay eggs inside the stems or leaves of submerged plants she finds it difficult to climb out again. Her mate then literally pulls her out.

One morning I saw a small Turtle sunning itself on a log floating in the creek. The commonest inhabitants of the water, however, were various humbler forms of pond and river life. Water-snails, water-beetles, water-boatmen and other aquatic creatures crawled and swam in hordes amongst the weeds in the shallows. These regions were also nurseries for several kinds of infant fish, slim or podgy, whiskered or clean-shaven, which darted hither and thither in shoals. In June crowds of tadpoles kept them company, but by July these had lost their tails, grown four legs and hopped ashore as baby frogs.

Two months earlier I had seen something of the origin of these little amphibians. Every evening in mid-May a loud, continuous, quavering noise, like the monotonous music of an orchestra of crickets, issued from a swamp near the creek. At first I thought it might come from a flock of birds, for it sounded like the "reeling" of English Night-jars. Then I realized that this was the love-song of a company of frogs. A mob of males were serenading their mistresses.

I went to inspect them. When I landed beside the swamp the chorus suddenly ceased. Looking down into the shallows, I saw amongst the water weeds an obscene sight. Everywhere individual frogs, pairs of frogs and trios of frogs lay about like the inmates of a brothel. Many males had scrambled on to females' backs and were avidly hugging them. In other cases two males were struggling, fighting and kicking for the possession of a female on to whom they both sought to climb. As they battled they squeaked angrily and their lungs inflated and deflated like bellows. The female sprawled lethargically beneath them, as if completely indifferent to what her suitors did to each other or to her.

Even the peaceful pairs looked more like all-in wrestlers than lovers. Mating frogs often lie thus together for hours and even days, without eating, before eggs are laid. To add to the filthiness of the scene, many females were horribly disfigured, with bodies swollen and throats blown up like balloons. For several of them the embrace of love had also been the embrace of death. Some were dying and others were already dead. Their corpses lay singly amongst the living couples, with lack-lustre, staring eyes, out-stretched legs and rotting bodies.

The paramount urge to mate had produced a mixture between a bawdy-house and a charnal-chamber. But in due course the result was a fresh surging of young life. In July the grass along the water's edge was alive with little jumping frogs.

Indeed the creek housed a menagerie of land and water animals. It was a playground for entomologists and icthyologists as well as a paradise for ornithologists.

2.

In July I saw a few species of birds which I had not seen before in the creek.

One morning two White-breasted Nuthatches were racing up and down the trunk of an Elm tree, exploring its deep grooves for grubs. They seemed to meet with gratifying success, for often they stopped to insert their strong, awl-like bills into the bark. The tree seemed particularly hospitable, since at the same time a Downy Woodpecker was similarly engaged on it.

In spite of a slight suggestion of deformity, owing to their large heads, long wings and short tails, White-breasted Nuthatches are trim little birds. Their black, blue-grey and white plumage, with a dash of chestnut under the tail, is pleasing. Their neat appearance is aided by the light swiftness of their movements. No other bird can travel so quickly up and down and round a tree trunk. Nor does a Nuthatch mind which way up it travels. It can climb a tree right-way-up or descend it upside-down with equal facility. White-breasted Nuthatches are hardy animals and stay in the Ottawa district all through the year. Their relatives the Red-breasted Nuthatches are much less common, though they are numerous as migrants in spring and autumn. I did not see any in Brewery Creek. No doubt they visit it sometimes, but their preference for pine trees, which are absent in the creek, makes them more usual elsewhere.

Every day in the middle of July three Little Green Herons came to feed in marshy ground close to the edge of the creek. They are the smallest true Herons in North America and are distinguishable by their dusky, glossy green plumage as well as by their size. A pair nested in the secluded part of the wood favoured also by the Northern Water-Thrushes. I found their nest after the young birds had flown, a rickety heap of sticks laid across two branches of an elm tree about twenty feet from the ground.

Often I disturbed the Herons feeding in the marsh. No wonder they favoured the spot, for it was an ideal fishing ground. Earlier in the year it had been a quiet inlet joined to the estuary of the creek. In its waters fish and frogs deposited their spawn. Then the level of the river sank and the connection between the inlet and the creek was broken by the appearance of a narrow, continuous piece of shore. When the young fish and tadpoles hatched they were trapped in shallow pools. The Herons could wade at random and gorge themselves on this dainty food to their hearts' and their stomachs' content. So rich were the fish-ponds that they provided regular fare also for two or three Bitterns.

I could silently paddle my canoe close to the Herons before they saw me. Then they rose hurriedly with harsh squawks and flew gracefully away, expressing their annoyance by raising their crests angrily when they alighted in the tree-tops. As soon as I turned my back and paddled away they flew again to their feeding ground. In the course of about a week's banquetting they and the Bitterns emptied it, and after that I saw the Herons no more.

Amongst the Waders who looked in at the creek in the latter half of the month was a Pectoral Sandpiper. In figure it was like a Spotted Sandpiper, but a size or two larger. In colour it was streaky brown above, striped brown on the breast and white on the belly. Pectoral Sandpipers start their autumn migration early. They nest on the Arctic tundra and then travel, some by way of the Mississippi valley and others down the Atlantic coast, to their winter quarters in Peru, Bolivia, Northern Chile, Argentina and Patagonia. This one rested and refreshed itself for a day on the Brewery Creek mud-flats in the middle of its gigantic journey.

No other new birds appeared in July this year, but one day in the previous year, 1944, an unusual creature flew over the creek. It was a Caspian Tern. The largest of the Terns, it is about the size of a Herring Gull and twice as big as a Common Tern. I am told that Common Terns migrate fairly regularly along the Ottawa River, but I looked in vain for them. I was disappointed, for the bird's slim, cigar-shaped body, deeply forked tail and fluttering, airy flight make it one of the most graceful animals in creation. However, although the heavy body, moderately forked tail and slow wing-beats of the Caspian Tern lacked the enchanting, magical quality of those lovely creatures, it had its compensation. A Caspian Tern in Ottawa has high scarcity value. Indeed, I believe that only one previous local record of a specimen exists.

3.

Song Sparrows in the nesting season have a rotten time. Their earlier nests are invariably built on the ground, where they easily fall a prey to enemies. Later in the summer, when the foliage on plants and shrubs has grown thick, they are sometimes elevated a foot or two above the earth. Even then, however, many of them come to a bad end. Mrs. Margaret Nice calculated that, counting eggs that were addled and chicks that died natural or violent deaths, more than 40% of the Song Sparrow offspring of her acquaintance were casualties.

That no doubt partly explains why each pair produces three and sometimes four broods in a season. Mass production is necessary for the proper preservation of the species. Nature has an uncanny, if sometimes blundering, way of adjusting these matters.

I have already described how the entire family of youngsters in my first Song Sparrow's nest were destroyed when a week old. At the beginning of July I found a second nest. It lay on top of a sheaf of tall grasses knocked down by a violent rainstorm. Except for a few wisps of grass sloping across it, the nest was in no way concealed. It was not sunk amongst the fallen grasses, but stood precariously balanced on them like a cup thrown casually there. However, it was firmly woven and in it lay four speckled eggs.

After a few days two chicks hatched. Nothing emerged from the other two eggs. They were addled. So already half the mother's original effort had been in vain.

Like many other parents who have appeared in this book, she was a courageous sitter. Her nest lay beside a path and I could easily approach close to it. But I never took her by surprise. Her mate kept watch in a tree above her and advised her of my approach. When she was still sitting on four eggs she slipped away soon after his initial warning. But after her two chicks hatched she invariably continued to sit even when I stood only three feet from her. Not moving a muscle nor stirring a feather, she eyed me intently. Only when I bent down to the nest did she pop quietly over its side and fly away.

When I approached the nest on the fifth day after the youngsters' appearance I heard no warning signal from their father. Then I saw that their mother was not sitting on the nest. Alas, there was no reason for her to do so! The nursery was empty. Its floor was pierced by a round hole bored by a murderer. Through it a Vole, a voracious meat-eater, had climbed to steal the chicks and eggs. When I picked up the nest I found a space tunnelled in the grass below, where the killer had prepared his plot. It was typical of the method and handiwork of a Vole, which always makes its attack from below.

A few days later I found a third Song Sparrow's nest. It too lay on the ground, half-concealed in a clump of grass. In it were four eggs. I need not prolong the agony again. For ten days I watched the nest and the set of four eggs was always complete. On the eleventh morning, however, when the chicks must have been close to hatching, the nest was empty. Its floor was soaked with fluid from the eggs, spilt when a Crow or some other enemy cracked them to make a meal. One or two chicks may have hatched before the tragedy occurred, in which case they went to add spice to the feast. From my observations the most dangerous period for the contents of nests is the first few days after young birds have hatched, before they learn to lie still when their parents are away on errands.

So the casualty rate in my first three Song Sparrows' nests, containing between them 13 eggs, was 100%.

I always hoped that I might chance upon a nest where one or more youngsters survived the dangers of childhood. At last I did so. One day in the last week in July I noticed a Song Sparrow fly from a thick clump of Purple Loose-strife growing in tall grass. Examining the site, I saw a newly built, still empty nest attached to the flower stalks two or three inches from the ground. Next morning an egg lay in it and on each succeeding day another egg appeared until the set contained four. Then the mother started sitting, well concealed in her bower of green leaves, purple flowers and rank grasses. She proved to be a champion incubator. All four chicks hatched and ten days later they safely left the nest.

Thus out of the total of seventeen Song Sparrows' eggs which I observed, 76.5% came to a bad end. I have no reason to suppose, however, that the casualty rate in the creek as a whole was higher than Mrs. Margaret Nice's 40%. I did not go out of my way to look for Song Sparrows' nests, because of the risk of inadvertently treading on them. I tended therefore to find only the less happily situated ones, those placed where they were evident not only to human eyes but to more hostile eyes as well. It is probably true that the nests most easily discovered by an unsystematic watcher like myself are also those most quickly seen by the Sparrows' enemies. Moreover, however careful one is when watching a nest, one cannot help leaving traces, such as footmarks in the grass, which may attract the attention of predatory birds or beasts and lead them to their quarry. For these reasons the casualties amongst my Song Sparrows were probably more numerous than amongst their better concealed neighbours. Anyway, as the summer advanced plenty of Song Sparrow fledglings appeared in the trees and bushes, clamouring to be fed by their hard-worked parents.

4.

During the first few days of July the Mystery of the Three Young Phoebes deepened. On July 1st I concluded that the fledgling—or whatever it was—sitting in the nest was dead, for it remained unstirring in exactly the same position as before. So inactive was it that when flies landed on it and strolled over it, it did not even wince. From its shape as well as its immobility it might have been a lump of earth or a stone. I wondered whether some strange accident had landed an inanimate object in the Phoebes' home. I could not make out its texture, for the light under the old mill was poor.

However, on reflection I concluded that it must be a bird. What else could be in the nest? I decided that it was one young Phoebe (not three) in the quill stage of growth—as dead as a door-nail.

Yet, whilst I made these observations, both parent birds sat in the branches of a tree close by, uttering quiet, restrained alarm calls. They were worried and obviously had a young family in the neighbourhood. It could hardly be anywhere except in the nest!

Next day my belief that the creature in the nest was dead was shaken. It had not changed its position, but had grown decidedly larger. So there must be life in the young bird yet. It definitely was a bird, for three or four small feathers now stuck up on top of its head. I began to form a theory that it was a young Cowbird who had kicked its step-brothers and sisters out of the nest. It still sat strangely motionless and I felt that there was something sinister about the nest and its occupant.

The parent birds, however, displayed their usual affectionate solicitude, flitting and perching in the trees a few yards away, eyeing me and calling gently. I thought that perhaps their warning notes made the youngster sit unmoving, so as not to betray its presence to a possible enemy.

Whilst they remained so close and talkative, hope of a happy ending to what otherwise seemed a mysterious tragedy persisted.

Next day the youngster in the nest squatted exactly as before, its mass unchanged in either size or shape. A few infant feathers still sprouted on its top-knot, but, so far as I could see, it had not altered its position in any detail in the previous twenty-four hours.

Elsewhere, however, I found something which solved part of the mystery. The ground below the mill was loose, dry earth sloping steeply into a jungle of bushes and grasses at the edge of the creek. Near the foot of this slope sat a young Phoebe, fully-fledged and alive, comfortably settled in the dust. It must have fallen out of the nest (or been forcibly ejected, if its companion was a Cowbird) several days earlier and rolled down the hill to continue its childhood there. By some miracle the youngster had escaped unhurt. Its parents continued to feed it and it waxed strong, grew quills, sprouted feathers and now looked almost ready to fly. It appeared completely content in its improvised earthen nest, doubtless assuming that to fall several feet from a high beam, crash to the ground, roll down a steep hill, fetch up at the bottom and resume existence there was a perfectly normal part of every young bird's experience.

It gazed calmly at me. The parent birds, however, became agitated when I stood near it and called fussily from boughs overhead. So I withdrew behind a shrub, where I continued to watch. Presently the mother bird flew under the mill. First she sped up to the nest-beam and paid a fleeting visit to her youngster there, then dropped down and fed the fledgling on the ground. She was clearly accustomed to do duty at both nurseries.

When I returned to the place that evening the fledgling still sat with unruffled composure on the ground. It had taken a little mild exercise during the day, for it was about a foot away from where it sat in the morning. Its juvenile plumage was complete except for long tail feathers.

Next morning it had gone. I searched the neighbourhood in vain. It had left its "home away from home" on the ground and flown to school in the trees, where it would learn to fly and feed itself and become completely independant. The parents had left with it. I could neither see nor hear them anywhere. They had deserted the immediate vicinity of the shed, where they had built their first nest, and the mill where they had built their second. Only the untidy, mossy fabric of that second nest remained as tangible evidence of their sojourn there—and in it still sat, as motionless and lifeless as a dummy, what appeared to be the figure of a fledgling.

I watched for a few days in the hope that the parents had not really finally departed and would come back to care for it. But they never did. The silhouette of the figure on the nest remained invariably the same. After a week I took a long stick and poked it down.

No wonder the parents had lost interest in it! It was a fully formed young Phoebe with a well grown head and body. Its plumage and wings were complete. It sat peacefully there, with its beak resting on the edge of the nest, as if in repose. But it was only a shell of a bird. Its eye-holes were empty and its frame was hollow. Its skin supporting the feathers was as dry and hard as parchment. Its eyes, flesh and internal organs had all been eaten.

So the Mystery of the Three Young Phoebes was two-thirds solved. One youngster had tumbled in infancy out of the nest. The second had been gruesomely killed. It was a clear case of murder. A verdict of "guilty" must be returned against the lice or other vermin which often infest a Phoebe's nest. This was a grim reminder of the penalty which parent Phoebes sometimes pay for not keeping their home clean. The youngster's death must have been a lingering one—death by a thousand bites.

Now I understood the meaning of the various developments which I had observed. The youngster was presumably still alive on the day when I noticed its sudden increase in size, the change being due to the bursting of its quills and the sprouting of its feathers. It was, however, already too weak to move. It may or may not have had a spark of life in it the next day when a parent Phoebe paid it a brief visit. By then, however, it must have been at least comatose, and perhaps it had already expired.

I never knew what happened to the third young Phoebe. If it tumbled out of the nest, it had not been killed, otherwise I should have found its corpse somewhere on the ground below. Perhaps it fell out and had the same good fortune as the second. These two may have been so maddened by nibbling lice that they jumped from the nest in desperation and thereby saved their lives.

Two days later I saw a young Phoebe which must have been one or the other of them. It was near the top of an Elm tree not far from the mill. In form it was an adult bird with tail feathers complete, but in plumage it was a juvenile in its first autumn dress. Its movements too betrayed exceeding youth. Although it flew successfully enough from branch to branch in search of food, its flight had a cautious, amateurish quality. When it darted after a passing insect its aerial evolutions lacked the light, graceful, dashing twists and turns of a mature Phoebe. Its progress through the air was ponderous and pedestrian, the first,

tentative, uncertain steps towards becoming an accomplished, professional Flycatcher.

But the youngster was on the way to becoming that. It
was on its own now, independent of parents. It had matri-
culated to the tree-tops with the whole free air as its world.
Time would correct all its youthful faults. Practice would
make perfect.

5.

I caught only occasional, casual glimpses of the later
life of most of the other species whom I had watched at
their nests.

The young Yellow Warblers remained dependant on
their parents for several days after they took wing. Many
family parties of them could be seen in the trees. The
juniors stayed perched on the boughs whilst their elders
conducted a ceaseless caterpillar hunt over the surrounding
territory. They chirped constantly to remind the parents
of their whereabouts and avidly received all the fruits
of the chase brought to them.

For a few weeks they remained in the modest, mostly
dull plumage which they acquired in the nest. Then this
costume began to wear out and in its place grew a more
splendid plumage, which for both sexes in the first winter
is like that of an adult female. By the middle of July I saw
several birds in whom this transformation was taking place.
Their wings and backs were still brown, but their crowns
were already olive-green and their faces and throats bright
yellow, whilst a yellow patch appeared also at the base of
their tails.

As June advanced the Northern Flickers whose nest was
hidden somewhere inside the mill flew more and more frequently in and out of the knot-hole in the window shutter.

211

They were evidently feeding hungry chicks. Early in July these visits became unnecessary, for half-a-dozen hale and hearty youngsters emerged to join their parents outside. Their plumage was already similar to that of an adult and they were a handsome and colourful company flying about together. Often they called to each other in loud, carefree, musical voices. There was a merriness, a light-headed gaiety about those calls which created a slight impression of inebriation. I was tempted to wonder whether the fledglings had been reared not in the old mill but in the ancient brewery itself, where they had found a vat and imbibed its contents not wisely but too well. The family stayed together for some time before drifting apart and away.

I think that a few pairs of Catbirds on the creek bank may have reared second broods. They continued to behave as if guarding the precious secret of eggs and chicks hidden somewhere in the foliage. But the leaves on the shrubs and trees were now so thick that searching for new nests amongst them would have been a tedious labour. I was content to watch the growth of members of the first broods. For some days after they left their nests they perched on neighbouring boughs, still dependant on their parents for being fed. Besides being tail-less they had the rather dishevelled look which characterizes many fledglings. Their first juvenile plumage was not so sleek as their second suit of feathers, which in all young birds soon replaces this first and is called their "juvenile autumn plumage". By the end of July they had generally assumed it, tails and all, and looked neat, slightly smaller editions of adult Catbirds.

Matters developed similarly with the Baltimore Orioles. During the early days of July every Elm tree seemed to have its quota of young Orioles perched amongst the branches, announcing their whereabouts by hungry calls. Each was visited regularly first by its mother and then by its father, bringing food. The older birds were anxious about the safety of their young. In that frame of mind they gave me a surprise. I had grown used to the idea that everything about an Oriole is beautiful: its appearance, its habits and its voice. I was astonished, therefore, on approaching a youngster to see an adult male—its parent—fly towards me, alight on a branch close by, face me challengingly and utter harsh, rattling, chattering cries. These alarm notes were ugly. In July they were the most commonly heard Oriole sounds, almost completely taking the place of the pleasant whistles and songs, expressive of domestic affection between husband and wife, which had filled the Elm trees with sweet music in June.

6.

When I last wrote about Savannah Sparrows these quiet, humble, self-effacing little birds were preparing to nest along Savannah Sparrow's Row. Let me briefly continue their tale. They are clever at concealing the sites of their nurseries. In June I used to see cock birds perched on stones and tufts of grass, often so inconspicuously that I should not have noticed them if they had not, at my approach, spoken tender words of warning to their mates sitting close on eggs. In each case the nest must have been in the grass somewhere near. But I could not find it. The hen bird never flew directly from it, but first ran stealthily and quietly, like a mouse, through the grass and only from a distance fluttered into view.

By the beginning of July several sets of eggs had

hatched. Parent birds kept coming and going on the errand of feeding their young. When they arrived at the nest their beaks were stuffed with food. Sometimes a large, juicy caterpillar dangled there; at other times the plump body and stiff wings of a hapless grasshopper protruded, and at yet other times the soft bodies of half-a-dozen small insects stuck out in all directions from the Sparrow's beak.

I felt sure that now I would find one or two nests. Surely if I sat still and watched carefully I would discover the place where one at least of the birds deposited its catch of meat. So, like Chaucer,

"There I sat down among the fairë flow'rs
And saw the birdës trip out of their bow'rs".

But in vain. I never on these occasions found the site of any of their bowers. Sometimes I lay patiently and cunningly still and quiet only a few yards from a place where two parents were accustomed to arrive with provisions, but they were always either more patient or more cunning than I. These little birds, who seemed so casual about their own safety, were cautious in the extreme about the safety of their progeny. They were fearless for themselves, allowing me to approach close to them as they sat singing on a wild flowering-stalk; but they were absolutely determined by hook or by crook to keep me as far as possible from their nests. Always detecting me, they were never deceived by my quiet stillness, however long it lasted. They fluttered from place to place or strolled to and fro in the grass, eyeing me suspiciously and muttering little protests at me, without relaxing their firm grip on the loads of insects filling their beaks. Sometimes they would maintain this vigilance for a long time and make no attempt to visit their nests until I

Photo by **W. V. Crich, F.R.P.S.**

BELTED KINGFISHER
"Bold and handsome."

grew impatient and moved away. At other times a bird would tire first and I saw it suddenly flutter into the air and dive into the grass further off. I knew that I would only make a fool of myself if I rose and went to inspect that spot, for the clever bird had deliberately alighted at a distance from its precious family. I could see blades of grass shaking and occasionally catch a fleeting glimpse of the creature's own mouse-like form—its head lowered and body crouched—as it stealthily made its way by tortuous paths to its home. Shortly afterwards it would rise again from the grass in some entirely different place, its beak empty of food, and fly away to fetch another load of insects. Often I thought that I had outwitted it and noticed the exact place where it fed its young. When it had left I strolled over and searched amongst the wild grass and plants—and found nothing. Probably I was not far wrong and an intensive hunt in the neighbourhood would have revealed the nest. But I was always fearful lest I should tread unwittingly upon it, so I never made a thorough search.

It was by luck that at last I found a nest, on July 9th. Walking along casually, I almost trod on it. Suddenly a Savannah Sparrow rushed from beneath a dock plant near my feet and ran away swiftly. One wing was raised stiffly above its back. Lifting a large dock leaf, I saw the nest on the ground. It was constructed of grass, like a Song Sparrow's nest. In it lay four eggs. They were smaller than a Song Sparrow's and their greenish-white pigment was largely covered with reddish-brown splashes.

That raising of a wing above her back was an attempt by the mother to decoy me away. Always when I disturbed her afterwards she gave a similar performance. Sometimes a wing was held more or less upright over her back, at other times it was stretched sideways and at other times both wings were raised. Sometimes the wing was held stiffly and at other times it vibrated or fluttered. Whilst running in this attitude the bird pursued an erratic, zig-zag course and occasionally at a distance from the nest ran round in little circles, as if she had gone crazy. No doubt this was all calculated to attract my attention and draw me away. The wily conduct of the Savannah Sparrow was in interesting contrast to the passive behaviour of the placid, undeceptive Song Sparrow.

Eventually four chicks hatched. Two days later the nest was nearly destroyed. A workman cut the grass and weeds over the whole area and the dock plant concealing the Sparrow family was laid low. The nest and its chicks were completely exposed. But when I visited it the next morning I found the mother, though no doubt dismayed, still bravely sitting. She watched me keenly, then slipped quietly away through the grass, doing mild decoy action. The quartette of youngsters gaped helplessly and blindly upwards. Feeling distressed at their exposure to danger, I tried to assist them and their parents by picking a large dock leaf and placing it over them in the same position as their previous protective covering.

But alas, next day one chick had disappeared. Only three remained. An enemy had carried off their brother or sister. The others lasted rather longer. Their quills appeared and feathers began to sprout. But not fast enough, oh not fast enough! One by one the youngsters were taken. On the sixth day only one was left. On the seventh I found the nest empty and the parents crying mournfully at their love's labour lost. It had been a sad case of,

Four little Savannah Sparrows
   Sitting on the lea.
A hawk pounced on one of them
   And then there were three.

Three little Savannah Sparrows,
   Gradually they grew.
One became a Vole's lunch
   And then there were two.

Two little Savannah Sparrows
   Blinking in the sun.
Down flew a Carrion Crow
   And then there was one.

One little Savannah Sparrow
   Just about to run
But a snake saw it first
   And then there was none.

7.

I never found the young Spotted Sandpipers who hatched from the nest amongst Evening Primroses. The parent in charge of them must have led them amongst bushes where I did not happen to go. I was lucky, however, with my Spotted Sandpiper families. As soon as I lost sight of one I promptly found another.

On July 1st I discovered my third Sandpiper's nest lying on rough, grassy ground where blue Chicory flowers blossomed in profusion. It contained two eggs. I presumed that the mother was in process of completing her clutch and that on the following day I should find three eggs. But there were still only two, so warm that the parents were evidently already incubating them.

That morning I found yet another Spotted Sandpiper's nest in the same area of ground, about thirty yards from the third. This one contained three eggs. A parent bird was sitting at the time and was taken by surprise. Leaping hurriedly from the nest, it uttered panic-stricken shrieks and screeches and, alighting a few feet away, immediately resorted to violent decoy action. It arched its body, drooped and fluttered its wings, fanned and depressed its tail and all the time continued to make a frightened, and indeed frightening, hullabaloo.

However, it did not keep this up for long. After half-a-minute it calmed down, strolled around in its ordinary, quiet fashion and then flew to the shore as if nothing untoward had occurred.

On the following afternoon both nests were threatened with destruction. Workmen came with scythes to cut the long grass and blooming Chicory. Over the whole area they shaved the earth clean of everything growing more than two inches high. Afterwards the place looked neat and tidy, but I was distressed to think of what had probably happened to the Sandpiper nests. They could hardly have escaped being trampled on and having their eggs smashed by the boots of men trudging systematically over the ground. At the best, if they had themselves avoided complete destruction, the tall grasses and wild flowers on which the birds counted for concealment would be shorn away.

I therefore approached the nests with apprehension. Both, by a miracle, were still intact. Their sets of eggs were complete and unscathed, but they lay wholly revealed to the sharp gaze of enemies. The defensive jungle surrounding them had disappeared and except, for one factor, they were almost as exposed as billiard balls in the middle

218

of a billiard table. That factor was their camouflage, their protective colouring. It was remarkably efficient, making them blend perfectly into the stubbley ground.

No parent birds, however, were anywhere in sight or hearing. They had been so disturbed and frightened by the grass-cutters' activities that they had fled. The eggs were all cool—abandoned.

Next morning the nest containing two eggs was still unvisited by the parents. The eggs were stone cold, utterly deserted. At the other nest also I saw no sign of a bird. The three eggs were in place as on the previous day. Trying to reconcile myself to the fact that they too would be deserted, I bent down to feel them. Could I be right, or was my imagination playing a trick on me? They felt warm. I picked one out to make sure. Yes, it had the distinct heat of an egg still being incubated. So the parents were persevering.

For a week afterwards I visited the nest every day. Both Sandpipers helped to incubate the eggs, at any rate during the first few days. Later I saw only one of them, probably the male,[1] who was invariably sitting. He was alert and wary, seeming to detect me as soon as my head rose above some mounds of earth which provided my nearest concealed approach, about thirty yards away. No doubt he was often helped by unsolicited signals given by other birds— the startled cry of a Killdeer, the cawing of a Crow or the staccato note of a Song Sparrow alarmed by my presence in the neigbourhood. In this way different species warn each other of the approach of a possible enemy.

No change occurred at the nest until July 11th, the tenth day after I discovered it. In the morning the clutch of

[1] For the rest of this narrative I shall assume that it was the male.

three eggs lay as usual. But in the afternoon things began to happen—and when things do happen in a Spotted Sandpiper's nest they happen quickly. I had a free afternoon and took my enchanting friend Diana MacDougall to see the nests, eggs and young birds in the creek. Perhaps I should explain that Diana is four years old.

The Spotted Sandpiper put on an excellent show for us. As we approached his nest, soon after four o'clock, he flew off the eggs, according to custom. As usual too, he alighted on the grass a few yards away and piped casually once or twice. Then his conduct became unusual. Instead of taking wing again and flying nonchalantly to the shore he stayed around, showing unprecedented anxiety. He walked to and fro, pacing nervously and uttering small cries of annoyance.

When we reached the nest and bent over it we saw what bothered him. Two of the eggs were there as usual, but the third had gone. In its place lay a baby Sandpiper, crouching flat on the ground, already instinctively trying, on hearing its father's alarm signals, to pretend that it was not there. The afternoon was brilliantly sunny, hot and dry, yet the chick was soaking wet. Its down stuck to its body as clammily as the hair of a schoolboy who uses generous quantities of hair-grease. It could not have left its egg more than a few minutes earlier, for the sun's strong rays would quickly dry it. Nevertheless every trace of its egg-shell had already disappeared, removed by the cautious parent to a safe distance.

Unlike all the newly hatched birds which I have described hitherto, this chick was prettily made. In figure it was a miniature replica of an adult Sandpiper, with correctly proportioned head and body. Its beak was a reasonably formidable toy model of the real thing. Its dark, bright eyes were open and I could see quite a large foot protruding underneath it. The youngster remained studiously motionless and unblinking as Diana and I looked at it.

Diana caught her breath with delight. In tones of the tenderest motherly solicitude she addressed a few remarks to the baby. She longed to stroke it gently with the tips of her fingers, but resisted temptation and stuck her hands resolutely behind her back. She was anxious not to frighten the little creature.

We saw a small hole in the broader end of each of the two remaining eggs. Evidently their chicks also were coming to life and seeking escape from confinement. Perhaps our presence was delaying the process. The parent bird was circling round us in great agitation and was certainly being prevented from assisting in his children's liberation. We decided to depart and leave them to it.

I returned three hours later. As soon as I came in sight of the nest the father flew off it. He behaved as he had done in the afternoon, alighting close by, strutting nervously in the grass and piping. Two different notes sounded in his voice: the first harsh and even strident, a note of anxiety and protest aimed at me; the second gentle and persuasive, a note of warning addressed to his family. As I walked nearer the nest he fluttered into the air, flew low over the grass, passed right above the nest and uttered subdued, conversational piping sounds as he did so. He was no doubt advising the chicks to lie absolutely motionless, and seeing for himself that they took the advice. His behaviour, though agitated, showed restraint. He did not indulge in any decoy action nor give way to the violent crying and wailing which accompanies that. He seemed reluctant to leave the immediate neighbourhood of the nest, wishing to keep an eye on his family and have the evidence of his own sight that no harm befell them. If he turned to lead me from the nest, some accident might occur whilst he was away. So he continued to pace restlessly in the grass a few yards off, calling continuously and every now and then bobbing his tail up and down.

I did not stay long. It was long enough, however, to see that all the eggs had disappeared, except for one small fragment of egg-shell dropped about six inches away. In their place sat three young Sandpipers. They were as pretty a sight as one could see, squatting close-packed side by side all facing in the same direction. They were perfectly formed, with neat little beaks, black eyes and bodies covered with soft down from the crowns of their heads to the tips of their tails. This thick, furry coat was dry and fluffy now, with a grey-brown ground colour, a black stripe on the sides of their faces running through each eye, and another long, broad black stripe stretching from their brows, over their heads, down their necks and along their backs to their tails. In design and texture they looked like minute tabby kittens.

Their colouring gave them excellent protection, making it hard to pick them out from their surroundings. To increase the difficulty they lay motionless, flattened as much as possible against the ground, gazing at me with un-blinking eyes.

When I returned an hour later the situation was unchanged. I only stayed for a few moments and then withdrew behind a tree to watch what the father would do. He had remained nearby, as before, betraying anxiety but making no attempt to decoy me away. Almost as soon as I left he leapt into the air, flew towards the nest and alighted a few yards from it. Bending low, he ran quickly to it, following the course of various dips in the ground, so as to expose himself as little as possible, like a soldier hurrying from shell-hole to shell-hole. He halted beside the nest, looked cautiously round in every direction, bobbed his hind-quarters several times up and down, piped reassuringly and then settled down to brood his family.

I visited the creek as usual early the next morning. From a great distance I could hear the parent Sandpiper crying in alarm. Hastening towards the nest, I saw a man walking close by with a dog frisking at his heels—enough to frighten the bird out of his wits. The man and the dog, however, passed on. But I stayed to add to the Sandpiper's troubles. He expressed his agitation by making a great shindy.

I went to the nest. It was empty. Six inches away, how-ever, a chick crouched unmoving in the grass. I lifted it in my hand. It remained there unperturbed, no doubt inno-cently wondering what was happening and merely obeying its instinct to stay still. When I replaced it on the ground it continued to "lie doggo", betraying no spark of life except in the light of its bright black eyes.

I saw no sign of the other chicks. Their father had already led them to some neighbouring patch of long grass, where they could hide. This third chick was probably the weakling of the family who needed more time to gather its strength and take its first walk over the rough ground. After all, less than fourteen hours had passed since the little family hatched.

Evidently the father had been trying to coax it away to greater safety. All the time that I stayed there he fussed around it and me, once more making no attempt to decoy me away.

An hour or so later I returned to the site of the nest. As the parent bird did not flutter into the air when I approached, I concluded that he and his infant had successfully travelled into hiding further away. Suddenly, however, he sprang from the ground only a few feet from me, screaming with alarm. He had been so engrossed with the youngster that he did not notice my return. There the chick lay, looking particularly helpless, for its father's departure had been so hurried that in getting off the ground he accidently kicked it over. It lay on its side, with one leg sticking comically into the air and its white, downy breast and belly exposed. In this awkward position it remained motionless. Its unstirring discomfort served no useful purpose, since its white belly, unlike its well camouflaged back, fully revealed it to the gaze of any passing enemy. So strong and unreasoning is its instinct to remain still when its parent utters an alarm note!

Meanwhile the father was trying to decoy me by action of a most violent kind. The contrast between his behaviour now and an hour earlier (when he had received plenty of notice of my approach) seemed to be further evidence that he only resorts to this extreme conduct when taken badly by surprise whilst guarding eggs or young. He humped his body, spread and quivered his wings, fanned his tail, screeched aloud to attract my attention and then started running over the ground away from the youngster. At first I pretended to take no notice. He promptly turned round, came back towards me, turned once more and again began to run away with every appearance of suffering acute agony. This time I followed him. He ran quickly

224

through the grass, never relaxing for a moment his awkward, strained, exhibitionist posture, nor ceasing his loud screams. Only when we were forty yards from the chick did he suddenly cease all his play-acting and resume a normal, quiet attitude. He looked up at me, jerked his tail impudently, piped almost cheerily as if to say, "I've fooled you!", spread his wings and flew back to his chick.

I returned to the site of the nest. The adult Sandpiper was still in the same place with his child. He fluttered into the air with rather gentler alarm calls than usual and I saw the chick rise and run more or less steadily through the short grass into the concealment of a patch of tall, wild flowers.

So at last it had really found its legs, was safely away from the nest and had started on the adventure of mobile life.

The capacity of young Spotted Sandpipers (and other similar species) to make long treks soon after hatching is remarkable. This Sandpiper family gave a good example of it. My next visit to them was that afternoon, almost exactly twenty-four hours after the youngsters had left their eggs. They were roaming about gaily a hundred yards from the nest!

I should not have found them, except that their zealous parent betrayed their whereabouts, as he did on many later occasions. He saw me as soon as I landed on the shore and immediately started the outcry which he used to make at the nest after the chicks hatched. I walked to where he was, on a path between crops of standing hay. I saw no chicks, but it was obvious from his behaviour that they were hidden somewhere very near. He seemed partly frightened and partly bold. His shrill cries had a frantic note, but whether it was an expression of panic in himself or an attempt to create it in me seemed a moot point. He kept fluttering into the air, sometimes at a discreet distance from me and at other times with an aggressive motion in my direction. Every few moments he alighted on the path and started to run along it, piping loudly. This effort to decoy me was mild, unaccompanied by those extravagant antics and contortions of the body which he exhibited when suddenly caught by surprise.

For a while I made no response to his appeals and he quickly abandoned each successive effort to draw me along the path. Instead he fluttered restlessly into the air again. He did not stay silent for a moment, all the time rending the silence with distressful pipings.

Then I walked along the path in the direction which he wished me to take. He looked a bit relieved as he flew slowly at my eye level a short way ahead of me, like a sprite coaxing me onwards. Every detail of his conduct was eloquent of anxiety. Yet still I had not set eyes on any of his young charges. I wanted to make sure that I was right in supposing that they were somewhere near, to discover whether all three chicks had so far survived and to see what they looked like and how they deported themselves at the end of their first day.

When I had followed him some way, therefore, I stopped and lay down in the long grass at a point where I could look back to the spot where I suspected the youngsters to be. At first he did not notice this manoeuvre and fluttered on. When he discovered that I was no longer following him he was perplexed. His call took on a new note of uncertainty, of interrogation, as he turned and cautiously retraced his passage through the air, searching for me. On seeing me lying in the grass he was very upset. His cries became shriller and louder. He alighted on the path in front of me and made a series of darting attacks at me, which he only checked each time when within a yard of my face. He never ceased to yell defiance and showed astonishing courage throughout this attempt to "shoo" me away.

I lay absolutely still. After all, what is sauce for the goose is sauce for the gander. If his chicks, when I approached them, assumed a motionless attitude in the hope of persuading me that they did not exist, I would now assume a similar attitude in the hope of persuading him that I too was non-existent. The trick worked. After a while his cries of protest became less strident and insistent. Soon he turned his back on me and began to wander slowly back to where his precious children were. His mind turned again to other aspects of their affairs and every now and then he stooped to catch an insect in his beak. He gathered quite a number of them. Was he collecting them to feed his babies? As he walked the tone of his voice altered. Distress gave way to mere disturbance and then disturbance changed to reassurance. Intervals of silence began to punctuate his sustained piping, giving it a new mood of restored calm.

Eventually he reached the youngsters. I could not see them, but the evidence of his voice was unmistakable. Its tone changed completely, suddenly becoming gentle, solicitous and affectionate, with a sweet cooing note in it. He was talking to his offspring.

After a while I rose and walked to where he was. Instantly he sounded his alarm call and fluttered into the air. Then I saw two chicks in a patch of grass at a fork of the path. They skedaddled across the path, looking like small balls of fluff on top of swiftly running legs. A third did not appear, so I was not sure whether the whole brood had survived.

One of the pair hid in the hay beside the path, but the other hesitated, then halted and tried to conceal itself in the middle of the bare earth. It looked very funny. Some whim of instinct made it squat motionless with its head lowered until the chin almost touched the ground and its tail tilted skywards, like a broken-down toy motor-car lacking fore-wheels. I stooped and picked it up. At first the pretty little thing stayed quietly in my hand, making no protest and betraying no agitation. I was able to admire at close quarters its cunningly patterned coat of down and to examine its limbs. Its feet were large, with three long and sensitive toes, like an artist's fingers. Its wings were rudimentary, mere fluffy, down-covered stumps.

When I raised it above ground level it showed signs of fright, shaking feebly those almost non-existent wings and uttering a few weak, high-pitched pipes. The father flew straight at me, fluttering his wings and screaming. I returned the youngster to mother earth, tucking it safely amongst the uncut hay, where no chance enemy could detect it. There it immediately resumed its posture of lifeless immobility.

The father then resorted to mild decoy action, eschewing all those extravagant wrigglings and shakings of the different members of his body which sometimes characterized the performance. He ran straight along the path, piping coaxingly to me in the hope that I would follow. This wish I gratified and he did not halt until he had led me a hundred yards away to the site of his old nest. His return to the region seemed direct and automatic, as if he naturally retraced his steps to such a familiar spot. There he loitered for a while, piping, bobbing and gathering morsels of food in his beak. Then he cocked an eye at me, favoured me with a farewell whistle and flew light-heartedly back to his children. I saw him drop into the long grass where they were.

Next morning the family had moved to other quarters about fifty yards away. They were now on the shore, not far from the water's edge. I did not see the chicks, but from their guardian's behaviour they were evidently hidden in a thick, isolated, grassy patch of Wild Lettuce, Sweet Clover and Purple Vetch surrounded by open ground. This rank little bit of vegetation gave them as good protection as if they had been housed behind the stone walls of a fortress. They were invisible even to a closely searching eye.

The father fussed a great deal as I approached. I was beginning to learn, however, that whatever might be said in favour of some of his qualities, his intelligence was severely limited. If I stood upright in his presence he showed extreme alarm and continued to express violent agitation as long as I remained standing. But if I sat down, part at least of his suspicion was removed and after a minute or two he grew calmer. If I sat not in the open but behind a bush or sapling—however near and obvious (one would have thought) to the most stupid mind—he was satisfied that the threat of my presence had been removed. After a few reminiscent protests he would quieten down completely and go about his usual occupations as if I did not exist.

By this simple device I was able to observe him as he kept guard over his young family. First he disappeared into the patch of wild flowers in search of them, no doubt anxious to assure himself of their safety. I could hear him calling them and gossiping with them in that affectionate, cooing voice of his. Then he reappeared at the edge of the flower patch, looked round, piped enquiringly as if to ask "Is anybody watching me?" and then strolled into the open. He at once started gathering food, jabbing his beak here and there at insects. After a few minutes of industrious hunting he returned to the nursery, calling to the infants as he disappeared in the tangle of Vetch.

Shortly afterwards he appeared again and resumed his hunting. Once more, when he had gathered a goodly quantity of insects he went back to the chicks. He repeated this process several times during the half-hour that I watched. I concluded that the youngsters were still incapable of collecting enough food for themselves and that he was feeding them. Only once did he move far away from the wild flowers, when he flew to the water's edge, presumably to get a drink. Otherwise he acted the sentry as well as the "bread-winner" with unwinking care. All this time no youngster appeared.

Next day the family had moved again, this time to a group of saplings and shrubs close to the water. When I arrived three chicks were roaming about on the shore, foraging for themselves. As soon as he spied me the father uttered his alarm call. The youngsters immediately recognized it as a signal to take cover and ran helter-skelter into clumps of Convolvulus carpeting the ground beneath the saplings. They were like infants who had become highly expert at toddling. This was the first time that I had seen all three since they left the nest and I was delighted to know that none of them had come to any harm.

For at least another fortnight after that the family kept together. The father stayed constantly with his children, keeping a careful guard over them and acting as their guide and tutor in all the problems which beset young Sandpipers

BLACK-CROWNED NIGHT HERON
"Immature birds are brown and cream coloured."

learning the ways of the world. They were sometimes in one part of the shore, sometimes in another, alternating between two or three favourite spots, making a grand tour of that little corner of the earth. I could always guess their whereabouts from the father's outcry at my appearance. He started his hullabaloo at once from the spot where he and they were, with no attempt to deceive me by moving quietly away until he could start his alarm call from a distance. This was due to his anxiety to warn his youngsters without delay of the aproach of a stranger, so that they could take instantaneous defence action. If they were on open ground they immediately raced for cover, which was usually not far away. If they were already amongst concealing grass or undergrowth, they at once "froze" into immobility.

It was by his voice that he commanded their actions. Its tone changed according to the situation. His first alarm calls were sharp and staccato, though comparatively restrained, with an unmistakeable note of warning. The chicks knew what to do when they heard it, and did it at once, as described above. If the danger which he spied drew closer his voice grew sharper and more insistent, emphasizing the need for his youngsters to be particularly careful not to give themselves away. If the danger came really close, the quality of his utterance changed again. It grew frenzied, violent and threatening—a loud sustained screeching aimed then (I concluded) not at conveying any message to his youngsters but at conveying one to me, the intruder. It was an effort to frighten me, to drive me away. If he succeeded in doing this, he followed me as I departed. If I did not retreat far or fast enough, he ran or flew ahead of me in an attempt to lead me to a safe distance. During this process his voice changed once more. The screeching ceased and he reverted to a continuous, monotonous reiteration of wild pipes or calls. These seemed to be aimed partly at attracting me onwards and partly at reporting back to his chicks where he was and what he was doing. The youngsters could not but conclude from his tones that they should still remain strictly in hiding. If he succeeded in conducting his dupe to what he considered a safe distance, he usually marked the moment by emitting one or two normal, reassuring whistles. This was probably a signal to the chicks that they could relax their vigilance. Soon afterwards he flew back to them, uttering contented pipings and, on arrival, greeting them with joyous, loving, crooning ejaculations.

If, on the other hand, he only succeeded in driving or leading me to a distance which he did not regard as entirely satisfactory, he continued to declare his concern by worried, sometimes querulous expostulations. Even if he decided, on the whole, to give me the benefit of the doubt and started to stroll back towards his family, he now and then expressed his uncertainty in a peevish, dissatisfied remark. Most of these sounds were unnecessary except as signals to the chicks. Their purpose was to keep them constantly informed on a situation as it developed.

As I have already described, he had a completely different set of tones for ordinary family conversation with them. His voice then assumed the sweet quality of a young mother addressing her babies. It was full of soft, fond, almost caressing notes bespeaking tender parental love. A little series of different noises and of different shades of tone in which these were uttered took the place of words. His phrase announcing that he was coming to see them, wherever they might at the moment be, was recognizably different from that which he employed when summoning them to come to him. Sometimes I heard their answering voices, small, eager pipings telling him where they were in the tangle of grasses and flowers.

His conduct with them was as charming as the tones of his voice when speaking to them. One morning when they were only a few days old they were foraging rather widely over an open space of ground. As soon as I appeared he uttered a warning to them and they at once started running to hide. Two of them reached cover safely, but somehow the third took a wrong turning and wandered further and further into the open. He thereupon called some endearment to it which made it promptly squat motionless on the ground. Then he walked to it, spread a wing over it and sat down to brood it.

On another occasion also they were scattered over the open ground when I arrived on the scene. I sat down behind a bush, but he caught sight of me as I did so. For a few moments he was nervous and uttered tentative notes of warning which caused the chicks to stop dead in their tracks. He peered anxiously in my direction and seemed uncertain whether to sound a full alarm note, which would send them rushing towards cover, or to give them the "all clear" signal and let them continue their carefree wanderings. Torn by doubt, he decided to compromise. He called in a gentle, conversational tone which must have been the equivalent of the "come hither" clucking of a mother-hen summoning her chicks, for they all ran to him. Then he raised both wings, whilst they ran under them. He settled down on top of the entire family and they remained in hiding there for a full minute.

On the fourth or fifth day of their existence his functions on their behalf changed. Hitherto he had spent much of his time collecting food for them and passing it to them.

Now, however, their skill at gathering their own provisions had become so great that they were each self-supporting. He need only hunt for himself. So from being intensely mobile he became rather immobile. Instead of forever chasing, often at a run, after insects and carrying them in beakfulls to his dependants, he usually stood stationary on a hillock or fallen log, from which he could keep a guardian eye on them whilst they hunted their own prey. During the early days he kept close to them. If he needed to fly to the water to slake his thirst, he stayed there only the minimum time necessary and then hurried back to his post. He was a thoroughly efficient sentinel, not even permitting other harmless adult Spotted Sandpipers, casual visitors to the scene, to come near the youngsters. Later, as their strength and capacity to look after themselves increased, he was a less indefatigable and conscientious sentry, permitting himself longer journeys in both space and time away from them. They were constantly in his mind, however. Wherever he was, he always still kept one eye on the look-out for any possible danger to them. At the slightest sign of it he came flying quickly back, with loud alarm calls, to their neighbourhood. If I were the danger, he would try to attract me away by mild decoy action. But he did not show the same all-consuming desire to succeeed as he used to. It was a more casual performance, almost a mere matter of form, for he had greater confidence in his offsprings' capacity to elude me by sprinting into cover.

Gradually they grew. It was amusing to see how in one respect they were unmistakably Spotted Sandpipers from the beginning. As soon as they mastered the use of their legs and left the nest they acquired the habit of bobbing their hindquarters up and down. This was in keeping with

234

their remarkable precocity in being able to walk and help to feed themselves when only half-day chicks. In other ways, however, they were obviously and charmingly juvenile. For the first few days they remained minute in size. They had the unsophisticated, innocent air of exceeding youth and the fluffy prettiness of many young animals. Although they were reasonably proficient on their lanky legs, occasionally, when coming up against an unexpected obstacle on the ground, they staggered as very young kittens and calves do.

As the days passed they put on size and weight, but it was a long time before they put off their down. When I last saw them they were seventeen days old. Each had grown to about the size of an adult Spotted Sandpiper, yet they were still almost completely covered with fluffy coats. Feathers had begun to grow on their wings, but they could not raise themselves from the ground for even a few inches of flight. Their only method of locomotion was running. This they could do well. They had developed an impressive turn of speed. It was almost a sprint.

The chicks then still formed a close family party and the faithful father still guarded them. That day I left Ottawa and did not return for almost a week. When I next visited the creek I could see no sign of them. Perhaps they had moved collectively elsewhere, where I did not happen to find them; or perhaps in the meantime the youngsters had become fully fledged and independent and the family had broken up. I think the latter was the case.

During much of this time I had been keeping an occasional eye on another party of young Spotted Sandpipers. I first discovered them when they were already fairly grownup. They lived on the opposite shore of the creek, where

235

vegetation grew more thickly and concealment was easier. Perhaps for this reason, but more likely because the chicks were already able to take reasonably good care of themselves, their guardian parent was less fussy and nervous than the first. It kept a regular watch over them, but was less noisily resentful of me. One of its favourite look-out posts was the top of a clump of wild flowers. It balanced neatly on their summit and there gained a wide view of the surroundings, like a sentry on a high watch-tower.

Judging by what I observed of the later development of this second family of chicks, I think that five or six days must elapse between the stage at which I last saw the first family and the time when the chicks would be sufficiently fledged and self-reliant to leave the care of their father. In other words, the youngsters probably stay with him for about three weeks after they hatch. During the first two weeks they remain clothed mainly in down with all the original markings: a grey-brown head, back and rump; black eye-stripe and line down the centre of the back from crown to tail; and speckless white throat, breast and underparts. At the end of a fortnight feathers begin to sprout, growing first on the mantle and wings. One youngster whom I saw could already lift itself from the ground and fly a few paces when its body was still downy except for fairly well developed wing plumage. Afterwards feathers develop on the flanks, crown and breast and finally on the neck, rump and tail. Before this last transformation the chicks can fly efficiently and are independant of their parents. One day I watched a couple of them who had just started off on their own. They flew restrainedly, in an experimental kind of way, from rock to rock. Their heads and bodies were neatly covered with new feathers, but round its neck each wore a little "ruff" of down.

236

Several other new families of Spotted Sandpipers were maturing in the district during July. By the end of the third week fully plumaged young birds began to appear, strolling and feeding by themselves on the shore and the log-rafts. Two features in particular distinguish them from their elders. First, their plumage had a brand-new, spick and span appearance. It was spotlessly clean and natty. Secondly, their breasts and underparts were pure white, lacking any sign of the scattering of dark dots which marks the adult bird and gives it its name of Spotted Sandpiper.

8.

The only other shore birds who nested in the creek were Killdeer Plovers. A few pairs acquired small scoops in the ground and laid in them their speckled eggs. I never found any of these. The parents' wariness was so thorough that they did not betray the location of their nests. No sitting birds allowed themselves to be caught napping. Either as a result of warnings from their mates or else as a result of their own sharp-eyed alertness, they always spied me long before I came near, ran off the nests and then, from some distance away, began the violent decoy antics which I have already described.

Killdeers are early nesters and before the end of June one or two family parties, consisting of two, three or four young birds with their parents, strolled on the shore and flew around the creek together. The plumage of fully fledged youngsters and of adult birds is similar.

Later, however, I saw some downy chicks. Sometimes Killdeers raise two broods in a season and possibly these were members of second families. On July 1st, for example, I came across a youngster on open ground far from cover. It was small and clothed entirely in furry down. Its upper parts were mottled brownish-grey and its face, neck and lower parts were mostly white. Black stripes in various parts of its head and body aided its camouflage and added incidentally to its prettiness.

Already this mite had acquired some of the habits of its elders, for it piped nervously and retreated before me in a series of alternate runs and halts. First it would sprint for quite a distance, then stop and squat close to the ground like an adult Killdeer, then rise impulsively and hasten again across a considerable space, then plump down once more. It maintained these tactics until at last it escaped into long grass. It seemed restless and temperamental compared with the Spotted Sandpiper chicks. At the same time its actions were evidently performed automatically and the difference between the two species was not so much one between conscious, well-formed character as between the dictates of their respective blind instincts.

All the time both parent Killdeers flew around, landed and ran over the ground excitedly, then flew for a space again—torn between anxiety to keep a close eye on their child and a desire to decoy me far away from it.

Next day, in another part of the shore, I saw two rather larger chicks together. Once or twice afterwards I caught glimpses of infant Killdeers, but they were elusive. By the middle of the month they had all grown up and assumed their juvenile plumage. Family parties could frequently be seen feeding and idling at the water's edge. The nervous, excitable side of their character had developed. Long before I was within any distance from which I might do them harm they uttered their alarm calls, rose in a group into the air and moved off with direct, graceful, long-winged flight like a squadron of small aeroplanes starting on a sortie.

9.

Another summer resident in the creek frequented the shore. This was the Belted Kingfisher. It is not a shore bird in the sense that Killdeers and Spotted Sandpipers are, but it takes up its habitation somewhere near water and is often seen perched on a post, rock or bough beside a lake or river.

To a visitor from Britain the Belted Kingfisher is at first a disappointing bird. The English Kingfisher has breath-taking beauty. Its distinction is not due to its figure, which appears squat and rather top-heavy, but to the colours of its plumage. The warm chestnut of its breast is rich adornment, but its chief glory is its shimmering, metallic blue head, back and wings. As Lord Grey wrote, "The bird flashes like a jewel as it flies."[1] Usually one catches only a glimpse of it, for it is a shy creature and passes with the swiftness of an arrow. Yet even one brief sight of such loveliness is unforgettable.

The Belted Kingfisher of North America is also dressed largely in blue. But it is a dull, slatey blue covering much of the bird's head, face, back, wings and tail. In places it is relieved by white and black spots and streaks. The blue is continued in a broad band across the bird's chest, whilst its neck, breast and underparts are white. In the female a rufous belt crosses the lower part of the breast below the blue band. These are really not bad decorations—except in comparison with the brilliant plumage of its namesake in Britain. Beside that, it is like prose compared with poetry.

However, what the Belted Kingfisher lacks in colouring it tries to make up in form. Here it gains some points over its English relative. Its wedge-shaped body is topped by a

[1] Viscount Grey of Falloden, *The Charm of Birds*. Hodder & Stoughton Ltd.

large head and the head is crowned by a magnificent crest. The general effect is bold and handsome.

As I have recorded earlier, I first caught sight of a male Kingfisher in the creek on March 30th. It appeared several times during April and by the middle of the month used to perch in a Willow tree overlooking the water with the air of one who has settled in. On the 28th I watched him flying accompanied by a female. During May and the early part of June the pair put in only occasional appearances, being too busy establishing their home to dawdle in the open. First they had to excavate their nest in some suitable place, a labour which usually occupies several days, for it is a long tunnel burrowed with beaks and claws into the creek bank. After that the female laid about half-a-dozen eggs in a chamber at the burrow's far end. Then she spent between two and three weeks incubating these, assisted throughout by her faithful spouse. I would have given a good deal to find their nest and to peer, somehow, inside it; but I never did. I think it was situated amongst dense undergrowth on a high slope of the creek bank.

In the latter part of June the male bird, and sometimes the female, began to appear more frequently. It was charming to see occasional demonstrations of the devotion which united them. Several times I watched them flying together. They would come dashing through the air with a rather care-free flight, travelling swiftly with various erratic, inconsequential twists and turns in their route. In this manner they circled widely round the boundaries of their domain, with no apparent object except *joie de vivre*. Now and then one would hesitate impulsively in the air, hover for a few moments with eyes staring keenly at the water below, then suddenly abandon the intention of fishing and hasten away to catch up its mate. They seemed to be revelling in some sort of escapade and occasionally one or the other of them expressed its feelings in a glad cry. Perhaps all this was just an outburst of healthy animal spirits, but they seemed like two lovers celebrating something or other—either their betrothal or their honeymoon or the birth of children.

Early in July one or the other of them could always be seen fishing in the estuary, indicating definitely that their chicks had hatched and were growing lustily. The parents had several ravenous mouths at home to feed. So they spent hours every day perched on lookout posts beside the water, scrutinizing keenly the aquatic life below them and plunging into its midst whenever a tempting fish swam into view.

At about the same time other Kingfisher families hatched all along the Ottawa River. Sometimes I paddled my canoe down stream to see the succession of adult Kingfishers spaced at more or less regular intervals in trees or on other vantage points along both banks. Each married couple had its territory and territorial waters and stayed within its boundaries, enjoying exclusive rights to fish its own area and that area alone. Occasionally a bird either unwittingly or for mischief crossed the line into a neighbour's property, but this never happened with impunity. The intruder was immediately attacked by the rightful owner and a vicious battle ensued. It only ended when the intruder had returned within his own domain.

The pair in the creek did a thorough job of fishing. No nook or corner of the shallow waters round the creek's edge escaped their searching eyes. In each part they had a few favourite look-out points, where they perched to watch and wait for their prey. Here it was a rock and there a wooden post sticking from the water; in one place it was an over-hanging branch of a tree and in another a fallen log jutting into the shallows. The birds would travel from one of them to the next, using each in turn.

They were patient anglers, sometimes sitting motionless for long periods with their keen eyes fixed on the moving waters below. I liked to watch one perched on top of a worn tree-stump. It looked like a piece of splendid, gro-tesque Gothic carving on a church pew-end, with bold, medieval blue, red, white and black paint still surviving on its squat body, massive head and fearsome beak.

When fishing from one of these look-out posts it plunged straight into the water on sighting its prey. But the utility of these posts was limited. They only gave access to the water immediately surrounding them. When a bird wished to explore the further, wider spaces of its fishing ground it adopted a nobler technique.

Its performance then was beautiful to behold. The Kingfisher would mount deliberately into the sky, climbing steeply with quick, vigorous wing-beats until it was fifty feet or more above the estuary. There it ceased to ascend and remained hovering like a hawk in the air. Its poise was perfect. Except for the wings, it remained so still that the details of its person could be studied through field-glasses as accurately as if it had been a lifeless, stuffed speci-men in a glass case. Its body slanted forwards at an angle of $45°$, its head was turned downwards and its beak pointed dagger-like towards the water below. Its small, rather dainty feet were drawn up into its breast with half-closed claws. Indeed, all these parts of its anatomy looked as if it were sitting calmly on a branch of a tree—but there was no branch! Its tree was thin air and it held itself there by the

242

action of its wings. They were in violent agitation, beating the atmosphere rapidly and powerfully.

Every now and then the bird ceased flapping its wings. It had spied a fish. With motionless, out-stretched pinions it quickly shifted its body into a horizontal position whilst its head and beak remained pointing downwards and its eyes continued to search the water below. For a second or two it stayed thus, still and tense, unmistakably a bird-of-prey poised for a pounce. If a puff of wind threatened to upset its position, a slight fanning or tilting of its tail held it in proper equilibrium. Once or twice I watched a Kingfisher perform this feat in quite a stiff breeze. I have seen Kestrel Hawks in Britain and various Terns all round the world do it, but somehow the achievement seemed more miraculous in an awkward-looking, top-heavy creature like a Belted Kingfisher than in those stream-lined birds.

This momentary, motionless hesitation in the air was usually the prelude to a headlong dive; but not always. Sometimes—no doubt because the fish far below either disappeared or was too large or too small for serious consideration—the bird decided not to plunge. It tilted itself upwards again and reverted to its previous position with swiftly beating wings and keenly searching eyes. Occasionally before doing this it dropped several feet through the air to get a closer view of the scene below. There it hung suspended, watchful and potent.

When it saw fair game below, it made up its mind in a flash to strike. Turning a quick half-somersault forwards, until it was upside-down with its whole weight concentrated behind its beak, it half closed its wings and dropped head-first through the air. Entering the water at breakneck speed, it disappeared in a white splash. Sometimes it did this into water only a foot or two deep, so presumably

243

it checked its fall with its wings or by some other bodily action at the moment of contact with the water.

After a few moments' total immersion it reappeared. I never saw an adult bird miss its target. Always when it emerged a minnow was held in its beak. It then flew low over the water, with a jaunty flourish to its wing-beats, and landed on the nearest convenient perching place. There it sat complacently for a short while with its catch bulging from its beak. Then, with a convulsive jerk of its head and neck, it swallowed and the fish disappeared. At least, the fish usually disappeared; but sometimes the bird caught a larger one than could easily be accommodated in its gullet. On those occasions several vigorous attempts at swallowing were necessary before the fish wholly disappeared. I liked to imagine the Kingfisher afterwards delighting its angling friends with tall yarns about the vast dimensions of the fish which it had caught.

The effort of diving, capturing and devouring its prey usually left the bird looking a bit untidy. Its crest appeared ruffled and its body feathers seemed fluffed out. So it soon set to work on its toilet, shaking its head, wriggling its body, quivering its wings and alternately pecking and stroking its feathers into place. All this it did with much energy. Sometimes it engaged in an even more thorough wash and brush-up, jumping several times in and out of the shallow water, with much splashing and flapping of its wings, and then carefully preening its feathers. When at last it was neat, sleek and comfortable again it settled down to rest for a while. All the time, however, it kept a sharp look-out on events in the creek, its head turning quickly now in this direction and now in that and its eyes missing nothing of what was going on around it.

After a while it uttered a harsh, rattling call, cast itself into the air and flew to another part of the creek. Mounting steeply skywards, it started the whole process of hovering, diving and fishing again.

By the middle of the month the young Kingfishers were sufficiently grown-up to leave their nest. One day five or six appeared, distributed round the shore on various rocks and tree stumps. Their plumage was in most respects similar to that of their parents, but was distinguishable by the breast bands being rusty-brown instead of slatey-blue. They called frequently to their parents, who answered from wherever they were catching the family meal. Their harsh cries and counter-cries sounded like a conversation between a company of rattles.

For many days they stayed together as a family party, the youngsters still dependant on their parents for being fed. I often came across the mother or father pushing a fish into an infant's mouth. Then the new generation began to learn to fish for themselves. It was amusing to see one hurl itself into the water with a mighty splash—and re-emerge with an empty beak. Gradually, however, their skill increased and their aim became more certain. In the end it was as deadly as their parents'. The half-dozen birds must have taken a fearful toll of the local stock of minnows. Several weeks passed, however, and July had become August before the youngsters became so self-supporting and independant that the family broke up and some of its members left their playground beside the Ottawa River.

10.

Many other species summered in the creek. I did not find the nests of them all, but judging by the pairs which

I saw regularly through June and July I think that about thirty different kinds of birds settled and bred there. Besides those which I have mentioned previously as nesting they included the Crow, Downy Woodpecker, Goldfinch (a very late nester), Red-eyed Vireo, Warbling Vireo, Redstart, House Wren, House Sparrow, Cedar Waxwing, Kingbird, Wood Peewee and Least Flycatcher.

II.

Summer began to wane and each day the sun made a shorter stay in the sky. The more sensitive birds felt a chill in the air and started to leave their breeding grounds for places with a more salubrious fall and winter climate. In fact, autumn migration began. The movement was apparent both by the departure of some species for the south and the arrival of others from the north.

In the early days of July large flocks of Tree Swallows came to the creek. They flew about ceaselessly, hour after hour, with little or no pause for rest. It might seem aimless, this perpetual fluttering round and round, up and down, often in the same small space of air. But in reality these flights had deep purpose. In the course of their manoeuvres, even if they never wandered further than a comparatively few yards from some centre, the Swallows travelled many scores of miles. Though they did not leave a certain limited area of the Ottawa River, they in effect traversed provinces. Whilst catching food they were also exercising their wings, strengthening them against the not far distant day when they would set out on the vast journey of autumn migration.

Not long after the middle of the month the sky was suddenly almost empty of them. The Tree Swallows had started off—the vanguard of the countless host of birds of

BLACK-CAPPED CHICKADEE
"Possession of the woods was gradually passing to regular
winter birds like . . . Chickadees."

many species who during the next three months would make the great trek.

Others were preparing to follow them. Cowbirds, for example, now gathered in small flocks. They strolled over the ground in decorous fashion, with no suggestion of that constant inclination to make love which had marked their earlier conduct. With them, as with the other birds, it was a case of "all passion spent". They were reserving their energies for a different type of grand undertaking.

At about the same time as the Tree Swallows departed, the first migrants from further north arrived. I have already mentioned the appearance of a Pectoral Sandpiper. Now flocks of Peeps—a nickname for both Least Sandpipers and Semipalmated Sandpipers—reappeared. Their favourite feeding grounds were the long rafts moored near to shore. Trees which in life, growing erect in the forest, were the homes of Warblers and other passerine birds now became in death, lying prostrate in the river, a resort of Waders. The Killdeers, Spotted Sandpipers and Peeps who frequented them in July were the forerunners of many other species who arrived later and chased along the logs after a harvest of insects which immersion in water forced from the wood.

By the end of July the flocks of Peeps had grown to considerable sizes. The little Sandpipers called excitedly to each other in high-pitched, twittering voices as they scurried over the logs. Often they rose into the air and flew in close formation round the creek. Their aerial manoeuvres then were graceful and precise. In unison they turned and twisted this way and that, like well-drilled soldiers. Their movements were swift and restless. They were possessed by an urge to travel. In the next few weeks it was to become infectious amongst multitudes of birds.

247

CHAPTER NINE

AUGUST

1.

FAMILY LIFE amongst almost all the birds had now passed beyond the nest stage. The young were adolescents. They were fully fledged and had ventured forth into the world.

A few still depended on their parents for being fed. Young Bronzed Grackles, for example, perched in the tree-tops and harshly summoned their hard-working mothers and fathers to appease their hunger. This seemed insatiable, but in fact it had a limit. One morning I heard a young Grackle squawking pathetically for food, as if it were suffering the worst tortures of starvation. As I caught sight of it high in an Elm tree a parent flew to it with a large slice of bread. The youngster grew almost uncontrollably excited. Craning its neck and opening its beak, it shrieked eagerly whilst the old bird landed on the branch beside it, gripped the bread in its claws and tore at it with its beak like a hawk dissecting carrion. As the parent broke each piece off it leaned over to the youngster and pushed the food far down its throat. As soon as the young bird had swallowed one morsel it started clamouring for more and the old bird tugged viciously again at the crust. After the seventh mouthful, however, the fledgling was satisfied. It fell silent, closed its beak, hopped away to another branch, shut its eyes and snoozed. The parent bird then fed itself on what was left of the bread.

Most youngsters, however, had now learned to feed themselves. None showed more deadly proficiency in securing food than young Black-crowned Night Herons. An occasional adult appeared in the creek in 1945; but in the previous year a pair nested there and I watched the young birds' later development. As their name implies, these Herons are most active after dark, yet their night life does not prevent them from appearing also at any hour of the day. I often saw a parent bird and two or three juveniles wading at the same time along the edge of the creek. They were distributed at different places along the shore, each fishing its own area.

Black-crowned Night Herons have not the grace and beauty of their cousins the Blue Herons and White Egrets. They are dumpier creatures, like their more distant relatives the Bitterns. But their bodies are prettily adorned. A mature bird's crown and back are black with a bottle-green gloss; its face, throat and breast are white and its flanks are pale grey. Growing from its head are two or three tapering white feathers so long that in a breeze they blow like streamers of stiff ribbon. Immature birds are brown and cream coloured, similar in appearance to adult Bitterns.

These Night Herons are less secretive birds than Bitterns, who do not often leave the concealing screen of reeds in which they nest, live and hunt. The Herons feed more in the open. Yet they too are shy and wary and take wing quickly when disturbed. They do this even if the intruder is still at a distance. But if a watcher in a canoe is patient and cunning and the contours and vegetation of a shoreline allow a concealed approach, he may steal surreptitiously upon a bird and enjoy an excellent view of its remarkable performance as a fisherman.

Several times in August 1944 I gained such views. For example, one morning I spied from afar a young bird hunting its breakfast. Approaching by a route where it could not see me, I got within a few yards before it noticed my canoe as I finally manoeuvred the boat just beyond the edge of a reed-bed. As soon as the Heron turned its severe gaze upon me I froze into stillness. The movement of the canoe had been so slow and silent, so almost imperceptible, that the bird, though taken by surprise, was not frightened. It eyed me curiously and suspiciously, however, as it stood ankle-deep in water, with its body upright, its neck at full stretch and its head alert. Fortunately the morning was calm and no breath of wind puffed the canoe. The craft floated motionless on the water and I sat motionless in the craft with the bird standing equally motionless a few yards away. After a full minute of puzzlement the Heron gave me the benefit of the doubt, concluding presumably that I was some odd, inanimate object innocently adrift in the creek.

However, it did not immediately resume active fishing. First it had to calm down from the slight alarm which I had caused it. Relaxing gradually from its attitude of tense, statuesque alertness, it contracted its elongated body and sank its head comfortably between hunched shoulders. Its neck disappeared and its body, which had looked slim and even lean when stretched to its full height, filled out and seemed plump. The Heron remained for a long time in this attitude of apparent repose. Yet it missed nothing of what was going on around it. It kept turning its head this way and that, observing minutely the scene, evidently determined that no further incident should take it by surprise. When its profile was turned to me I saw the black pupils and yellow irises of its eyes glaring with magnificent, fierce brilliance.

For a considerable time it stood thus relaxed, yet observant. Then a movement below the surface of the water at its feet attracted its attention. Instantly its head shot forward and its neck stretched to its full length, like a telescope suddenly opening. The bird now faced me and I saw the beautiful, cunning pattern of its fore-plumage. Alternate broad brown and yellow stripes stretched from its chin, down its neck and over its breast and belly to its thighs. They were like the marks of a yellow tabby cat—or of a tiger. And just as a tiger's coat makes it invisible amongst the sunshine and shadows of a bamboo jungle, so the Night Heron's plumage provides perfect camouflage in the smaller jungle of the reeds at a river's edge. Bitterns have similar protective colouring.

The Heron, remembering its hunger, forgot me and once more began to fish. No Highland gillie ever stalked a deer more skilfully. The bird waded stealthily through the shallow water, each step a carefully calculated effort. Picking a foot deliberately from the mud, it raised it quietly through the water, stretched the lanky limb slowly forward and set the foot cautiously down again a long pace ahead. Then it gradually moved its weight from the back leg to the front leg and with equal deliberation took another unhurried step. Thus the Heron progressed through the shallows with its neck extended, its head pointed searchingly forward and its eyes concentrated on events below the water's surface.

Suddenly it caught sight of a fish. It halted, shot its neck out to its utmost length and lowered its head. The sharp sword of its beak was held threateningly ready.

Its long, narrow head looked then like a snake's and its whole attitude as it stood poised for the strike seemed reptilian rather than avian. An instant later, with a swift yet easy movement, its bill dipped into the water and withdrew again with a fish gripped in its mandibles. Jerking its head slightly, the bird tossed its catch into its gullet and swallowed.

This was the usual procedure. Sometimes, however, the Heron caught sight of a fish not ahead of it but immediately below it, swimming past its legs. Then with one sharp, instantaneous movement it plunged its beak deep into the water. As often as not in these circumstances it missed its quarry. The method of the cautious stalk, followed by the slinky stretch of the neck and quick pounce of the head was more efficient as well as more characteristic. It never failed to make a kill.

2.

Most young birds had become capable fliers by the beginning of August. Some, however, were still uncertain performers. One morning I watched two fledgling Kingbirds who appeared to be taking lessons from their parents. I am told that young birds can fly without being taught, but that they need tutoring in the art of feeding themselves. So perhaps these young Kingbirds were learning flycatching rather than flying. They were perched in the top branches of a Willow Tree, above the nest which they had recently left. In another tree twenty yards away were their parents, calling encouragingly to them. But the youngsters stayed discreetly where they were. Every now and then one of the adult birds rose in the air and made a short demonstration flight, fluttering and hovering between the two trees, calling shrilly all the time, as if to say, "Look at me. This is how it's done. Now you try."

For a long while the pupils refused to budge. Then of a sudden one leaped upwards, tumbled awkwardly in the air for a moment, righted itself and hurried on rapidly flapping wings across to its parents' tree. It landed clumsily, but this slight defect was overlooked by the overjoyed mother and father. They hastened to the branch where their offspring now perched and in excited and prolonged twitterings appeared to be offering their congratulations.

Afterwards they turned to encourage the other youngster. They tried every means of coaxing it to make a maiden flight. But it held firmly to the opinion that discretion is the better part of valour and stayed obstinately where it was.

3.

Not every young bird had parents to teach it. One day I saw a Tree Swallow resting on the gunwale of an empty rowing-boat moored in the creek. Its sooty brown instead of steely, blue-black plumage betrayed its youth. From a little distance away I watched it through field glasses. As it showed no sign of alarm I paddled the canoe cautiously toward it and was surprised when it let me approach so close that I could have stretched out my hand and touched it. Tree Swallows are always tame, trustful birds, but this one seemed to exhibit those qualities to excess.

At first I thought that it must be hurt. It did not, however, become agitated and struggle to move away, as a wounded bird would have done. It stayed where it was with perfect *sang-froid*. If I had been a fellow-Swallow sidling up to it, it could not have looked at me with less troubled, bright eyes.

Then I realized that the young Swallow was not really interested in me at all. It was watching intently a crowd of other Swallows flying overhead. They were almost all Bank Swallows, expert flyers fluttering, swerving and swooping with joyous abandon in the summer air above the water. The youngster on the gunwale of the rowing-boat cocked its head sideways and gazed skywards whenever one of them passed close by. It watched the performer, I thought, with a touch of envious admiration. I had seen a similar look in the eyes of a schoolboy at the Oval cricket ground in London, watching Jack Hobbs score a faultless century. No doubt the same wonder lighted the faces of American boys gazing at Joe Di Maggio playing in World Series baseball games in New York.

Suddenly the young Tree Swallow stood up and hurled itself recklessly from the boat. For a moment its balance in the thin air was unsteady, but its wings beat bravely and bore it higher. It began to circle round. The effort was more painstaking than easy, it was amateurish rather than professional. Yet the trial was successful. The bird stayed in the air for a couple of minutes, then dropped down and settled again on the boat at my side. I was tempted to burst into encouraging applause and to pat my little companion on the back.

Several times it repeated the experiment, never staying in the air for more than a few minutes and always returning to rest on the same perch. It was indifferent to my presence, its whole attention being concentrated on something of vital and paramount importance to it. It was trying desperately to emulate the graceful and confident manoeuvres of the Swallows overhead.

The youngster was still there when I left, and when I returned the next morning it was also in the same place.

So far as I could see, no adult bird acted as its guardian or teacher. Almost all the other Tree Swallows had left the creek. By some accident this one had been separated from its parents before its education was complete. Now it was left to fend for itself, to fight alone the early battle of life. I never saw a creature look so utterly and pathetically orphaned.

When next I passed that way it had gone.

4.

The little Tree Swallow's solitude had been all the more marked because Bank Swallows were flying around in large numbers. Like the flocks of Tree Swallows earlier, they were preparing to migrate. Of all American Swallows they make the most prodigious journey. Tree Swallows fly to Florida for the winter, but Bank Swallows do not finally come to rest until they have landed in Brazil.

In the evenings especially they gave pretty exhibitions of mass flying. A crowd of them in loose, ever changing formation would skim low over the water, then climb and fall about in the air. No individual ever pursued a straight course for more than a second. It was as if they were all buffeted by a storm and found difficulty in holding their positions in the air. Yet no breeze blew. In reality, I suppose, they were hawking for flies. Usually they came in a succession of small parties or droves, rising and falling like scatterings of autumn leaves stirred up by puffs of wind.

Amongst the flocks of Bank Swallows were occasional Barn Swallows and Purple Martins. It was enchanting to see one of them swoop down to the surface of the river, lower its head whilst in full flight, take a sip of water and rise again, leaving only tiny ripples to mark the spot. Chimney Swifts, too, often joined in these evening exercises.

Sometimes they were present in large numbers, cleaving the air in wide circles and screaming excitedly as they flew.

All these beautiful Swallows and Swifts left Brewery Creek before the end of August. By then many other species also had started on their journeys. In the early days of the month the banks of the creek seemed much less populated by birds. This was partly because, for the time being, bird song had almost completely ceased. The spate of summer singing connected with the ownership of territory and pairing was over and the slight recurrence of song which occurs in autumn had not yet begun.

The principal reason for the comparative silence amongst the trees and shrubs, however, was that the birds themselves were departing in considerable numbers. This did not yet mean that whole species, other than the Swallows, disappeared. The individual families who had nested in the creek left, but for several weeks afterwards their places were taken by fresh waves of birds of the same species, who had bred further north and now stopped in the creek for a few hours or a few days on their way south.

Amongst those who went were, of course, the new generation of young birds. It was astonishing to think that these youngsters were now to undertake such immense journeys. A few weeks earlier they had been non-existent or were mere embryo creatures tightly folded in egg-shell. Now, without any previous experience or tutoring, they were to travel hundreds or thousands of miles to places where the had never been before. Their journeys would be accomplished with faultless direction, some travelling in the company of adult birds, others making the flight by themselves with no guide except compelling and unerring instinct. This migration of young birds is one of the most astonishing achievements in Nature and illustrates better than anything else the governing part which inherited instinct plays in bird life.

Yellow Warblers were amongst the first to go. The families hatched and bred in the creek left in the first few days of August. Afterwards a few parties of other Yellow Warblers arrived from further north, to rest and refresh themselves before flying on. I saw the last on August 30th, which is, I believe, a late date for their autumn departure from the Ottawa district.

Other Warblers who had nested in the creek or its neighbourhood stayed longer. They flitted amongst the foliage as prettily and restlessly as ever. Most sprightly amongst them were the American Redstarts. As they flew from bough to bough they constantly drooped their wings and fanned their tails, as if to show off their beauty. This action gave them something of the airy appearance of butterflies.

The autumn and winter plumages of juvenile and adult Warblers are often quite different from those of mature birds in spring and summer. These variations can be confusing and make identification difficult. By August the Chestnut-sided Warblers, for example, had assumed a fresh colour scheme. It was gay. Their heads and backs were bright lemon-green, a white ring encircled their eyes and their lower parts were white. The adult birds retained something of the chestnut splash on each flank, but the youngsters showed no hint of it. Old and young alike had the yellowish bars on their wings.

Northern Water-Thrushes had moved from the deep undergrowth and could occasionally be seen walking briskly on the shore. They chose a place beneath over-

257

hanging trees, where stones, logs and driftwood were scattered and the creek water rippled and swirled over shingle as if it were a skittish brook. The edge of running water is their favourite haunt. They remained shy, not showing themselves more than they could help. So they preserved an air of mystery as well as an appearance of beauty, which always made me think of them as Water Spirits inhabiting the creek.

About the middle of August these summer residents were reinforced by other Warblers who had nested in the northern forests. Tennessee Warblers, Myrtle Warblers, Black and White Warblers, Magnolia Warblers and Mourning Warblers all appeared in the creek in August. I had seen the first three species on their way through in the Spring, but the last two were new to me.

Magnolia Warblers and Mourning Warblers have as bold and bizarre colouring as any of their relatives. The former used to be called Black and Yellow Warblers. In spring the male's upper parts are largely blackish with white patches on the wings and tail, whilst his underparts are yellow heavily striped with black. The female is similarly marked but has no stripes on her breast. In autumn their backs change to brown and the male's yellow underparts lose some of their fine stripes. This was the condition of the August birds in the creek.

The male Mourning Warbler is mostly olive above and yellow below. But his head and neck are covered by a grey hood which turns to black crepe on his throat and upper breast, where it contrasts sharply with his yellow lower parts. The female lacks this sombre black adornment, her whole hood being smokey grey. In autumn the throats of both sexes become paler.

From the middle of August onwards successive waves of these Warblers kept flitting through the creek. That month they came in considerable numbers, yet they were only the vanguard of even larger contingents of their own and other species who, as I shall record, flocked southwards in September and the first ten days of October. Canada was being almost emptied of Warblers, for—apart from a few on the southern Atlantic and Pacific coasts—none stay in the Dominion during the winter.

Wood Peewees and Least Flycatchers stopped in the creek throughout August and into September. Phoebes remained much longer. Towards the end of August a new member of the Flycatcher family came—a Crested Flycatcher. This species, normally forest dwelling, breeds in the Ottawa district. As I have recorded earlier, a pair nested in the woods beside Mackay Lake. But none had so far appeared in Brewery Creek, at any rate whilst I was watching. The Crested Flycatcher is the largest and handsomest of Canadian Flycatchers, with a distinctly crested head, a long beak and colourful plumage. Its upper parts are brownish olive, its wings are crossed by two light bars, its throat and breast are grey, its belly yellow and its tail rufous. It is a cheerful bird who likes to perch on a high branch of a tree and entertain spectators by its loud whistles.

Other newcomers to the creek in August were a Rock Dove and two Mourning Doves. They did not stay long. The Rock Dove alighted on the shore, pecked at morsels of food for a while and then, startled by something, flew away. The characteristically shy Mourning Doves did not even come to earth. As they passed swiftly overhead, however, their long wings and pointed tails revealed their

identity. Almost equally typical of these gentle, affectionate creatures was the fact that two of them travelled
together. They are said to remain in pairs all through the
year.

One of the most attractive sights late in the month was
a family of House Wrens. Their nest was somewhere in
the neighbourhood. On two or three occasions after the
chicks were fledged I came upon them in the early mornings, before they left the bough on which they roosted for the
night. The place was a regular Wren dormitory. The
parent birds and four fledglings were perched side by side
on the bough, like a row of soldiers on parade. When they
were awake and had shaken themselves into alertness for
the new day, the father and mother hopped away and busied
themselves hunting breakfast for their youngsters. The
latter stayed in formation on the bough and, as their parents
caught grubs, were fed one by one.

One evening a parent Wren gave a demonstration of
the sharp eyesight which birds possess. Three or four members of the family were flitting amongst some saplings,
chattering to each other as they went. A Sparrow Hawk
flew overhead and alighted high in an Elm tree a considerable distance away. As soon as the falcon settled
one of the Wrens uttered a sharp note of warning. The
others immediately fell silent and remained still wherever
they were. So long as the Hawk stayed in the tree—which
was for several minutes—the sentinel Wren kept monotonously repeated its alarm note. But as soon as the bird of
prey left it ceased this pother. All the Wrens promptly
resumed their chatter and normal activities.

Other Hawks came to the creek in August. One day
the Waders on the shore were greatly agitated. They ran
and flew about restlessly, never settling long in one spot

and constantly uttering unhappy cries. The cause was a Marsh Hawk with the reddish-brown, streaked body, white rump and barred tail of a female or a youngster of the species. With easy, leisurely flight—a few ponderous wing-beats alternating with periods of sailing on motionless, half-raised wings—it floated to and fro low over the ground, quartering the area deliberately as it searched for food. The Waders need not have worried. Although earlier in the summer Marsh Hawks do sometimes steal their chicks, by August young shore birds are too large and tough to be tempting. The Hawk was hunting for field mice, which abounded there and often attracted it to the creek.

Some Waders also gave me my first warning of the approach of a more famous bird of prey. One morning a group of Killdeers and a Belted Kingfisher suddenly rose in noisy alarm from the shore and hastened away. They had keen eyes, for when I looked skywards I saw that the bird who had frightened them was still some distance off. It travelled quickly, however, and as it flew over the creek its medium size, sharply pointed wings, rather long, unspread tail and darkly "moustached" cheeks showed it to be a Duck Hawk or Peregrine Falcon. As this redoubtable creature passed above the wood small passerine birds rose from the tree-tops in scattering flight. One of them had the courage, foolishness or impertinence to chase it for a few moments. A Crow also followed it for a while, as if to see it safely off the premises. The falcon flew straight on, ignoring all these demonstrations of concern, treating its fellow creatures with contemptuous disdain.

Although a pair of Peregrines have regularly built their aerie and reared their young on a high cornice of the Sun Life Building in Montreal, no such record exists for an

261

Ottawa roof. So this bird was no doubt a transient. I was thrilled to include it in the list of Brewery Creek visitors, since the Peregrine is one of the most exciting members of bird society. For courage and skill in the hunt it has few equals and no superiors. Its favourite method of making a kill is to climb to a great height in the heavens, cruise there until it detects suitable game in the air below, and then drop head-first with half-closed wings "like a thunderbolt" on its prey. The force of its death-blow as it strikes the victim in mid-air is such that, in Forbush's words, even "large birds, ordinarily very tenacious of life, are killed as if struck by lightning".

Occasionally the falcon amuses itself by catching insects like beetles and dragon-flies, but for the most part it feeds on birds. Its taste is catholic, for it will take anything from Phoebes and Bluebirds to Duck and Grouse. Sometimes it even power-dives at a wild goose. Its noble status amongst birds of prey was recognized centuries ago, in the age of chivalry, when it was the *faucon gentil* reserved for the exclusive use of kings, knights and ladies induling in the sport of hawking.

5.

The association of birds with flowers sometimes produces sights of perfect loveliness. One day I saw a bright male Yellow Warbler perched on a cluster of gleaming red Sumach fruits. On another occasion a party of Goldfinches stopped to feed amongst blue Chicory flowers and from them moved with gay, undulating flight to a patch of pale-lemon Evening Primroses. Several times I watched piebald Downy and Hairy Woodpeckers hopping up the tall stalks of Great Mulleins, hunting insects amongst their yellow

Photo by Dr. Arthur A. Allen

BLUEBIRD
"The Spirit of Happiness."

flowers and green seed-pods. Such sights were exceedingly pretty in the brilliant August sunshine.

Several new flowers bloomed that month. Marsh Skull-cap, Water Hemlock, Swamp Milkweed, Yellow Loose-strife, Silver Weed, Yellow Toadflax, Asters and several kinds of Goldenrod all came out. These are late flowers and their blossoming itself indicated that summer was nearly spent. A few of the earlier flowers persisted, managing to produce fresh crops of blooms. But before the end of August they had mostly faded. Such masses of them were dead that the creek's banks looked like a grave-yard of wild flowers.

As with the plants, so also with the trees. The leaves began to wither and fall.

6.

The parties of Killdeers and Spotted, Semipalmated and Least Sandpipers on the creek banks were soon reinforced by other Waders. August was a month of shore birds, for this is the busiest period of their autumn migrations.

Killdeers were the most self-assertive amongst them, a characteristic due not to conceit but to nervousness. Whenever I or any other strange animal came near they worked themselves into a frenzy of excitement. They piped their alarm calls constantly, crying "Wolf" (so to speak) so often that although they thoroughly frightened themselves and hastened away each time on sharp, quick-beating wings, they never alarmed anybody else. The other Waders merely looked up for a moment, made a mental note that it was only those foolish, nerve-wracked Killdeers once more making a lot of fuss about nothing, and returned to their feeding.

263

The first newcomer to the shore in August was a Great Blue Heron, who arrived on the 3rd. Afterwards several more came. They had spent the summer in the noisy, crowded society of a heronry on some lonely lake. Now they abandoned communal life for individual existence. The Great Blue Heron, like most other Herons, thus reverses the process of many birds, who divide into isolated pairs in the breeding season but come together again and form large flocks in the autumn and winter.

The leisurely, powerful and graceful wing-beats of the Great Blue Heron make its flight seem particularly effortless. This quality and the bird's large size and beautiful carriage in the air give it a touch of majesty. Its dignity is no less impressive when it stands on the ground. Then its lanky legs, shapely body, long neck, narrow head and large beak compose a handsome figure. Sometimes when fishing it stands for long periods at a river's edge, as motionless as a statue, waiting patiently for an unsuspecting meal to swim within its reach. At other times it stalks its prey with furtive movements like those of the Black-crowned Night Heron. Wading in the shallows, it looks like a water giraffe. One morning I watched two fishing in deeper water. When their heads shot forwards and downwards to capture fish the birds disappeared completely from view, except for the humps of their backs protruding like slate-blue islands above the surface of the water.

A few days later a party of Sanderlings ran over the shore. These small grey, white and rust-coloured Sandpipers are vivacious creatures. Their customary habitat is the sea-shore, where they scurry swiftly amongst advancing and receding waves, probing the hard, wet sand for crustaceans and other beach insects on which they feed. Small flocks of them visited the creek several times in August and September.

On the same day two Solitary Sandpipers appeared. They are only "solitary" in comparison with many of their Wader cousins, who gather in immense companies. Larger than Spotted Sandpipers but smaller than Yellow-legs, their plumage is dark on their backs and white on their under-parts. Their grace on foot and on the wing is such that one would write about them in superlatives, were they not excelled in form and movement by two other shore birds, the Greater and Lesser Yellow-legs.

About the middle of the month these pretty creatures began to appear. First came small parties of Lesser Yellow-legs and later the Greater species joined them. The two are so similar in everything except size that the same description applies generally to them both. They have the most beautiful proportions of all the Waders who came to Brewery Creek. Their lanky, yellow legs, neat bodies shaped like perfectly cut morning coats, slender necks, pretty heads and fine, long bills are exquisite. Their mostly grey and white plumage is delicately streaked and speckled and their manners are in keeping with this excellent taste of their dress. In flight their long necks and beaks stretch forward, their wings curve in two graceful arcs and their stilt-like legs extend far beyond their tails. On the ground they walk elegantly and nonchalantly, and they are dainty feeders. Sometimes a dozen or more picked their way together along the shore. It would be impossible to see a more gracious group of animals. Their call is as sweet as their appearance—a plaintive, tremulous whistle like a yodel.

The principal differences between the two species are

first that the bill of the Greater Yellow-legs is slightly up-
tilted whilst that of the Lesser is straight, and second that
whereas the former bird measures more than a foot long
the latter is a few inches shorter.

The generic French name for all shore birds is Alouette.
It is of Yellow-legs that the famous song, beloved by
French-speaking Canadians, is sung:—

> Alouette, gentille Alouette,
> Alouette, je te plumerai,
> Je te plumerai le cou,
> Je te plumerai le cou,
>   Et le cou
>   Et les pattes
>   Et le dos
>   Et le nez
>   Et le bec
>   Et la tête
>   Etc., etc.

Although the law forbids shooting Yellow-legs, they are
much sought after as game birds in parts of Quebec. Not
that they give any particular satisfaction to a true epicure.
Their flesh, I am told, is less tasty than that of a Woodcock
or a Wilson's Snipe. In the autumn, however, they grow
fat and are tempting to some sportsmen. Occasionally in
September one of these law-breakers came to the creek to
shoot them. I hated to see such lovely creatures killed and
once, in my desire to save a little flock of them, stepped
from behind some bushes and offered myself to their perse-
cutor as a substitute. I explained that he could as lawfully
shoot me as the shore birds. With his gun half raised he
looked me up and down in disgust—and whilst he did so
the Yellow-legs flew jauntily away.

266

One morning towards the end of August two Semi-palmated Plovers and two immature Ruddy Turnstones arrived together on a lonely piece of shore. One Plover immediately balanced itself on a single leg, drew the other up beneath its body, tucked its head under a wing and fell asleep. It was tired after its long night journey. The other was more hungry than sleepy. It stayed very much awake and scurried about, hunting for food. The Turnstones also started breakfasting, living up to their name by turning loose stones over with their beaks and nibbling the insects exposed beneath. The quartette stayed in the creek all day and in the evening continued their journey southward.

Sometimes a Bittern flew from the reeds by the shore. The only other visitor was a Wilson's Snipe. One day I saw it feeding in the mud at the water's edge. However, it only permitted me a brief glimpse, being on this occasion even more wary than a party of Killdeers close by. Long before they set up their customary hullabaloo at my approach, it saw me and plunged swiftly into concealment in a clump of weeds. I did not see any other Snipe in the creek this year, but in October 1944 a number of these attractive game birds stayed there for several days. I shall therefore write of them in the chapter describing that month.

7.

In August the first migrating wild duck also appeared. For several days at the beginning of the month a Red-breasted Merganser and a Golden-eye kept each other company in the creek. Whenever I visited it they were swimming or flying together like inseparable "buddies". One morning a newcomer swam near them. It was so bashful and dived to conceal itself so frequently that for a while I could not identify it. Then I saw that it was a Horned Grebe, the only member of the Grebe clan who ever visited the creek whilst I was there.

In the middle of the month a party of seven Common Mergansers arrived and stayed for several days. The reader may recollect that this species was amongst the first to appear in spring and that one or two males and females spent some time in the creek in March and April. Since then the birds had mated, nested and reared young. Perhaps this company arriving in August was the family of a pair whom I had seen four months earlier.

It was now difficult to distinguish between the drakes and the ducks and between the old generation and the new. Through the summer the drakes moult into "eclipse" plumage, and the Mergansers were at the climax of this process. At that time the dresses of adult males and of the young of both sexes are similar to that of mature females, who do not change the style of their costumes with the seasons. All the birds therefore appeared more or less alike.

Probably, however, the father of the family was not present. A Merganser drake deserts his duck when she is incubating their eggs and leaves further family cares and responsibilities to her. This little party in Brewery Creek, therefore, was probably a mother and her brood of full-grown offspring.

Usually when I arrived at sunrise they were snoozing. Most of them sat blissfully unconscious on the shore, or on rocks or log-booms protruding from the water, with their heads tucked under their wings. One or two, however, stood wakefully surveying the scene, doing sentry duty. When I approached they communicated news of my presence to the sleepy-heads beside them and the whole party rose, waddled to the water's edge, slipped quietly in and swam away from shore.

Before long they started fishing. When so engaged they swam half submerged, like Loons, and dived frequently. With a quick, smooth, forward movement they leaped clear of the water, curved gracefully in the air and plunged headfirst into the depths. A Merganser swims more swiftly under water than on the surface and its long saw-bill is perfectly adapted for catching fish.

Every now and then one of the birds interrupted its fishing to perform its morning ablutions. This was a complicated and thorough business. Floating on the water, it first turned back its head to peck and stroke its wing feathers and then rolled over on one side like a toy yacht capsizing. Exposing most of its white tummy, it shook one leg with abandon in the air and industriously scratched and smoothed its breast feathers with its bill. After that it righted itself and completed the toilet by raising its body out of the water until it seemed to be sitting on its tail. Poised thus on the water's surface it vigorously flapped its wings.

On the same day as these Mergansers appeared, a dozen Blue-winged Teal arrived. Next day their number had doubled and by the end of August the flock had increased to sixty birds. I have already explained that Blue-winged Teal are delicate, warm-weather creatures. Just as they were the last of the duck to come north in Spring, so now they were the first to retreat south in autumn. As soon as the young are able to fly "or even before that"[1] they begin to gather in flocks, filled with apprehension at the suggestion

[1] F. H. Kortright—*The Ducks, Geese and Swans of North America*. American Wild Life Institute.

of chill in the air and with instinctive yearning for the hot sun of Central and South America.

The flock in the creek was gathering to start their journey. They always swam in a close crowd together, making an animated company. A few birds would swim placidly, but most were busy guzzling. Unlike Mergansers, they are surface feeders, not diving duck. Craning their necks forwards and dipping their beaks and faces into the water, they would shovel out morsels of weeds and insects floating just below the surface. Occasionally, when the food lay deeper, they tipped forward in a half-somersault, stood on their heads in the water and tugged with their beaks at whatever tempted them below. Always in the early mornings some birds in the flock were engaged in cleaning their feathers by nibbles, pokes and strokes of various parts of their plumage. Every now and then one would raise itself, balance on its feet and tail in the water and shake its wings.

All the Teal were in eclipse or juvenile plumage. It was difficult to distinguish the drakes from the ducks and the old birds from the young. Occasionally a male showed a pale remnant of the white patches which adorn his face in spring and summer. Otherwise they all appeared like ducks. Each member of the flock, however, regardless of sex or age, wore large, bright, chalky-blue areas on their forewings.

This lovely decoration was revealed in flight. When the flock was startled and took wing it moved in as close-packed formation as it kept when swimming. The sixty-odd birds' aerial evolutions, executed with fair precision, were a beautiful sight.

One day some Black Duck flew into the creek and on another occasion two Hooded Mergansers were swimming there. Sometimes a party of Red-breasted Mergansers arrived, whilst Golden-eye were frequent visitors. All these wild fowl nest in the Ottawa valley. No duck from the distant breeding grounds had yet come south. But these local residents made a brave show. Family parties and flocks of most of the species that I have mentioned could be seen in different parts of the creek at the same time. They swam in separate formations, like compact companies of different ships. Here was a flotilla of Mergansers, there a squadron of Golden-eye and somewhere else a grand fleet of Blue-winged Teal. The shooting season had not yet begun and the birds were surprisingly and charmingly trustful. They often let me paddle my canoe close to them. There I would let the craft drift as I sat watching the various water-fowl through field-glasses, as a monarch might inspect the ships in some great naval review.

Overhead flew escorts of Gulls. They were returning from their nesting colonies on various surrounding lakes or along the St. Lawrence River. As the month advanced their numbers increased steadily, until sometimes a hundred of them were circling in the air or standing in rows on logs floating in the water. Their peevish cries added wildness to the scene. Grey and white adult Herring Gulls were accompanied by their brown offspring. Occasionally a few Bonaparte's Gulls fluttered into the creek and towards the end of the month two or three Ring-billed Gulls appeared.

This gathering of water birds was another sign that the year was past its prime and slowly dying.

CHAPTER TEN

SEPTEMBER

I.

THE PACE of autumn migration quickened in the early part of September. Almost every day new birds travelling south broke their journeys in the creek. As the month progressed their numbers increased until one had the impression of vast armies of birds on the move, of a steady retreat of life from the north as the threat of winter advanced.

Many in the vanguard of these forces had not come from any great distance. At the furthest they had spent the summer in the coniferous forests and wild lakes of the middle-north, and journeys of only a few score or a few hundred miles brought them to Brewery Creek. Most of the species of the real north—the Barren Lands which lie beyond all forests, the solitary coasts of Hudson Bay and the remote Arctic Archipelago—came later. Some, like the shore birds I have mentioned, had already passed through and a few more arrived in September. But most did not appear until October or November.

Amongst the September arrivals were several species who had visited the creek on their northward journeys in the spring. For example White-throated Sparrows, White-crowned Sparrows, Black-capped Chickadees, Purple Finches, Slate-coloured Juncos and Nashville Warblers reappeared in the second half of the month. With them came more than twenty species which I had not noticed in the creek before. In order that the record in this book may be complete I shall mention them all. But I shall assume (no doubt correctly) that by now the reader is thoroughly bored with descriptions of birds' plumage and behaviour and shall—except in a few cases—make only a brief comment on each species. Some of the newcomers tarried for a few days or a few weeks in the creek, but most of them were birds of passage who stayed only a few hours. They will fly through these pages as swiftly as they passed through the creek. If anyone desires further information about them, he can find it in one of the excellent reference books which are available.

Early in the month two new Woodpeckers appeared. The first was a rare bird in the Ottawa district, a Red-headed Woodpecker. Several members of the family have a red patch somewhere on their crowns, but this alone has an entirely red head and face.

The other Woodpecker was the bearer of a charming, if somewhat disconcerting, name. Superficially the Yellow-bellied Sapsucker might be confused with either the Hairy or the Downy Woodpecker. But it is slightly smaller than the former, slightly larger than the latter and has a few distinguishing features on its plumage. The most reliable is the large, longitudinal white patch on its black wings. In spite of the bird's name, the yellowish tint on its belly is not always apparent. Its sap-sucking propensities, on the other hand, are constant and sometimes make the bird a dangerous enemy of trees. Undue numbers of the species in a district may result in too much of the life-giving sap of valuable trees being consumed. Then they are a pest and the only way to deal with them is with a gun. This is sad, for few malefactors look so innocent and enchanting.

Towards the end of August some much smaller creatures, who also live and find their food on tree trunks, appeared—Brown Creepers. The bird's mottled brown and whitish plumage blends so well with the bark of trees that it would be hard to detect, if it stayed still. But it hardly ever does. Alighting near the bottom of a trunk it creeps methodically upwards, hesitating for a moment now and then to pick out an insect with its sharp, curved bill, then climbing further until it arrives near the top of the tree. It promptly flies to the bottom of the next tree and starts to ascend again. So it progresses through a wood, perpetually flying down and climbing up, apparently blessed with boundless energy.

Ever since March Red-winged Blackbirds had inhabited the creek. Their individual family lives being now over for another year, they formed into flocks and gossipped unceasingly in the tree-tops or on the shore. The males' epaulettes looked the worse for wear, the autumn moult having tarnished them and in many cases left little of their earlier red and yellow splendour. In the first week of August the Redwings were joined by flocks of Rusty Blackbirds. In their habit of travelling in large and noisy parties the two species were similar. The size and figures of the individual birds were also alike, but the straw-coloured eyes and rusty brown feather-ends which in the fall obscure much of the Rusties' black plumage, distinguished them from their companions.

The most persistent September singer was a Warbling Vireo. Often its continuous, languid and charming utterance sounded high in a tree. Sometimes a Red-eyed Vireo also appeared. Towards the end of the month two other Vireos arrived. One, the Philadelphia Vireo, had paid a brief visit to the creek in the spring. Its yellowish breast and underparts distinguished it from its cousins. The other was the prettiest and most gaily coloured of the Vireos—a Solitary or Blue-headed Vireo. Either name is appropriate. Often in September and October I saw one of these birds. It was almost always alone, flitting and perching in some unfrequented part of the wood, as if it shunned company. Its ashy-blue crown and face were pleasing, but its most recognizable marks were two white rings round its eyes connected by a white line above its beak. These gave the bird's face a quaint appearance, as if it were wearing a pair of *pince-nez* spectacles. A greenish back, white underparts suffused with yellow and olive, and two prominent white wing-bars completed the Blue-headed Vireo's attractive dress.

I have already mentioned the return of various species of Warblers in August and of Nashville Warblers in September. In the middle of the month several members of this large family who were new to me arrived in the creek. They included Parula Warblers, Black-throated Green Warblers, Black-throated Blue Warblers, Blackburnian Warblers, Maryland Yellowthroats and an Oven-bird. Most of these decorative creatures were in flocks which passed in waves through the trees and shrubs above the shore. Agile and pretty, they were constantly on the move. I doubt whether many of them stayed in the district more than a few hours. Yet they seemed ever present, for each flock was soon succeeded by another. They were wise to hurry, for they had far to go. Their autumn journeys would not end until they had crossed the United States, and in some cases the Gulf of Mexico too, and arrived in Central and South America.

Only the Oven-bird was not in a flock. I found it in solitary occupation of a quiet, shady part of the wood.

275

Usually it is a ground bird, but this one was perched several feet up on the branch of a maple tree. It seemed as astonished to see me in the neighbourhood as I was to see it in that situation, and it eyed me inquisitively. Though it was not alarmed, it felt uncertain what to make of me. When it decided that wisdom required it to move, it did not fly away, but merely walked with careful steps further along the bough. There it turned and stared at me again. Like its near relative the Water-Thrush, its figure and plumage appeared like those of a neat and dapper little Thrush. But neither bird really belongs to that family.

Like the Oven-bird, the Maryland Yellowthroat does not normally ascend to the tree-top heights which most Warblers attain. It keeps close to the ground, moving more or less surreptitiously amongst the tall, rank grasses and other lowly vegetation in marshland. One morning I was admiring a clump of Broad-leaved Arrowheads growing by the water's edge. They grew thickly, their beautiful white-petalled, golden-centred flowers partly hidden in a forest of their sharp-pointed leaves. In a breeze the leaves sway this way and that; but no breeze stirred them that morning. Yet now and then a leaf shook fitfully, as if a minor earthquake were disturbing its foundations. I supposed that a frog or other aquatic animal was swimming in the water and colliding every now and then with a leaf-stalk. Then the true author of these tremors betrayed itself. A bird-note issued from the hidden undergrowth—a harsh scolding sound like the curse of a Wren. I watched carefully. But for a long time the bird stayed invisible, its passage marked only by the trembling of a succession of leaves. At last, however, I saw it—a brilliantly marked cock Maryland Yellowthroat. It was conspicuous by the distinctive black

276

mask across its forehead, eyes and cheeks, its green back and the lemon-yellow throat from which it gets its name.

For two or three weeks these birds were amongst the commonest in the creek, little parties of them inhabiting various patches of dead wild flowers in the rough meadow-land.

On a later occasion a Wren-like voice coming from a Dogwood bush turned out to belong to the most charming of actual Wrens. The Winter Wren is darker and smaller than the House Wren, with a stubbier tail held absurdly erect. According to Mr. Taverner it is "perhaps the finest songster in the northern woods." Unfortunately the creek did not inspire it to song, but its abrupt, nervous exclamation, "Chirr," led me to it and enabled me to see this tiny, shy, exquisite creature.

On about the same date two equally small migrants appeared—the Ruby-crowned Kinglet and the Golden-crowned Kinglet. I had seen the former but not the latter in the creek in spring. Wren-like in build and Chickadee-like in habits, their bodies seemed filled with miraculous energy for their diminutive size. As they travelled and searched for food they showed all the agility of trapezists, perching sometimes the right way up and at other times the wrong way up as they fluttered from twig to twig. During the next two months little parties of both species were a common and delightful sight along the river bank.

Other newcomers to the creek in September were two of the most beautifully coloured Canadian birds, the Scarlet Tanager and the Bluebird. For several days a number of Tanagers remained in the creek, often in the company of Crested Flycatchers. They were to some extent disappointing, for the male's strikingly handsome spring plumage had moulted and become similar to the female's more modest dress. Not that the latter is to be despised. Its green back, yellowish breast and dusky wings are charming; yet they are positively plain compared with the brilliant scarlet body and intense black wings and tails which grace the cocks earlier in the year.

Only one Bluebird visited the creek. The species prefer more open country and I can only suppose that this solitary representative honoured the creek with a visit in order that it might secure a place in this book. Bluebirds are sticklers for their rights. They will battle stoutly against intruders on their feeding grounds and nesting sites. Alas, they often fight a losing battle. As I have remarked before, Starlings are the Bluebirds' worst enemies and anything that can properly be done to aid and abet the native against the immigrant should be done. Canada would lose a precious treasure if its beloved little Bluebirds became scarce. In its spring plumage the cock bird is like a gem. Its heavenly blue head, back, wings and tail, chestnut-red throat, breast and flanks and white lower parts are deliciously beautiful. The bird which visited the creek was a hen, which—with all due respect to the sex—was disappointing. Its colouring was a paler edition of that of its sire. However, a glimpse of a Bluebird of any kind is more enchanting than a dozen other pleasant sights put together. The bright loveliness of its body not only delights the eye but also warms the heart, because of the bird's fame as the Spirit of Happiness.

Another fine creature whose predominant colour is blue came several times to the creek in the latter part of the month. Its harsh cry when a Hawk made a playful dive at it first drew my attention to a Blue Jay. Its crested head, ample figure and blue, black and white plumage are extremely

278

SNOWY OWL
"A bird of noble distinction."

becoming. But its behaviour hardly conforms with its splendid raiment. It is a mischievous bird—a blusterer, a mimic and a thief. At the same time it has many virtues, being gay, intelligent, hardy and devoted to its family. In fact, it is an engaging rascal.

Three Thrushes and three Hawks completed the list of September migrants who were new to me. A Wood Thrush, a Hermit Thrust and an Olive-backed Thrush appeared at various times in quiet corners of the wood. In the air overhead a Broad-winged Hawk, a Sharp-shinned Hawk and a Cooper's Hawk all came to hunt.

Thus the variety of land birds to be seen at the end of September was about as great as at the height of the summer. Yet the species composing the assembly were almost entirely different. In two months an immense shifting of population had occurred.

2.

On the shore the change was not yet so marked. Peeps, Spotted Sandpipers, Solitary Sandpipers, Pectoral Sandpipers, Sanderlings and Greater and Lesser Yellow-legs came and went. Sometimes a Bittern or a Black-crowned Night Heron joined them. A Belted Kingfisher was almost invariably perched on the bank or hovering over the water.

Before the end of the month, however, other birds began to appear. One evening three shore birds flew in and landed on a log-raft. When they arrived I was some distance away and was not sure of their identity. Paddling my canoe cautiously towards them, I stopped every now and then to watch them through field-glasses. However, I need not have been so careful. It is true that as I came very close they did show signs of doubt about me, but it was an uncertainty without fear or suspicion—merely a natural inquisitiveness to learn what sort of fellow-creature I was. When I stopped the canoe three yards from them they eyed me with keen, calm interest, not retreating so much as one pace. On the contrary, when a gentle breeze blew my canoe slowly nearer to them and bumped it into the boom on which they stood, one of the birds, unable to contain its curiosity any longer, ran towards the craft intending to come aboard. Unfortunately the canoe sheered away from the boom again. The bird, perplexed by the boat's inability to make up its mind where to stay, hesitated, then turned and ran back to its companions. From a few yards off they all continued to stare enquiringly at me.

I wish my boat had not been so precipitate in breaking contact with that boom. I would have enjoyed taking an American Golden Plover or a Black-bellied Plover for a canoe ride. By now I knew that the three new arrivals belonged to one or other of these species. Their Plover figures, with beautifully speckled brown-and-cream backs, solid black faces, throats and breasts—surprisingly black for so late in the season—and large, dark, gentle eyes like a small doe's, could belong to no other birds. In their autumn plumage the general appearance of the two species is similar. Certain marks, however, distinguish them from one another and my problem was to discover these.

It did not prove difficult. The birds quickly became accustomed to me and began to behave as if no stranger were present. Strolling along the log-raft, they sipped water from the river, scratched themselves and performed unconcernedly close by me even more private functions. Their tameness was charming. I tried to startle them and make them fly, so that I could identify them by catching sight of the colours of their rumps and axillars, which differ in the two species. But they would not be frightened. First I banged the canoe paddle on the gunwale near them, but in vain. They took not the slightest notice. Then I addressed them aloud, asking politely, "Will you please be so good as to fly a few yards further away, so that I may see your rumps and axillars?" But they still refused to be startled.

After a while, however, they spread their wings slightly in order to flutter from one log to another. Then I saw their sharply barred tail feathers and light-coloured rumps, evidence tipping the scales in favour of their being Black-bellied Plovers. The issue was definitely settled when one of them inadvertently stepped off a log into a patch of mud. Sinking knee deep into the slime, it became alarmed and raised its wings to flap itself out of its uncomfortable position. This action revealed the dark under-wing patch of its black axillars, unmistakably different from the American Golden Plover's grey axillars. Later I got clear views, through field-glasses, of hind-toes on all the birds' feet, a small detail which is absent on the feet of the other Plover.

I watched them for a long time. No doubt their trust-fulness was due to the fact that they had not seen a human being for several months. Nesting on the tundra of the Arctic coast, they had no remembered experience of Man. My canoe and I floating on the waters of the creek were as little a matter for alarm as a seal rising from the waves in Hudson Strait. Only when they renewed contact with civilization during their winter stay in the southern United States and Central and South America would they learn the unhappy lesson that it is prudent to be frightened of men.

They stayed two days on the log-raft and then continued

their journey south. Migrating Golden Plovers also visit the creek occasionally, but I never spotted one. An Upland Plover, however, I did see. About the size of a Greater Yellow-legs, it is buff-coloured with a medium-sized, straight bill. Its name is not scientifically correct, for the bird is in reality a Sandpiper.

3.

One day in September 1944 I saw a particularly attractive creature under somewhat inauspicious circumstances. Like the Plovers, it came from the far north.

As I paddled my canoe to the creek that morning the absolute peace of Nature had a comforting quality, like a blessing. The sky and earth were serene and the water was as smooth as polished marble. From afar I saw a noble gathering of wildfowl in the creek, rather further out from the shore than usual. It included Mergansers, Golden-eye and Blue-winged Teal. I promised myself an excellent morning's bird-watching, though the duck seemed restless and perturbed.

Then a gun-shot broke the silence. The birds leapt into wild movement, splashing from the water and circling overhead in panic-stricken flight.

I had forgotten the date. It was September the 9th. Duck-shooting had begun. My heart turned sick. I felt angry with the men who had arrived to destroy an experience of such perfect beauty as visiting the creek in the early morning. I reflected sadly how hitherto the duck had been confiding and almost tame, so that they let me approach close to them—and how they would never show that trust again. It was bitter to realize that from now on they and I would be enemies.

I paddled into the creek and landed. Across the water on the opposite bank I saw two sportsmen. They crouched half-hidden in long grass behind a "hide", dressed in rough clothes, with unshaven faces and the unfriendly look of men searching for something to kill. One held a gun across his knees and the other sat ready to act as a retriever.

I regarded them with intense dislike. This was of course unreasonable. Men who are free beings—as they all should be—develop various tastes. Many different characters compose a community, and God presumably made them all. He feels as compassionate towards the duck-shooter as He does towards the duck-watcher. My pleasure in studying birds alive was not morally superior to those sportsmen's pleasure in shooting them dead. Morals did not enter into the matter at all. I preferred one form of activity, they preferred another, and we each pursued our own particular pleasure selfishly.

Nevertheless, I personally took an unfavourable view of those men. Trying to forget them and the destruction which they were doing amongst the wild duck, I stayed on shore and watched some Warblers flitting amongst the trees. Every now and then a gun-shot rang out. Each time I felt distressed, especially when I heard the thrilling whistle of Golden-eyes' wings as they sped in fright overhead.

Glancing towards them, I suddenly noticed a strange bird in the creek. It was fluttering playfully just above the surface of the water, indifferent to the danger around it. Its movements were so airy and graceful that at first I took it for a Swallow. Then I realized that it was too large for that, and also that its wing-beats had a different rhythm from a Swallow's. In any case it disposed of the Swallow theory by alighting and swimming on the water. What

283

could it be? It was too tiny for a small Gull or Tern. Instinctively I knew its nature, although I had never before set eyes on such a bird.

Excited, I hastened to the canoe and pushed out from shore. The bird was swimming in the centre of a wide expanse of open water, about a hundred yards away. Paddling cautiously towards it, I stopped after every few strokes, partly to study it carefully through field-glasses lest it took fright and flew away before I came near, and partly in the hope that it might get accustomed to my presence and stay. For that reason I took almost ten minutes to get really close to it. To my delight it showed complete unconcern at my approach and allowed me to come within a few feet of it. Through my glasses I could examine it as clearly as if it had been sitting on my hand.

As I gazed at the little bird—less than eight inches long— and studied its markings another gunshot rang out. I did not move nor interrupt my ornithological concentration, for I realized that the sportsmen must have seen my slow, deliberate progress from the shore to the centre of the creek. They would doubtless avoid aiming their gun in my direction.

A moment later shots fell all around me, like a shower of raindrops pattering suddenly on the water. The sound was startlingly reminiscent, transporting me instantly in imagination from Canada in September 1944 to England in September 1941. Pieces of shrapnel had sounded like that when they fell around me in the streets during the London Blitz. Instinctively for a moment I felt the old mixture of apprehension and elation at being out at nights in that battle. Then I recollected where I was. This was not the Strand on a bomb-shattered evening. It was the

Ottawa River on a peaceful morning. I felt annoyed. Those men on the shore were damnably careless. In the Battle of London one had expected danger and worn a tin hat. Here I had not supposed such protection to be necessary. It would be ridiculous if I could not pursue the lawful hobby of bird-watching in the capital city of Canada without wearing a shrapnel helmet.

To hell with those murderous gun-men anyway! Perhaps their weapon had strayed accidentally in my direction, but it seemed more likely that they were taking a pot-shot at me as an inducement to me to leave their hunting ground. Whichever explanation was correct, I would not move. The little bird whom I was watching remained serenely undisturbed by the hail of shot falling round it. It continued to dart this way and that in its search for food. Why should I show any more concern? If, incidentally, my presence frightened the wild-duck and prevented them from returning to be slaughtered, so much the better. Laughing to myself, I continued to stare through my field-glasses at the trim body, slender neck, small head and rapier-like bill of the delightful creature in front of me.

It was a Northern Phalarope. Three species of Phalaropes live in North America. Two of them—the Red and the Northern—breed on the Arctic coasts and islands and are unusual visitors inland even on migration. The Wilson's Phalarope's favourite breeding ground is on the prairie, where it is a common sight on lakes and pools.

Phalaropes have the forms of Waders, but they are more than waders. They are also swimmers. Mr. Taverner says that they are "the only shore birds that habitually swim". Mr. Forbush refers to them as "swimming Sandpipers". One of their family names is "Sea Snipe" and many of them spend the whole winter on the ocean. Their aquatic skill is highly professional. They are completely at home on water and are often found swimming buoyantly hundreds of miles out at sea.

The Northern Phalarope in the creek treated me to a charming exhibition of its extraordinary idiosyncrasies as a swimmer. Floating high in the water, it seemed to sit *on* rather than *in* it, like a piece of thistledown or a ball of fluff. A Phalarope's plumage is thick, like a Gull's, with plenty of under-down, which explains why its small, light body is so buoyant. My bird bobbed about like a lively cork, never staying still for a moment. Its favourite manoeuvre was to swim quickly forwards, then hesitate and spin round and round in a small space, like a whirligig. This is a typical Phalarope performance, being its method of hunting food. As it turns itself round, kicking with its slightly webbed feet, it so churns up the water that many of the small aquatic animals on which it feeds are brought to the surface. The bird I watched had considerable success, for its long, fine, awl-shaped bill dipped constantly into the water to pick out food.

When the Phalarope swam forward it went with surprising speed for such a small, light creature, and when it whirligigged round its movement was also astonishingly rapid. It gave an impression of perpetual motion. Every now and then it stretched its wings, rose a few inches into the air, flew a short distance with flickering, Wader-like wing-beats and alighted and started its spinning-top action again.

The marks and colours of its plumage indicated that it was a hen. I was glad, for this meant that I had the privilege of gazing upon one of the most remarkable and masterful representatives of the sex. Female Phalaropes are larger and more brightly coloured than the males. The contradiction to what is customary in avian society does not stop there. Phalaropes provide the classic example of the matriarchal system in bird life, which we have already noticed in the case of Spotted Sandpipers. The hen Phalarope woos the cock. Moreover, almost all the offices usually performed by a female are performed by her meek and subservient mate. He makes the nest. It is true that she condescends to visit it and lay their eggs. But with that her duties are over. He incubates the eggs, hatches the young and rears them.

I visited the creek again that evening, to see whether the Phalarope was still there. It was in the same place giving the same exquisitely graceful and pretty exhibition of swimming and whirling about. It had evidently stayed there all day and was once more entirely unconcerned by my arrival. For a wild creature it was unbelievably tame, allowing me several times to paddle right up to it and almost touch it before it flew away. Even then it only flitted twenty or thirty yards before alighting and resuming its feeding.

I do not know whether it was still there on the following morning. That same night I had to leave Ottawa. Next day an even more important migration was taking place in Canada. Mr. Winston Churchill was arriving from England and he was to be followed a few hours later from the United States by President Roosevelt. With them would come flocks of Admirals, Generals and Air Marshals, all gathering to join in the second Quebec Conference. I flew to Halifax to meet Mr. Churchill and accompany him to Quebec.

After ten days I returned to Ottawa and visited Brewery Creek. There was no sign of the Northern Phalarope.

Probably by then it was swimming and spinning on the broad waters of the Atlantic Ocean.

4.

Early in September some Green-winged Teal visited the creek. About the same size as Blue-winged Teal, they lacked light wing patches. Except for them, no new species of wild duck arrived that month. But the population of previously established species kept changing. At the beginning of the month, for example, the large flock of sixty Blue-winged Teal took off for the south. Occasionally afterwards smaller flocks appeared, but I saw the last of them on September 22nd.

Once or twice some Mallards flew in. Parties of Mergansers and Golden-eye were commoner. They had become much more wary since shooting began. As soon as I came into view now, even when I was still a long way off, they started to swim apprehensively away from me and soon afterwards took wing, circled round once or twice overhead and alighted on a distant part of the water.

Nothing could be more beautiful than these wild, headlong flights of duck. In the evening especially they were awe-inspiring. Sometimes I sat in my canoe on the water as the sun was setting. If any wind had blown during the afternoon, it dropped at that hour when day was slipping into night. The water was smooth and the peace of Nature could not be deeper. As the sun dipped below the horizon the colours faded from sky and earth and river. The shadows of night advanced across the scene and soon everything was obscured in half-darkness.

Then the silence would be broken by a rushing of wild wings overhead and the stillness be disturbed by forms of duck moving rapidly across the sky. They might be a party of Mergansers or Mallards or Golden-eye. Their figures were mere shadows, black silhouettes hurtling through the dusk. Hardly appearing to have substance, they seemed like disembodied spirits fleeing through an unreal other-world. They expressed perfectly the eternal freedom and beauty of wild life.

CHAPTER ELEVEN

OCTOBER

I.

No SIGN is more symptomatic of autumn than the flocking of birds and no species gathers in larger assemblies than do Starlings. Near the creek grew a wood which was an ideal place for their roosting. For many weeks already a huge crowd had gathered there in the evenings. From a distance its chatter, contributed by thousands of throats talking in hundreds of trees, sounded like the steady murmur of sea washing upon a pebbly beach. But as one drew nearer it became much more raucous.

One evening early in October a section of this great Parliament of Starlings gathered for preliminary discussions in a group of trees beside the creek. Thousands of them blackened the branches, like a football crowd filling tiers of seats in a stadium. I sat in my canoe below and marvelled at their multitude. Their incessant gossiping was almost deafening, like the noise of a super monkey-house in a tree-tops Zoo.

Suddenly, as if at a signal, they were silent. A strange peace fell upon the air as the whole flock rose simultaneously into the sky. A few moments later I heard the swish of thousands of wings when the mass of birds passed over my head to join the even larger company already settled in their customary roosting place.

As the days passed the flock grew larger, until it must have included tens of thousands of Starlings. Towards sunset one could see many parties of dozens and scores and hundreds of birds flying in from every direction to join the assembly. Occasionally some unexpected sound startled the settled mob. Then they rose in a crowd into the air. Reluctant to leave the immediate neighbourhood of their dormitory, they flew around it not far above tree level, performing aerial manoeuvres with military sweep and precision. They flew so closely wing to wing that in the fading light the massed formation of birds looked like columns of dense smoke first pouring up from the trees and then floating in a black cloud which drifted this way and that above them.

This flock of Starlings in Brewery Creek reminded me of a flock which a few years ago settled in St. James's Park in London. I am indebted to my friend Sir Patrick Duff, now United Kingdom High Commissioner in New Zealand, for the following tale. He was then Permanent Secretary to the Office of Works and therefore responsible for maintaining the amenities of the Park.

A huge company of Starlings decided to roost at nights in the trees and shrubs of an island where many of the Park's splendid collection of wild fowl nested. This was as bad as a visitation of locusts, for the birds would destroy the island vegetation and threaten one of the Park's most attractive features.

The authorities in the Office of Works held a council of war to consider what they could do to get rid of the Starlings. The problem was baffling, for many thousands of birds were involved. Shooting them was out of the question since this would rouse the British public's sentimental attachment to feathered creatures and perhaps lead to awkward questions in the House of Commons. An attempt to poison them *en masse* would probably only end in many Mallards, Widgeon, Tufted Ducks and other water-fowl also being destroyed. Depriving the Starlings of their roosting perches by cutting down the trees would defeat its own purpose, since the object in view was to save the trees.

Then someone had an ingenious idea. He proposed that one night after the Starlings had gone to bed the fire-brigades from the surrounding boroughs should assemble beside the lake. They should do this stealthily, so that the birds received no warning of their presence. Their hoses should all be trained on the island and, at a given signal, shower upon it an unprecedented deluge of water. The entire flock of Starlings would be knocked over like nine-pins and drowned.

At the appointed hour the firemen gathered. From hiding places behind bushes and trees they watched the flock of Starlings collect from the four quarters of the heavens. For a while the birds maintained a lively conversation. Every fresh contingent of arrivals in the dormitory was greeted with an outburst of chatter. But at last the flock fell silent and the firemen knew that every member of it was caught in their trap.

The signal for action was given. Dozens of hoses simultaneously flung fountains of water at their target. At the same instant, however, the multitude of birds rose into the sky. When the deluge descended on the island a few moments later all the roosting places were empty.

The incident illustrates the acute sense of hearing and power of rapid action of a flock of Starlings. They evidently heard a sound connected with turning on the hoses, took alarm and instantly, with that unanimity which is so remarkable in large companies of birds, resorted to flight.

That was not the end of the story. The huge flock circled uncertainly overhead for a while and then made off along the Mall towards Buckingham Palace. They spent the night on the statue to Queen Victoria in front of the Palace gates. By the morning they had made such a mess of the monument that the Government had to spend £200 to have it cleaned.

2.

In October many other species gathered in flocks. During the first half of the month the wild shrubberies and edges of woodland on the creek bank were occupied by large parties of passerine birds. Some were coming together for the autumn journey south whilst others were forming the companies in which they would spend the winter in the district.

Commonest amongst them were various kinds of Sparrows. Large numbers of Song Sparrows, Savannah Sparrows, White-throated Sparrows and White-crowned Sparrows congregated early in the month. With them were flocks of Slate-coloured Juncos and parties of Purple Finches. They hopped and flitted restlessly amongst the weeds, bushes and trees, feeding and conversing amongst themselves. The white head-stripes, yellow eye-spots and white dickies of the White-throated Sparrows and the black and white head-stripes of the White-crowned Sparrows were gay. The immature birds, which were plentiful, had not these distinguishing marks.

Gay too were some of their voices. For a few days, especially when the sun was shining, they indulged in autumn singing. Generally this was a comparatively feeble echo of their earlier song. A White-throated Sparrow, for

example, would start boldly into its celebrated phrase—
"Sweet, sweet, Canada, Canada, Canada"—but after the
first couple of notes its voice would grow weak and in a few
more notes trail away to nothing. Often I heard the song
confidently started, but I never heard it continued beyond
"Sweet, sweet, Canada, Can . . ."

The Song Sparrows too only sang snatches of their earlier, challenging music. For a day or two the Purple
Finches seemed to be in stronger voice. Their song was not
only loud but sustained, the "lovely warble somewhat like
that of a Warbling Vireo, but richer and more vigorous"
described by Forbush. Listening to it, one might suppose
that all the evidences of autumn in the surrounding landscape were false and that the Purple Finches alone were
right in proclaiming the arrival of spring.

Occasionally a Chipping Sparrow and a House Sparrow
appeared. Then came three species which I had not seen
previously in the creek. Numerous Vesper Sparrows were
conspicuous by their white outer tail-feathers, unique
amongst common brown Sparrows. A stout, dark, grey-
breasted Swamp Sparrow stayed for a while in a reed bed.
A few days later some Fox Sparrows were easily recognizable by their large size and heavy breast stripes as well as
by their loud, sharp, almost explosive alarm note.

The list of Sparrows was completed by the arrival on
the 10th of several Tree Sparrows. Meanwhile flocks of
other birds were also passing through the creek. One
morning a small party of American Pipits walked and ran
along the shore. As they moved they frequently teetered
their tails, like Water-Thrushes. Without any particular distinction of plumage, they were sleek, graceful, good-looking
birds.

Photo by W. V. Crich, F.R.P.S.

RED-EYED VIREO

"The nests . . . were bound to each branch of the fork by the finest of all threads—cobwebs."

Most of the Warblers had already gone south, though early in the month I met an occasional Nashville Warbler, Magnolia Warbler, Wilson's Warbler and Black-throated Green Warbler in the wood. Myrtle Warblers, however, now arrived in considerable flocks. In spite of their bright yellow crowns, shoulder patches and rumps, they appeared rather untidy and dowdy compared with the neat and brilliantly coloured figures of other members of their family. But they are amongst the most likeable of the Warblers. They have what human beings call "personality", being fearless, vivacious and companionable. Never in the least concerned at my presence, they darted in dozens close around me, with half-Warblerish, half-Flycatcherish flutterings as they hunted for food. They gave me the same sense of being intimate with them as did the Yellow Warblers. As they moved about they often spoke to each other, uttering a pleasant, cheerful "Pee-ep", no doubt a signal to keep the members of the flock together.

They were so abundant that sometimes the words of a rude limerick jingled through my mind. These concerned a young woman who shared with the classical heroine Leda an inclination to fall in love with a strange animal. In her case it was not a swan but a turtle.

> There was a young lady called Myrtle
> Who had an affair with a Turtle,

the verse went. I forget the next two lines, but the last observed,

> Which shows that Myrtle was fertile.

I was interested to see from the large flocks of Myrtle Warblers that they shared with their namesake the blessed virtue of fertility.

The last Myrtle Warblers left the creek on the 14th. After that I saw only one more Warbler, who appeared on the following day. It flew about restlessly near the ground, perching now and then on a flower stalk or in a low shrub. Whenever it perched it jerked its tail, Sandpiper-fashion. This action, combined with its yellowish breast, was the unmistakable mark of a Palm Warbler. It stayed forlornly for a whole day in the creek, then disappeared.

The last of the Vireos—a Blue-headed Vireo—also left in the middle of the month. At about the same time I caught my final glimpses of two species who were common throughout the summer and have played a prominent part in this book. Every day until the 10th one or two Phoebes sat in the trees beside the old mill. Assuming them to be (as I believe they were) the adult pair whose nesting adventures had been enacted there, they remained faithful to the place for more than six months. On the 11th they were absent and I never saw them again. They must have left during the previous night.

All this time a few Catbirds had stayed in the creek, but I saw the last of them on the 13th. Birds which were not hardy enough to stand the Canadian winter were rapidly disappearing.

In the middle of the month a severe storm of wind and rain blew through the creek. When I visited the place next morning I found that its blast had achieved three things. First, it blew many of the autumn leaves off the trees; second, it blew most of the passerine migrants away to the south; and third, as I shall describe later, it blew a fresh migration of wildfowl into the creek.

Amongst the land birds whom it drove southwards were almost all the Sparrows. No large flocks of them appeared afterwards. Some species left altogether, not to reappear until the following spring. Until the end of the month, however, White-throated Sparrows and Song Sparrows continued passing through in small parties. Occasionally one or two House Sparrows strayed from the warmth of city eaves and chimney-pots, where they spend the winter. Tree Sparrows, on the other hand, were often to be seen in considerable flocks. They are hardy birds and at least a few stay in the Ottawa neighbourhood right through the cold months. One day towards the end of October quite a company of them beside the creek suddenly burst into their strong and sweet warbling song.

Red-winged and Rusty Blackbirds continued to visit the creek in noisy flocks right through October. Parties of Robins also occasionally appeared. Now and then a Crow flew solemnly by. But possession of the woods was gradually passing to regular winter birds like Goldfinches and Chickadees.

3.

In October 1944 I saw two birds who did not reappear in 1945. Both are, I am told, uncommon in the Ottawa district. The first was a Yellow-billed Cuckoo, a more unusual creature than its relative the Black-billed Cuckoo whom I saw in the following spring.

I was first attracted to it by its loud cry, "Kaow-kaow-kaow", issuing from the middle of a thick clump of trees. Not being familiar with the call, I went to investigate. The bird, however, saw me and slipped unobtrusively away to other trees. It is a shy creature and for some time successfully eluded me. Once or twice as it flew silently and almost sinuously from tree to tree in a jungle of vegetation near the water's edge I caught tantalizing glimpses of its slim form and long tail with black, white-tipped outer feathers. At last by patience and stealth, I got an excellent view of it perched in the half-light and half-shadow of dappled sunshine penetrating bushes partly stripped of leaves. Its head was well lit and I saw at once the black upper mandible and yellow lower mandible of its rather ferocious, curving bill. In its beak dangled a hairy caterpillar, like a catkin. Such hairy caterpillar fare is a Cuckoo speciality. More fastidious birds cannot swallow the bristly coats of these insects, but Cuckoos manage to do so. Indeed, the interior of a dead Cuckoo's stomach is often so lined with these bristles that the stomach itself appears to be growing fur.

Of Black-billed and Yellow-billed Cuckoos Mr. Taverner writes, "In regard to their parental duties our birds show considerably more realization of responsibility than the European (Cuckoos). They are slightly parasitic in their habits, that is, they occasionally drop their eggs in the nests of other birds and shelve upon them the cares of raising their young, but the practice is not common and is perhaps only accidental."

The other unusual bird whom I saw was a Bohemian Waxwing. Although these Waxwings are common to the Old as well as the New World, their name does not indicate any particular geographic association with the ancient Kingdom and modern Republic of Bohemia. It is merely a romantic reference to the bird's irregular, wandering habits, a trait which it is supposed to share with Bohemians. We are accustomed to a similar description attaching to human beings who lead restless, vagabond lives. Attractive though some of these latter "Bohemians" are, none of them within my ken is as decorative as the Bohemian Waxwing. Like its relative, the Cedar Waxwing, it has a gay, exotic appearance. Its high, sharp-pointed crest; the black bars passing through its eyes and across its brown head; its black chin, fawn-coloured body and tail with tail feathers edged by bright orange "as if dipped in paint"; and the brilliantly coloured appendages, like drops of red sealing-wax, on its secondary wing feathers and sometimes also its tail make a striking combination. Except for certain little differences it is similarly marked to the Cedar Waxwing. For example, small white bars on the closed wings of the bird which I saw established it as a member of the former species. Its finery, however, was not as pleasing as it would have been earlier in the season, for it was tarnished by the autumn moult.

4.

Shore birds were not plentiful in October. This was not because the season was late but because the water was high. The river was fuller than usual in the fall and various stretches of muddy bank in the creek, which had been a favourite resting and feeding ground for migrating waders when I watched in the previous year, were covered. As there was less shore in October 1945, so there were fewer shore birds.

Occasionally Killdeers, Yellow-legs and Sanderlings appeared. A few Spotted Sandpipers came often, but none of them wore spots on their breasts. The adult birds had all migrated, leaving these youngsters to find their own way south. Sometimes a Great Blue Heron was fishing in the shallows and one or two Belted Kingfishers were almost invariably present.

Before the end of the month, however, all these species except two had gone. I saw my last Killdeer on the 10th, my last Spotted Sandpiper on the 13th, my last Kingfisher on the 21st and my last Sanderling on the 22nd. Only Great Blue Herons and Yellow-legs stayed through October and into November.

As I have said, in 1944 shore birds were commoner. One morning about the middle of October a Wilson's Snipe put in an appearance. It was feeding with some Killdeers on the shore. As it strolled over the damp, soft ground it often stopped to bury its long beak deep in the mud. Needless to say, something perturbed the Killdeers. They were nervous and seemed incapable of staying quiet for more than a few moments. Constantly they ran a few swift paces along the shore, then halted, bobbed their bodies violently up and down and cried pathetically. I could not see what agitated them, unless it were a small party of Rusty Blackbirds who kept flying to and fro near the water's edge.

Amidst all this excitement the Snipe remained calm. But it behaved prudently. Whenever the Killdeers raised an alarm it stopped feeding and squatted quietly amongst the grass tufts on the shore. There it stayed absolutely motionless, relying instinctively on its clever camouflage for protection, until it decided that danger was past.

A few days later half-a-dozen Wilson's Snipe visited the creek. They were scattered at different places along the shore, all busy feeding. Some walked on the mud and others waded in the shallows. They were quiet-mannered and had a secretive air, as if they realized that they were favourite targets for sportsmen and must avoid attracting hostile eyes.

They stayed in the creek through the rest of the month and for a few days into November. Sometimes I got excel-

300

lent, close-up views of one or other of them. One morning, for example, I managed to bring my canoe slowly—as if it were a bit of driftwood—within a few yards of a Snipe and to jam it conveniently between two protruding rocks in the water whilst I studied the bird. Puzzled by this strange phenomenon, the Snipe stopped feeding, stood stock still and eyed me keenly. It stayed immobile for several minutes. Through my field-glasses, adjusted almost to their shortest range of vision, I got a perfect sight of it. It had beauty of marking rather than of form. Its beak, almost three inches long, seemed out of proportion to its squat body and short legs, but its plumage was finely speckled and striped with woodland colours—browns, ochre and white.

It would probably have remained motionless for an indefinite period. But I wanted to see it fly. So, I lifted a hand into the air to frighten it. Instantly it rose, flew without any fuss or sound into a nearby reed-bed and disappeared.

On a second morning I disturbed another Snipe feeding in the mud just above the water line. Startled, it ceased feeding, ran quickly to a patch of faded brown grass and weeds close by, flopped into it and sat as still as a statue. The bird seemed completely confident that its camouflage provided perfect concealment. Though I approached closer and closer and it eyed me keenly, it remained calm and unmoving. Its estimate of the value of its markings was correct. I would not have detected the bird even at very close quarters had I not seen it from afar and carefully watched its every subsequent movement. Its composure was remarkable. At least, so it seemed. It may really have felt horribly frightened and its heart may have been beating with furious agitation. Outwardly, however, it remained serene. Only when I brought my canoe so close that I could have touched it with my paddle did it suddenly rise, fly low over the ground and plunge into a clump of reeds further along the shore.

This quiet, self-controlled behaviour of a Wilson's Snipe is in pleasant contrast to the excitability of a Killdeer. Nor is the difference due to the circumstance that the Snipe can instinctively behave with greater calm because its protective colouring is more efficient than that of the other bird. The Killdeer's marking is also an effective piece of camouflage. The difference can only be explained by a contrast in the natures of the two species. It is an interesting demonstration that different birds have different temperaments and that it takes all sorts of birds to make a world.

5.

None of the wild-fowl who came to the creek in the two previous months had travelled from any great distance. They had probably bred somewhere in the Ottawa valley. Now, however, duck from the further north began to appear.

On October 5th the first two arrived, a couple of Surf Scoters. The principal breeding ground in America of these sportive sea ducks is the Arctic coast of north-western Canada and the basin of the Mackenzie River. The birds were now migrating to their winter residence on the Atlantic coast, somewhere between the Bay of Fundy and Florida.

The two in the creek were youngsters, presumably making the journey for the first time. Their blackish-brown colour with two obscure white patches on each side of the head might have been marks of adult females. But the absence of a whitish patch on the back of their heads established them as juveniles. Their large, bulbous bills, conspicuously punctured by nostrils stamped them with unmistakable Scoter ugliness.

I was able to approach close to them. This was not because, like the Black-bellied Plovers and the Northern Phalarope, they were unafraid of me. On the contrary, they showed agitation and endeavoured to outpace me as they swam away through wind-swept, choppy water. I followed in the canoe, gaining steadily on them and drawing closer. Then they dived to escape me. This they did quickly but heavily, with considerable splashes. As they sank their wings were half-open, for they use both wings and feet to swim under water. They remained below for some time and emerged again at a distance from where they disappeared. These tactics they repeated several times, but I followed them and eventually almost caught up with them. Then they tried to rise from the water in flight, but failed. I ceased paddling, lifted my field-glasses to my eyes and got excellent close-up views of them.

I had pursued them down-wind. Now they turned to face the breeze, which was blowing fairly strongly. At once I saw that they felt more comfortable. Spreading their wings, they started flopping along the river with much lashing of water and slowly increasing acceleration. Gradually, with a great effort, they got clear of the water and rose into the air. Their flight was then strong and swift.

As Mr. Arthur Cleveland Bent's *Life Histories of North American Wildfowl* observes, a Surf Scoter "rises heavily from the surface of the water and experiences considerable difficulty in doing so unless there is some wind, which it must face in order to rise. This necessity of rising against the wind is well understood by gunners, who take advantage of it to approach a flock of bedded birds from the windward, forcing the birds to rise toward the boat and thus come a little nearer".

As their name suggests, Surf Scoters feel most at home in a shallow sea where white-capped breakers race towards the shore. They ride the water confidently, allowing themselves to be carried far up the side of each succeeding wave. As the wave rises and its crest overbalances and breaks into flying spray, the birds dive into it and "scoot" through to the comparatively calm water on the other side. They do this over and over again, through breaker after breaker, as if it were a regular sport.

The two Scoters in the creek stayed several days, but no more wild duck appeared until after the middle of the month. Then they came in large numbers. I have already referred to the storm of wind and rain on the 15th which blasted most of the leaves off the trees, blew away many of the small land birds and brought a fresh lot of wild-fowl to the creek. This last effect, like the others, was instantaneous. For more than a week no duck whatever had appeared in the creek. But on the morning of the 16th half-a-dozen Mergansers, a Greater Scaup duck, two Surf Scoters and some American Scoters were swimming there. From then onwards the numbers and species of duck increased steadily until their immense movement of migration waned about three weeks later.

The American Scoters on this occasion were immature birds, distinguishable from young Surf Scoters by the whole of their cheeks and chins being whitish. A few days later a party of nearly twenty adult drakes flew into the creek,

304

sombre creatures with all-black plumage relieved only by a butter-yellow swelling at the base of their bills.

Red-breasted and Common Mergansers often came to the creek. As the month advanced their flocks became larger. One morning a company of almost fifty flew close over my head and splashed on to the water nearby. They immediately started fishing. They all dived at about the same time, stayed under water for the same period and reappeared more or less simultaneously. In this way they progressed right across the estuary, like a flotilla of submarines at exercise.

Green-winged Teal, Ring-necked Duck, Golden-eye, Mallards, Hooded Mergansers, Greater and Lesser Scaups, Buffle-heads and Pintails came and went, some singly, some in pairs and some in considerable parties.

One morning a flock of about forty Black Duck flew into the creek and alighted in a cloud of spray on the water. They swam, as they had flown, in close-packed formation, looking from a distance like a large, dark patch of solid substance floating there. "The most sagacious, wary and wildest of all ducks[1]," they were alert and restless. After swimming for five minutes, they rose into the air again as abruptly as they had alighted and flew off in a close-knit mass of flying bodies. Gradually the compactness of the flock broke. They spaced themselves and eventually formed a long, straggling line of wildfowl.

Two species which I had not noticed in the creek before appeared. More than once a party of Redheads were present and one afternoon a score of Canvas-backs flew over in arrow-head formation. Making a bee-line for the

[1] F. H. Kortright, *Ducks, Geese and Swans of North America*. American Wild Life Institute.

Houses of Parliament, they passed right over the Peace Tower.

When I arrived in the creek early on the 21st an Old Squaw duck was there. Here indeed was a visitor from the top of the world! The Old Squaws' principal breeding grounds are on the tundra along the Arctic coast from western Alaska to north-east Labrador, on all the Arctic Islands and round the coasts of Greenland and Iceland. The visitor to Brewery Creek that morning was a sweet, dumpy, piebald little creature. Swimming around aimlessly, she appeared perplexed and lost, as if wondering what to make of these restricted waters with citified surroundings after the spacious, empty solitudes of the far north. At my approach she showed not the slightest alarm. She even evinced a certain amount of curiosity, eyeing me with an engagingly trustful gaze when I came near her. She allowed me to approach so close that I did not need field-glasses to study her markings. If only all wild duck were as tame, the problems of identification would be simple!

She was soon joined by a drake in his elegant winter dress. His short bill and round head had an air of breeding, but his greatest distinction was his streamer-like central tail feathers, between eight and ten inches long. His white and black plumage was "racy" of the Arctic, appearing especially designed to match snow-fields, ice-bergs and dark cliffs. He seemed lethargic, spending much time floating lazily wherever the current took him. But occasionally he and his companion engaged in a burst of activity, diving after food or making short flights round the creek. Their dives were short but efficient. They appeared most at home, however, when they flew. Then they lost their air of being not quite sure of themselves, flying low above the water with a beautiful, confident, swift flight driven by strong, regular wing beats.

On a later morning half-a-dozen Old Squaws came. At the same time a young Common Loon was on the water. Its disposition was the reverse of theirs, for it was shy in the extreme. I had the greatest difficulty in getting near to it, and after once succeeding was never allowed to repeat the success. The Loon kept diving to elude me, outwitting me regularly by staying long and swimming far under water, constantly changing its direction. In the end it simply submerged and disappeared altogether. I do not know where it went. I never saw it again either that morning or on any subsequent day.

When several flocks of these various creatures were in the creek at the same time, swimming, diving and flying around, they looked like a gay regatta of wild-fowl. I never crossed the river in the latter half of October without seeing half-a-dozen parties of duck. With them were always two or three species of Gulls and occasionally some Double-crested Cormorants. No sight could be more exhilarating than these river and ocean birds gathered in large numbers.

One day towards the end of the month a flock of about two hundred Canada Geese flew overhead. They were not spaced in their famous, stately, arrow-head formation, but flew in a compact, irregular bunch. This is their custom when flying round their feeding grounds or making only short flights. Even so the majesty of the birds was apparent and the leisurely, powerful beat of their great wings was beautiful.

Soon afterwards their migration began. I did not see any of the massive flocks, but on the 28th a fisherman on the river told me that through the previous evening and early that morning he had watched multitudes flying over. Their honking, he said, was very loud. So many thousands of birds were present that sometimes they filled vast spaces of sky.

6.

October is the loveliest Canadian month. For some time frosts have been stealing down at night from the north and forcing that sad crisis in the woods—the death of the leaves. Nothing in Nature is more memorable than the transformation which then takes place. The funeral rites of the Canadian trees are celebrated with pageantry of startling gorgeousness. Gradually the dark, sultry green of the summer foliage is changed into many lighter, gayer, more vivid hues. Each day the wonder grows until in the first half of October it reaches its climax.

The whole Ottawa valley then is a field of blazing colours. On a sunlit day it appears as if the Creator had accidentally dropped the contents of His paint-box from heaven and spilled them across the landscape. The earth is like a huge artist's palette. Masses of dark evergreens, pale green, russets, pinks, reds, crimsons, scarlets, yellows, orange and gold are splashed everywhere. Through this splendour flows the sapphire river and overhead is the blue sky.

Brewery Creek took its place in this brilliant scene. It is impossible to describe the many different tints of its trees. Maples provided the dominant colours. The Red and Silver Maples turned crimson and yellow respectively. Some Silver Maples even, not content with a simple adornment, wore red, yellow and green leaves all at the same time. Other rich colours vied with these. The deep, warm scarlet of Sumach positively glowed. Elm trees turned russet, Dogwood bushes became purpley-red and Rose-coloured Raspberry leaves went greeny-yellow. The fine, thin leaves of Willows and the broad leaves of Cottonwood and Sugar Maples remained green. Only later did they turn to orange and gold.

Autumn flowers added their delicate artistry to the picture. At the beginning of the month plumes of Golden-rod still bloomed on the banks of the creek. Here and there a sprig of comely blue Chicory flowers showed. White and blue Asters grew in tall clumps and Yellow Toad Flax was scattered over the ground.

I know of only one other season in one other country which compares in beauty with the Canadian fall. It is the English spring. The two seasons evoke different thoughts and emotions. The one cries "Hail!" and the other says "Farewell!" The one is concerned with birth and the other with death. One expresses joy and the other sorrow. Their moods contrast widely. But for sheer, aesthetic beauty they are peers in perfection.

The moment of supreme glory in the Canadian autumn, however, does not last long. In a few days it is past. Wind and rain strip the boughs of their frail leaves. The trees' fine raiment grows ever more scanty, dropping in brilliant rags upon the ground. For a brief while the beauty lingers there. Scores of thousands of fallen leaves cover the earth with a deep carpet. No Persian rug woven by human hands can rival this fabric made by the Supreme Artist from dying leaves. Its exquisite beauty is due in part to its many delicate colours and partly to the pattern of its differently shaped leaves interlaced with each other.

For two days after the storm in the middle of the month this carpet remained vivid. It was soft and soundless to walk upon. Then the leaves faded and dried. The last foliage lingering on the trees also died. The subdued, autumnal voices of a few remaining Sparrows and Juncos whispered amongst the bushes. The gossiping of Chickadees and chattering of Starlings could likewise be heard. But the principal sound was the frequent, dry clatter of late leaves falling and striking twigs as they descended. Soon most of the trees were completely bare. On only a few did shocks of orange foliage still cling, like brave flags flying at the end of a battle.

In the bare trees relics of birds' summer residences were starkly revealed. Battered by wind and rain, many abandoned nests clung to the branches. Their architecture was varied. Suspended at the ends of drooping Elms were the long, fibre bags woven by Baltimore Orioles. The nests of Robins and Catbirds were set on the tops of their boughs. Others, like those of Yellow Warblers, were tied to the upright stems of bushes. Yet others were slung below supporting branches. Amongst these the homes of Red-eyed Vireos were particularly charming. Inserted under forking twigs, these small, dainty, cup-shaped structures were bound to each branch of the fork by the finest of all threads—cobwebs. Nevertheless, these bonds proved so strong that the nests survived all the autumn storms. They were a gallant, if dilapidated sight, these Ancient Monuments of the bird world.

7.

On October 24th some well-known heralds of winter appeared—half-a-dozen Snow Buntings. It was a raw, cold

TREE SPARROW
"Braved the rigours of the season."

morning, but the harsh conditions did not worry them. They roamed amongst the stones on shore, indifferent to a biting wind. Their arrival was timely, for that night the first snow fell and next morning it lay half-an-inch deep on the ground. In a few hours it melted, but two days later small, thin, fragile panes of ice appeared in the creek, floating in the shallow, quiet waters along the edges of the shore.

Winter was nudging Autumn off the scene.

CHAPTER TWELVE

NOVEMBER

I.

SOME MORNINGS in November were blown in by storms of wind. They nearly blew me to Kingdom Come. Canoeing on those occasions was not so easy as it might be. I should have put a stone in the craft's bow to steady it, but invariably forgot to do so. The boat rocked and frolicked on the waves like a raving lunatic. Occasionally it even developed a suicidal mania, showing a passionate disposition to capsize. This tendency I had to discourage with a firm hand. Sometimes I found it difficult to keep my temper. I wanted to take my paddle and smack the canoe where it would hurt most. But that—as is so often the case in such chastisements—would have hurt me more than it did the boat. A moment's hasty violence might have proved fatal. Instead I had to humour the canoe, to coax it, almost to caress it. I had to induce it to keep its dear little nose pointing into the wind. I admit that sometimes whilst doing so with apparent calm I was swearing at the craft at the top of my voice. I said some very direct things to it, offering disparaging remarks about its ancestry, accusing it of various improper practices and making dogmatic statements about where it would go when it left this world. Fortunately these observations were lost in the howling wind.

Conditions were worst when the breeze blew directly along the river. One morning I was forced up stream as

far as the Inter-Provincial Bridge, half-a-mile above Earnscliffe, before reaching the opposite shore.

On other mornings there was no breath of wind. Instead a white mist hung over the glassy water. Sometimes
it lay in a solid, even mass. Wherever I paddled its thickness was uniform, unyielding, baffling, and I could not get
my bearings. At other times the mist lay in wisps and
coils. Its thickness was variable and clear holes and passages appeared in it. Then it was fun chasing along the
passages to see where they would lead. Occasionally I came
across wild duck swimming in the mist, like unsubstantial
bird-shadows floating in grey space. They were as surprised
at my sudden appearance as I was at theirs.

But those were exceptional days. Most mornings the
weather was cold and clear. The days were growing
shorter. Even at the beginning of November the light was
insufficient for bird watching until after 7 o'clock. Sometimes at that hour the temperature was still several degrees
below freezing and a beautiful powdering of frost covered
every tree and shrub and blade of grass. All Nature seemed
exquisitely fragile, as if it were made of thin, white Venetian
glass. When the sun rose it gave a sparkle to the scene but
could not banish the chill from the air. Those cold, crisp
November mornings were some of the best in the year.

2.

Only the tough guys amongst the birds could stand
these conditions. Some Red-winged Blackbirds, Rusty
Blackbirds and Song Sparrows stayed for the first few days
of November and then fled to a warmer climate. Tree
Sparrows, Slate-coloured Juncos and Ruby- and Golden-
crowned Kinglets braved the rigours of the season longer,

but I did not see any of them after the middle of the month. After that only the true winter birds were left.

They were a merry as well as a hardy company. Their presence was all the more precious because of the comparative absence of living creatures in the freezing world. They seemed more vivacious because of the still, dead landscape around them.

Even Starlings acquired charm. This was partly due to their having now assumed their winter plumage, attractively speckled in black, buff and white with green and purple reflections on the glossy feathers. It is a decorative, pleasing dress. But also, as the winter deepened and bird voices grew fewer, the constantly cheerful whistling and chattering of Starlings seemed more companionable. These despised immigrants somehow came into their own.

Every now and then a spick-and-span, black-and-white Hairy or Downy Woodpecker travelled through the wood. As it flew from tree to tree, hammering and boring for insects, it uttered a sharp, whinnying cry. That call and the tapping of its beak on the tree trunks marked its progress. Like most other birds, it seemed possessed by an insatiable hunger and spent all its waking hours hunting for food. In winter the shorter days require that birds should feed more quickly so as to take in enough fuel to keep their temperatures at a robust level.

Woodpeckers hunted alone, but most birds moved about in flocks. None were more lively than the parties of Black-capped Chickadees. From a distance I could hear their conversation. As they drew nearer it grew louder, until two or three dozen birds were flitting, hopping and performing acrobatics in the trees around me. Their powers of balancing were remarkable. Giddiness meant nothing

314

to them, for they could perch the right-way up or upside-down with equal readiness. Nor did they seem to know fear, at least of Man. So indifferent were they to my presence that occasionally one of them, if my face happened to be on the line of flight between the place where it was and the place where it wished to be, flitted impertinently right under my nose.

As they travelled, searching each tree in turn for food, they talked continuously to one another. Their usual remark was the characteristic "Chickadee-dee-dee", but their phrases varied. What did their different expressions mean? Why did a bird say one thing at one time and another at another?

After the first heavy snowfall a flock of thirty or forty Goldfinches often came to feed on the seeds in a meadow of faded wild Chicory and Golden-rod. The plants looked gaunt and cold growing from a continuous white snow field. They now lacked their blue and yellow flowers and the cock Finches had lost their brilliant summer plumage. They were soberly clad like the hens, except that they sported yellow shoulder patches. Their tinkling voices, however, were as gay as ever and sounded often as they flew from place to place.

One morning whilst I watched this party of Gold-finches they were joined at their meal by about twenty Redpolls. Common Redpolls and Greater Redpolls were both present. They flew in with the same cheerful manner as the Goldfinches and made a similar massed attack on the flower stalks. But their red crowns, dusky chins and striped flanks immediately distinguished them.

As they fed on the crop of plants protruding from the snow a larger bird alighted on a bare tree nearby. The crowd of Goldfinches and Redpolls immediately rose in alarm. Flying in a loose bunch round and round in the air above the tree, they chattered continuously to each other and seemed undecided what to do.

The intruder was a Northern Shrike. Through my glasses I studied its black, grey and white plumage and its trim body, alert eyes and cruel beak. But the Butcher Bird was not bent on murder that morning. Evidently it was not hungry, for it gave no sign of desiring to attack the smaller birds. After a while it uttered a harsh cry and flew away.

Several times Snow Buntings came to the creek. Their white and black plumage had lost its spring freshness and was tinted with brown. But when they spread their wings and fluttered into the air they still appeared mostly white birds, worthy of their nickname "Snowflakes". Unlike snowflakes, however, they were noisy, often addressing each other in tinkling, whistling voices.

One morning towards the end of the month a flock of nearly forty small birds were foraging amongst weeds jutting from the snow on shore. Some of them were Snow Buntings and at first I presumed them all to belong to that species. Then a member of the party made a remark which did not sound to me like a Bunting observation—a dry, rattling "Chirr". Looking through field-glasses, I saw from its dark wings that it was a Lapland Longspur. The flock turned out to be composed in equal parts of these two different cold-weather birds.

One other name completes the list of hardy land birds who came to the creek in November. As I walked one morning on a newly laid carpet of snow in the maple wood a large bird left a tree ahead of me. In spite of its obvious heaviness, its flight was as silent as a shadow's. It manoeuvred quickly amongst the intertwining branches and before I could fix my glasses on it disappeared. Obviously it was an Owl. But what kind of Owl? I felt tantalized at not discovering its exact identity, especially as I suspected that it might be the far-famed Snowy member of the family.

Next morning I walked cautiously towards the group of trees where it had perched, hoping to see it there again. I was disappointed when they proved untenanted. Then I almost jumped with fright when I saw the Owl in a nearer tree, a dozen yards away, gazing fixedly at me. It was larger than I had expected, being about two feet long. Its grotesque, flat face, hooked beak and large, staring eyes seemed forbidding. It did not blink nor stir. Except for the fierce light in its eyes, it might have been a stuffed specimen.

Slowly, so as not to startle it, I raised my glasses and adjusted them to the right focus. It did not move a feather and for several minutes we scrutinized each other. The bird's identity was now plain. Alas, it had not the yellow eyes, dark bill and white plumage of a Snowy Owl. Its brown-black eyes and yellowish beak and the pattern of stripes on its body revealed it as a Barred Owl. The twin dials of its face were light grey and half-covered with brown concentric rings; its near-white breast was darkly barred as if it wore several necklaces; its belly was striped and splashed lengthwise and its feathered feet were flecked with dusky spots to the edges of its long talons.

After a while I moved further away and slowly walked a half-circle round the bird to see the colour of its upper parts. Its back, wings and tail were sepia-brown spotted and barred with buff. The effect was rich. I never saw the

317

back of the Owl's head, for wherever I moved its eyes and full face followed me. The head swivelled round easily. When I stood immediately behind it the face gazing at me from above the folded wings gave the bird an absurd, twisted, back-to-front appearance.

So long as I did nothing to disturb it, it remained composed—except for those intently staring eyes. Sometimes when I stayed still for a while it even paid me the compliment of trustfully closing them and snoozing. But if my movements alarmed it, it launched itself on the air and fled. Its noiseless flight seemed magical. This is made possible by the softness of its feathers and is an example of Nature's adaptation of the equipment of an animal to its particular needs. An owl's night hunting requires a silent approach to its victims.

For three days the Barred Owl stayed in the creek. Each morning I found it on the same spot on the same bough of the same tree, perched close to the trunk. Probably it would have stayed there much longer. But on the third day I thoughtlessly spoke of it to a man who, I later discovered, collected stuffed birds as trophies. Next morning the Owl was gone. I never found it again in the creek. But a week later I saw it perched on a bit of wood in the workshop of my excellent friend Hector Bedard, the taxidermist in Rockcliffe. I thought that the poor bird's glass eyes looked at me reproachfully.

3.

The shore was almost empty of birds in November. The last Yellow-legs yodelled "Good-bye" to the creek on the 3rd and hastened towards its winter quarters in the Deep South and beyond. On the 18th a Great Blue Heron alighted at the water's edge, but soon made off again. Except for these the shore was deserted.

Waterfowl were more plentiful. At various times eight different species appeared. I had hoped that a ninth might come. Each year migrating King Eiders travel up the St. Lawrence as far as Montreal and occasionally a few wander along the Ottawa River to visit the Canadian capital. I should have enjoyed a glimpse of the drake's extraordinarily ugly face. But unfortunately in 1945 these birds gave Ottawa a miss.

However, a species that was new to me did appear. A small party of White-winged Scoters were on the water one day. I first suspected their identity when I noticed their large size and it was confirmed when they took wing and showed white speculums.

Surf Scoters and Greater Scaup appeared sometimes. A Black Duck came once and Red-breasted Mergansers flew in two or three times. Old-squaws came more frequently. They always looked picturesque. One morning I saw a pair through a veil of mist. I approached close to them, but they did not stir. The water was calm and they sat absolutely motionless upon it. Their neat figures, exotically designed plumage and perfect tranquility made them appear, through the misty atmosphere, like ducks in a classical Chinese painting.

All these Duck left the creek before the last week of the month. After that only American Mergansers and Golden-eye were left. The Mergansers swam and fished in parties of about half-a-dozen. The Golden-eye were sometimes more numerous. At the end of the month a flock of about twenty spent a few days in the creek and its vicinity, travelling always in a crowd. They were shy and wild and would

319

not allow me to get anywhere near them. As I paddled about they kept flying in and out of the creek, settling on the water for a while, then taking alarm and rushing into the air again. The whistle of their wings was sharp and loud. I watched them through field-glasses. A few showed the white cheek marks of drakes passing out of "eclipse" plumage into their smart winter dresses; so the cycle of their lives was beginning again.

They are remarkably hardy birds, these Golden-eye. For example, the thermometer on the morning of November 27th recorded 16° of frost. I had to tear the canoe's padlock and chain free from thick moorings of ice which had nailed them to the wharf during the night. When I crossed the river and tried to enter the creek I found the entrance barred by an ice-field. Yet on the river nearby several American Golden-eye swam. The water must have been perishingly cold, but they did not care a damn.

CHAPTER THIRTEEN

DECEMBER

I.

When I went out on December 1st the sun was rising into a clear sky. The thermometer, however, stood at 12° and the frosty air had a sharp cutting edge. The Ottawa was mostly frozen. Whereas on the previous day a broad and noble river flowed unrestricted, now only a few large channels of free water remained and the rest lay imprisoned beneath a vast, polished, steel-like sheet of ice.

Nevertheless, the ice beside the wharf at Earnscliffe was thin. Launching my canoe through it, I forced a way into the largest passage of open water, hoping that the whole ice-field might prove brittle and weak and that I could get across to the creek. Two-thirds of the way across, however, where the water becomes more sluggish towards the Quebec shore, the canoe struck ice which it could not break. A solid rink of it, half-an-inch or more thick, covered the rest of the way. It was too firm to paddle through and too fragile to walk upon. I had to abandon the journey and turn back.

By next morning Winter had so increased its grip upon the river that children on the Quebec side were playing ice-hockey some way from shore.

During the next week the temperature varied and conditions on the river varied with it. Some days the central channel was completely free of ice, but wide, jagged margins of ice too thick to penetrate with a canoe always stretched along either shore. Covered with snow, they provided neat white borders to the wild, grey river.

On land snow lay several inches deep and the landscape had assumed a Christmasy aspect. The clustered roofs of Hull and the fields, farm buildings and copses in the country beyond were clothed in white from head to foot. On the horizon the wooded Gatineau Hills were coloured like pieces of blue and white porcelain.

Then on December 8th a thaw began. Next morning the river was open, except for occasional ice-floes travelling down stream. Its ice borders melted until they were as thin and easily torn as paper. I crossed to the creek on the mornings of the 9th and 10th, landing each time and walking through snowy meadows and woods. The snow remained deep enough for winter sports. Having canoed on the river on the morning of the 9th, I skied on land in the afternoon and canoed again the following day.

2.

Few birds enlivened the creek on those mornings. A few Starlings, a party of Black-capped Chickadees and a flock of American Goldfinches were the only old friends whom I met on shore. However, two new winter residents appeared, the last comers of the year. In the maple wood I came across a cock Evening Grosbeak. Its big, whitish bill, yellow forehead, yellowish body and white-patched, black wings distinguished it from its rosy-red relative, the Pine Grosbeak. The latter must also have visited the creek sometimes in December, but I never had the good fortune to see it there.

The other newcomer did not actually cross the air, land or water boundaries into the creek itself. But I count it in the list of Brewery Creek birds because I was standing on the shore there when I caught sight of it. That is a reasonable enough excuse for completing my list with the name of a bird of noble distinction. My heart leaped when I saw it, for this was the realization of an especially cherished ambition.

The bird suddenly sailed into view above a neighbouring field, flying not more than fifty feet up in the air as its eyes searched the earth for food. Its round head, bulky figure, majestic wing span and plumage as white as the snow on the ground below could belong to only one creature—a Snowy Owl. I could scarcely believe my eyes and immediately fixed my field-glasses on it. The fewness and smallness of the dark brown splashes on its white body indicated that it was an adult male. Mature females and juveniles of both sexes are more generously speckled and barred with spots and streaks.

The Owl flew slowly and as silently as a giant moth across the field, over a wood and out of sight. It never came near enough for me to detect its savage yellow eyes, its dark, short beak hooded like a Roman nose and its long talons. But that hardly mattered. Enough it was that I had been privileged to catch even a passing glimpse of this uncommon and magnificent creature, a member of that exclusive society which inhabits the Polar regions, associate of White Whales, White Foxes and Polar Bears.

Snowy Owls are not regular winter visitors to Ottawa. They are birds of the Arctic tundra who generally stay throughout the year beyond the limits of considerable human settlements. But occasionally disease or some other mishap amongst mice and lemmings—their principal foodstuff—so reduces the numbers of these animals in the far north that hunger forces the Owls south in search of more liberal supplies of rodents. Then Canadian cities and rat-infested places in the northern United States become the haunts of Snowy Owls. 1945 was one of those years when famine conditions in the Arctic brought the birds south. An invasion of them occurred in the Ottawa neighbour-hood, more than sixty Snowy Owls being recorded there in December.

That I should see one of them was a splendid climax to my bird-watching in Brewery Creek.

3.

On the water only two kinds of wild duck now appeared—American Mergansers and Golden-eye. A pair of the former and a dozen of the latter were usually swim-ming and diving whenever the water was open. Overhead fluttered a few Herring Gulls. So the year had gone almost full cycle and the scene was much like that which I had observed in early March. Then only Mergansers and Golden-eye fished amongst the ice-floes on the wintry creek, whilst Gulls glided overhead. Now again these three hardy birds were left in sole possession of the freezing cold water.

The prospect was the same, yet different. In March the year had been young, the earth was waking from slumber and a promise of spring was in the air. Now the year was worn and senile. Slowly the earth was sinking into a coma, slipping into its long winter sleep.

4.

On the morning of December 11th the river was covered with ice from shore to shore. Only a few small pools of free water remained. Canoeing was impossible. At last the time had come to lay aside my paddle and prepare snow-shoes for their winter's work.

324

A canoe is a perfect craft in the Canadian spring and summer and autumn, for its body and spirit alike are responsive to the pleasures of out-door life in those open seasons. No other inanimate object has so much the quality of a living creature. It moves beneath you like a horse, speeding smoothly and gracefully forward when the water is calm, jogging on a choppy surface like a trotting nag, prancing on rougher water with the regular rhythm of a canter and leaping over long ocean rollers like a steeple-chaser jumping hurdles. It is as sensitive, too, as a well-trained horse to its master's guiding hand. The slightest flick of the paddle to left or right wins instant response in the desired direction. Of course, like other creatures with sensitive natures, it has its bad moods. Certain winds will throw it out of humour and make it so obstinate that you find difficulty in forcing it into a direction which it does not wish to take. But you must forgive these little idiosyn-cracies. After all, wind can sometimes afflict and upset even the kindliest people. And not all winds bring out the worst in a canoe. Some breezes improve its temper and send it speeding more swiftly and gaily than ever upon its way.

It has other qualities which are virtues in the outdoor world where one studies birds and beasts. It is noiseless and furtive, is able to run or creep or halt at a moment's notice, and can insinuate itself through narrow spaces. Above all, wild creatures are apt to regard it as one of them-selves. They do not resent its intrusion so long as its advance is tactful. When it first appears they may eye it suspiciously for a while, but if it moves forward gently they are inclined to acquiesce in its near approach.

Yes, a canoe is an incomparable companion in the Cana-dian spring and summer and autumn. But in winter it is helpless. When the lakes and rivers freeze life flees from its limbs. Its body grows paralyzed and its spirit dies. Like many animals then, it must hide itself away. Since it cannot migrate like a Swallow, it hibernates like a Bear.

Reluctantly on December 11th I saw my canoe tucked away in a boat-house for the winter. It was sad to think that we would never again keep each other company. When the Ottawa River unfroze next spring I should be far away, journeying towards new duties and recreations in Malaya. However, the canoe and I had enjoyed a good year. We had glided and frolicked our way up and down the river, and ventured into every nook and cranny of Brewery Creek, from March 21st until December 10th. Almost nine months of continuous canoeing! Not bad!

After seeing the canoe borne to its winter grave I stood in the garden at Earnscliffe and looked across the river to Brewery Creek. That enchanting place seemed of a sudden horribly distant and unapproachable. I saw the ice binding its waters. Not even Mergansers and Golden-eye could alight there now.

Yet one species of bird still would not desert the place. Herring Gulls stayed around. One swam in a small pool of open water on the river close by me. It seemed perplexed by its surroundings. Paddling agitatedly with its feet, it swam quickly first in this direction and then in that until, each time, further progress was barred by an edge of encircling ice. Whenever it met this obstacle it turned sharply and speeded in the opposite direction. I could almost hear it muttering to the ice,

"Don't fence me in."

Raising my field glasses, I gazed into Brewery Creek. A few Gulls flew restlessly to and fro above its ice-field.

Now and then they alighted or walked or slid uncertainly on its strange, slippery floor. I could see that they never lost the appearance of grave dignity which Herring Gulls always assume. But they also betrayed that they were painfully surprised. They seemed to be saying to themselves that the world had become an odd and disconcerting place to live in, but that they supposed they must make the best of it.

To my human mind this seemed an appropriate comment on affairs at the close of the year which had seen the explosion of the first atomic bomb.

That was my last impression of bird life in Brewery Creek.

INDEX

A

Audubon, James, 94-6, 107

B

Bent, A. C., 30, 141, 303-4
Bittern, 202, 249, 267, 279
  American, 116
Blackbird, 41, 56, 60
  American, 36
  English, 36
  Red-winged, 31, 35-6, 60, 66,
    111-12, 124, 138, 168,
    274, 297, 313
  Rusty, 60, 274, 297, 300, 313
Bluebird, 25, 26, 32, 262, 277-8
Bobolink, 108, 110
Breeding, 14-19
Buffle-head, 55, 84, 86-91, 93,
  305
Bunting, 14
  Snow, 24, 310-11, 316
Butterflies
  Camberwell Beauty, 38
  Mourning Cloak, 38
  Swallowtail, 198
  Tiger Swallowtail, 198
  Viceroy, 198

C

Calvert, George, Lord Baltimore,
  111
Canada Bird, 99
Canary, Wild, 113
Canvas-back, 305
Catbird, 108, 109-10, 121, 126,
  138-9, 176-81, 212, 296,
  310
Chamberlain, Neville, 7, 8

Chickadee, 277, 297, 310
  Black-capped, 98, 120, 314-15,
    322
Chicken, Prairie, 146
Churchill, Winston, 287
Cormorant, Double-crested, 104,
  307
Cowbird, 31, 41-5, 60, 124-5,
  136, 165-7, 168, 207, 208,
  247
Creeper, Brown, 274
Crow, 26, 27, 29, 60, 123-4,
  168, 177, 205, 219, 246,
  261, 297
Cuckoo, 121, 298
  Black-billed, 120-1, 297, 298
  English, 45
  Yellow-billed, 297-8

D

Damsel flies, 199
Dove, Mourning, 259-60
  Rock, 259
Dragon-fly, 198
Duck, 5, 83, 94, 126, 262
  Black, 56, 84, 87, 270, 305,
    319
  Buffle-head, 55, 84, 86-91, 93,
    305
  Canvas-back, 305
  Eider, King, 319
  Golden-eye, 32, 59, 84, 86,
    91, 151, 267, 271, 282,
    283, 288, 289, 305, 319-
    20, 324, 326
  American, 31, 47-50, 83,
    87, 320
  Mallard, 56, 84, 288-9, 305

Duck
  Old-squaw, 56, 84, 86, 306-7,
    319
  Pintail, 32, 305
  Redhead, 305
  Ring-necked, 56, 84, 86, 87,
    91, 305
  Scaup, Greater, 107, 304, 305,
    319
    Lesser, 55, 85-6, 92, 107,
      305
  Scoter, American, 304-5
    Surf, 302-4, 319
    White-winged, 319
  Teal, Blue-winged, 106-7,
    269-70, 271, 282, 288
    Green-winged, 288, 305
  Wood, 56, 85, 91, 151-2

E

Egret, White, 249
Eider, King, 319

F

Falcon, 100
  Peregrine, 261-2
Finch, 6, 14
  Purple, 55, 58, 272, 293, 294
Flicker, 60
  Northern, 20, 32, 66-9, 126,
    127-33, 167-76, 186,
    211-12
Flycatcher, 45, 119, 120
  Crested, 168, 259, 277
  Least, 120, 246, 259
Forbush, E. H., 64, 262, 285,
  294
Friedman, Dr. Herbert, 43
Frogs, 199-200

G

Golden-eye, 32, 59, 84, 86, 91,
  151, 267, 271, 282, 283,

Golden-eye
  288, 289, 305, 319-20,
  324, 326
  American, 31, 47-50, 83, 87,
    320
Goldfinch, 246, 262, 297,
  315-16
  American, 29, 112-13, 322
Goose, 83, 93, 262
  American Brant, 119
  Canada, 56, 307
  Common Canada, 93-6
Grackle, 177
  Bronzed, 29, 36-7, 60, 66,
    123, 138, 248
Grebe, Horned, 268
Grey, Viscount, of Falloden, 7,
  106, 239
Grosbeak, 23
  Evening, 322
  Pine, 322
  Rose-breasted, 113
Grouse, 262
Gulls, 177, 271, 284, 286, 307,
  326-7
  Bonaparte's, 104, 105, 106,
    271
  Glaucous, 104, 106
  Herring, 29, 60, 92-3, 105,
    106, 203, 271, 324, 326,
    327
  Ring-billed, 55, 92, 105, 106,
    271

H

Hawk, 260, 278
  American Sparrow, 100
  Broad-winged, 279
  Cooper's, 279
  Duck, 261-2
  Kestrel, 243
  Marsh, 261

Hawk
  Pigeon, 55, 56
  Sharp-shinned, 279
  Sparrow, 260
Heron, 18
  Black-crowned Night, 116,
    249-52, 264, 279
  Great Blue, 249, 264, 299,
    300, 318
  Little Green, 202
Howard, Dr. Elliott, 17
Hummingbird, 98
  Ruby-throated, 13, 121-3
Huxley, Dr. Julian, 81

J

Jay, Blue, 278-9
Junco, 310
  Slate-coloured, 32, 55, 57,
    272, 293, 313

K

Killdeer, 29, 37-8, 59, 72-82,
    116, 117, 192, 193, 194,
    219, 237-8, 239, 247, 261,
    263, 267, 299, 300, 302
  American, 76
Kingbird, 119, 246, 252-3
Kingfisher, 300
  Belted, 32, 239-45, 261, 279,
    299
  English, 239
Kinglet, 98
  Golden-crowned, 99, 277, 313
  Ruby-crowned, 98-9, 277, 313
Kittiwake, 106
Kortright, F. H., 269, 305

L

Lady Beetles, 198
Lapland Longspur, 316

Lark, Horned, 27-8
Linnaeus, 111
Lloyd, Hoyes, 102-4
Loon, 269
  Common, 117-18, 307

M

Mallard, 56, 84, 288-9, 305
Martin, Purple, 150, 255
Mathews, F. Schuyler, 109, 110
Meadowlark, 32, 60, 124
Merganser, 32, 59, 85, 282,
    288, 289, 304, 326
  American, 30-1, 47, 83, 84,
    85, 319, 324
  Common, 268-9, 305
  Hooded, 151-2, 270, 305
  Red-breasted, 56, 85, 267,
    271, 305, 319
Migration, 10-13, 256-7
Mockingbird, 109, 121

N

Nice, Mrs. Margaret, 61, 204
Nighthawk, 150-1
Nightjar, English, 200
Nuthatch, Red-breasted, 201
  White-breasted, 201

O

Old-squaw, 56, 84, 86, 306-7,
    319
Oriole, Baltimore, 111-12, 126,
    139, 181-90, 196, 212-13,
    310
Oven-bird, 103, 275-6
Owl, 5
  Barred, 317-18
  Saw-whet, 5
  Snowy, 317, 323-4
Oyster-catchers, 77

P

Peabody Bird, 99
Peep *see* Sandpiper
Peewee, Eastern Wood, 120
    Wood, 246, 259
Peterson, Roger Tory, 101, 106
Phalarope, Northern, 285, 286-8, 303
    Red, 285
    Wilson's, 285
Pheasant, 149, 168
Phoebe, 20, 31, 45-7, 60, 69-72, 126, 133-5, 156-7, 206-11, 259, 262, 296
Pintail, 32, 305
Pipit, American, 294
Plover, 37, 280, 282
    American Golden, 13, 280, 281, 282
    Black-bellied, 115, 280-1, 303
    Green, 81
    Ring, 76-80
    Semipalmated, 110, 116, 267
    Upland, 282

Q

Quebec Conference, Second, 287

R

Rail, Virginia, 168
Redpoll, 23
    Common, 315-6
    Greater, 315-6
Redstart, 246
    American, 102, 103, 168, 257
Robin, 29-30, 35-6, 60, 66, 100, 125, 196, 297, 310
Rook, English, 18
Roosevelt, F. D., 287
Ruffs, 146

S

Sanderling, 264, 279, 299, 300
Sandpiper, 247, 279, 282, 285
    Least, 116, 150, 247, 263
    Pectoral, 202-3, 247, 279
    Red-backed, 117
    Semipalmated, 116, 150, 247, 263
    Solitary, 265, 279
    Spotted, 5, 20, 56, 72, 116, 126, 139-47, 151, 190-5, 203, 217-37, 238, 239, 247, 263, 265, 279, 287, 299, 300
Sapsucker, Yellow-bellied, 6, 273
Scaup, Greater, 107, 304, 305, 319
    Lesser, 55, 85-6, 92, 107, 305
Scoter, American, 304-5
    Surf, 302-4, 319
    White-winged, 319
Shrike, Northern, 23, 316
Siskin, Pine, 26
Skylark, English, 28, 143
Snipe, 267
    Wilson's, 266, 267, 300-2
Sparrow, 5, 24, 44, 57, 58, 104, 112, 116, 186, 294, 296-7, 310
    Chipping, 99-100, 294
    English, 114
    Field, 56, 57
    Fox, 294
    House, 114, 133, 187, 246, 294, 297
    Savannah, 55, 58, 63-6, 126, 213-17, 293
    Song, 15, 29, 33, 34, 39-41, 51, 52, 60-2, 63, 64, 126-7, 138, 152-3, 161, 168, 203-6, 215, 216, 219, 293, 294, 297, 313

Sparrow
  Swamp, 168, 294
  Tree, 32, 55, 57, 60, 294, 297, 313
  Vesper, 294
  White-crowned, 112, 293
  White-throated, 99, 168, 293-4, 272, 297
Starling, 25-6, 27, 29, 60, 66, 114, 123, 133, 138, 196, 278, 290-3, 310, 314, 322
Swallow, 150, 256, 283
  Bank, 108, 254, 255
  Barn, 56, 59, 108, 255
  Cliff, 18
  Tree, 32, 56, 58-9, 66, 108, 246, 253-5
Swan, 94, 118
Swift, 256
  Chimney, 108, 255-6

T

Tanager, Scarlet, 277-8
Taverner, P. A., 37, 114, 277, 285, 298
Teal, Blue-winged, 106-7, 269-70, 271, 282, 288
  Green-winged, 288, 305
Tern, 243, 284
  Arctic, 12
  Caspian, 203
  Common, 203
Thrasher, Brown, 121
Thrush, 30, 36, 112, 276
  Hermit, 279
  Olive-backed, 279
  Wilson's, 112, 154-6
  Wood, 279
Turnstone, Common, 114-15
  Ruddy, 114-15, 267

V

Veery, 112, 126, 154-6, 168, 177
Vireo, 6, 44
  Blue-headed, 275, 296
  Philadelphia, 120, 274
  Red-eyed, 120, 246, 274, 310
  Solitary, 275
  Warbling, 120, 246, 274, 294

W

Waders, 147, 247, 260-1, 263, 265, 285
Wagtail, Grey, 7
Warbler, 5, 6, 13, 44, 98, 100-4, 151, 186, 257-9, 275, 276, 283, 295
  Bay-breasted, 102, 103
  Blackburnian, 103, 275
  Black and White, 101, 103, 258
  Black and Yellow, 258
  Black-poll, 101, 102, 103
  Black-throated Blue, 103, 275
  Black-throated Green, 103, 275, 295
  Canada, 102, 103
  Cape May, 102, 103
  Chestnut-sided, 102, 103, 257
  Magnolia, 103, 258, 295
  Mourning, 103, 258
  Myrtle, 101, 103, 104, 258, 295-6
  Nashville, 102, 103, 272, 275, 295
  Palm, 104, 296
  Parula, 103, 275
  Tennessee, 102, 103, 258
  Wilson's, 102, 103, 295
  Wood, 101
  Yellow, 44, 101, 103, 126,

Warbler
  Yellow
    135-8, 139, 157-67, 178,
    211, 257, 262, 295, 310
Water-thrush, 104, 276, 294
  Northern, 151, 202, 257
Waxwing, Bohemian, 298-9
  Cedar, 120, 186, 246, 299
Whip-poor-will, 5
Wood, William, 122
Woodcock, 266
Woodpecker, 56, 66, 273
  Arctic Three-toed, 23
  Downy, 55, 56, 112, 201,
    246, 262, 273, 314

Woodpecker
  Golden-winged, 67
  Hairy, 56, 98, 112, 262, 273,
    314
  Red-headed, 273
Wren, 98, 276
  House, 106, 246, 260, 277
  Winter, 277

Y

Yellow-legs, 265, 299, 300, 318
  Greater, 265-6, 279, 282
  Lesser, 265-6, 279
Yellow-throat, Maryland, 103,
    168, 275, 276-7